BY THURSTON CLARKE

BALLANTINE BOOKS   NEW YORK

Searching

FOR

PARADISE

A JOURNEY AMONG
THE LAST REAL ISLANDS

THURSTON CLARKE

Formerly titled *Searching for Crusoe*

FOR ANTONIA

A Ballantine Book
Published by The Ballantine Publishing Group

Copyright © 2001 by Thurston Clarke

www.ballantinebooks.com

Library of Congress Cataloging-in-Publication Data is available upon request.

ISBN 0-345-43510-9

Cover design by Min Choi
Cover photo © David Lawrence/Panoramic*Images*

Manufactured in the United States of America

First Trade Paperback Edition: January 2002

10   9   8   7   6   5   4   3   2   1

CONTENTS

INTRODUCTION:

THE FOUR BROTHERS

If I look east from my house above Lake Champlain, I can see four of the least promising islands you could imagine. They are called the Four Brothers and are mostly gray cliffs, rocky beaches, and skeletal trees picked clean by gulls and cormorants. But from the way they excite people you would think they were Maui, Mykonos, Tahiti, and Capri. When Thoreau wrote how even the smallest and barest island in the Merrimack River possessed an "undefined and mysterious charm," he could have been describing the effect the Brothers have on anyone seeing them for the first time. My guests invariably ask who owns them, if anyone lives on them, and if they can go ashore. I explain that the islands are a bird sanctuary and describe rocks frosted with guano and beaches littered with dead gulls. My guests ignore me. An island not worth a visit is inconceivable.

I tell them the Astor family once owned these islands and planned to build a mansion on the largest until an Astor and his wife were shipwrecked on it for twenty-seven hours, but this story only adds to the Brothers' appeal.

In winter, people inquire about skating or skiing out to them and I warn about the currents and pressure ridges that make Lake Champlain treacherous even when it appears solidly frozen. They promise to take cellular phones. In summer, we go sailing and my guests steer for the Brothers, or row out by themselves; they return with blistered hands and aching backs, but raving about the views of the Adirondacks and Green Mountains and speaking as if they had somehow discovered these islands, becoming instant Crusoes.

No other story, of course, haunts a geographic feature the way *Robinson Crusoe* haunts islands, even small, lake-locked ones. Mark Twain's Huckleberry Finn owns the Mississippi, but not the Nile or Amazon. The Congo, but only the Congo, is Conrad's. Walden Pond belongs to Thoreau, and Odysseus has the Mediterranean. But the shadow of Daniel Defoe's Robinson Crusoe falls over every island. Crusoe persuades us that islands are more liberating than confining, more contemplative than lonely, and that they are holy ground where we meet God more easily because we have been, like him, "removed from all the wickedness of the world."

Robinson Crusoe is one of Western literature's greatest stories. No other novel has produced so many imitations and adaptations. There have been two hundred English editions and six hundred foreign ones, in almost any language you can imagine, so that when a Burmese lands on an island in the Mergui Archipelago, or a Panamanian canoes to one of the San Blas islands, he or she arrives, like someone going ashore on the Four Brothers, carrying Crusoe.

James Joyce believed that Crusoe's "manly independence, unconscious cruelty, persistence, and slow yet efficient intelligence" defined the Anglo-Saxon spirit, and that whoever read Defoe's book would fall under its prophetic spell. One summer, I took Joyce's advice and reread it, searching for an explanation for the most passionate and enduring geographic love affair of all time—the one between mankind and islands. In it I met the most influential dead white European male of all, the man behind the Boy Scouts, Outward Bound, and the Peace Corps, and the first modern Solitary Man, the model for T. E. Lawrence, James Bond, and Dirty Harry. I learned that even the most inept (white) man has untapped skills and talents. I saw, foreshadowed, the imperialists and tycoons responsible for centuries of enlightenment, progress, and prosperity—or, if you prefer, racism, exploitation, and misery. I brushed against the insular obsession of the tycoon searching for an island where he can proclaim himself, as Crusoe did, "King and lord of all."

I sometimes looked up from *Crusoe* to the Four Brothers, and as whitecapped waves smashed into their cliffs and tornadoes of gulls swirled over them, I thought of all the archipelagoes and atolls, low islands and high islands, cannibal islands and friendly islands, prison, pleasure, desert, and jungle islands that haunt my memory and dreams. There was Fishers Island, where I spent some of my boyhood summers, and Campobello, the Canadian island where Franklin D. Roosevelt spent his. There was Patmos, with its mountaintop monastery; Christmas Island, with its palm-shrouded graveyards of nuclear test equipment; and Jura, the island in the Hebrides I think finally made me an islomane, someone who, according to that famous island-lover Lawrence Durrell, experiences an "indescribable intoxication" at finding himself in "a little world surrounded by the sea."

I could go on about what I liked about Jura and tell you about my friendship with Jamie and Damaris Fletcher, who own the farmhouse where George Orwell wrote *Nineteen Eighty-Four*, or about the whirlpool that gives any voyage around the island a satisfying frisson of danger, or how I was happy walking across the moors by myself but never missed an opportunity to join a forty-five-minute drive to the one pub. I could tell you all this and more, but it would not explain precisely why Jura and these other islands bewitched me, or why I always imagine myself escaping to an island after a tragedy or catastrophe, or why my island memories are more vivid and sharp than my mainland ones. Finally, I would have to admit that my attraction to islands remains, like Thoreau's to the islands in the Merrimack River, somewhat undefined and mysterious.

I suspect I arrive on an island assuming it will be haunted by its history because my memories of a 1955 trip to Nantucket are of cobblestone streets, tumbledown mansions with banging shutters, and the fog-shrouded cemeteries where my mother searched for our whaling captain ancestors.

I suspect that any personal connection with an island makes it a potential soul mate, and that my mother's friendship with George Orwell heightened my attraction to Jura. She had taken the *Île de France* to England in 1938 to satisfy her late husband's request that his ashes be scattered midway between the United States and Britain. The day after she arrived in London, Orwell picked her up in the British Museum. She charmed him by saying she had whispered "Bon voyage" as the urn tumbled into the North Atlantic. He charmed her by taking her to the Changing of the Guard to giggle at the tall guardsmen marching to the nursery rhyme cadence of the "Dance of the Hours." They met several times afterwards and if he admitted to being married, which he was, she does not remember it. She knew him by his real name, Eric Blair, and recognized him as George Orwell only when she saw the photograph that appeared above his obituary.

I think I size up every new island as a potential refuge because of my experience in a sailing camp on Long Island Sound. It was run by "the Captain," a greedy old salt who had taken fees from twice as many students as his sailboats could handle. We spent hours on glassy Long Island Sound, sitting in motorboats, waiting our turn to be transferred to one of the Captain's few dinghies, plagued by thirst and then by full bladders. One day, we persuaded a counselor to land us on an uninhabited island where we scattered into the scrub and poison ivy and hid—anything to escape bobbing in that oily brown water.

I believe I became concerned at an early age about islands disappearing because if I walked a hundred yards through the woods behind my boyhood home I reached the retirement house of Brigadier General Leslie Groves, former director of the Manhattan Project, the wartime program that developed the atomic bomb. I thought he resembled Santa Claus, and I liked him because he was the only elderly man in the neighborhood who was nice to children. I once repaid him for his many kindnesses by placing a whoopee cushion on his favorite chair during a neighborhood party. This boyhood prank was out of character, but it occurred at a time when I was fascinated by the bomb, drawing mushroom-cloud doodles in school notebooks and staring into car headlights so I could experience the blinding light that might one day incinerate my father at his desk in New York City. I believed Hiroshima and Nagasaki had been a fair payback for Pearl Harbor, but the postwar tests that had turned twenty-six beautiful islands on Bikini Atoll into nuclear wastelands had shocked a boy whose favorite books were *Peter Pan*, *Mysterious Island*, *Treasure Island*, and *Robinson Crusoe*.

The French philosopher Jean-Jacques Rousseau launched this tradition of desert island literature for children by choosing *Robinson Crusoe* as the first book his son would read and predicting it would be read "with delight, so long as our taste is unspoiled." My daughters adore island books and have read *Lord of the Flies*, *Swallows and Amazons*, and *Swiss Family Robinson*, among others. On the day I left for Jura, my daughter Edwina was finishing R. M. Ballantyne's *The Coral Island*, a Victorian retelling of the Crusoe story in which three boys are shipwrecked on a Pacific island more beautiful than the one Defoe gave Crusoe. They live a splendid outdoor life, hunting pigs, talking late around campfires, and swimming at a "sandy beach of dazzling whiteness." There are no adults and no rules. On islands, Edwina says, kids get to do what they want.

But which came first, the island books, or islomania? Does Edwina love islands because of these books, or do they appeal to an islomania as innate as a fear of snakes? Did George Orwell move to Jura because his friend David Astor told him about an empty farmhouse on a neighboring estate, or because of the *Odyssey*, *The Tempest*, *Treasure Island*, and *Robinson Crusoe*?

You will not find "islomania" in a dictionary, but the phenomenon exists just the same. It explains why an anonymous donor contributed

£750,000 to help the sixty inhabitants of Eigg buy their Hebridean island, why a private island is the final jewel in the crown of a multimillionaire, why Jimmy Buffett ballads and Caribbean cruises are popular, why 800,000 visitors a year cram themselves onto tiny Mykonos, and why the top "dream vacation" for men surveyed by *Psychology Today* was "being marooned on a tropical island with several members of the opposite sex."

I know islomania exists because I have met people gripped by it. In 1985, I spent a week on Christmas Island, a Central Pacific atoll belonging to Kiribati. The main island was 125 miles of scorching salt flats covered with palm, heliotrope, and rusting military equipment and surrounded by a boiling sea, a treacherous reef, and so many gray sharks no one went swimming without a billy club. The government officials posted from Tarawa had to be there; so did the copra cutters working on five-year contracts, and the incorrigible prisoners incarcerated in a jail that is the Devil's Island of Kiribati. But how to explain John Bryden? He was a large, good-natured Scotsman with a sun-scorched complexion who lived with his wife and children in a cinder-block house and earned a living repairing trucks and hauling cargo. He had come from Britain to work as an agricultural officer on Fanning, a nearby island, and after his contract expired he moved to Christmas Island instead of returning home. As we sat drinking beer one afternoon, staring at the yellowing fronds of some drought-plagued palm trees, he said, "It's not a pretty island, is it? And as you've found, there's nowhere to swim. I tried jogging but it's too bloody hot. But I've been here five years, so I guess it isn't all bad."

The sun fell, the mosquitoes attacked, and the room darkened until we were silhouettes. I asked him why he stayed. He gave a deep sigh. The year before, four British technical advisers posted briefly to Christmas Island had become such bitter enemies they refused to speak and ate at separate tables in the hotel. They reminded him how much he loathed confrontations, feuding, and any kind of unpleasantness, and he supposed that was why he liked friendly islands like this one.

A second British islomane, Eric Bailey, had been district commissioner for Christmas Island and had written *The Christmas Island Story*, a thin but lavishly illustrated volume that was clearly the work of a man obsessed by islands. I met him on Abemama, another Kiribati atoll, where he had retired and become the only foreign resident. He went around shirtless, wore a blue lavalava, lived with his native wife in a palm-thatch lean-to, and accepted whatever setbacks Abemama offered with the nonchalance of a hippie. Abemama was prettier than Christmas Island but his life on it was a hard one, particularly for a man in his late seventies. His vegetables were stunted, his English cucumbers had died on the vine, and his fishing nets were rotting because his arthritis prevented him from pulling them out of the water every day. He perplexed the Abemamans. They were kind people, so they worried about him. Where were his children? they wondered. His relatives? Why was he here? Later, after visiting more islands and meeting people like him, I realized he was simply mad for islands.

The appetite for islands and more islands is so insatiable that icebergs, clouds, and mirages have been misidentified as new ones. In the 1920s, *Bartholomew's Great Survey Atlas,* the bible of British cartography, still showed the Anson Archipelago, a nonexistent chain of islands between Hawaii and Japan named after Lord Anson, who had seen them only on the charts of a Spanish galleon he had seized off the Philippines in the eighteenth century. Until the 1980s, the JRO Globus of Munich globes that were a feature of Lufthansa ticket offices around the world placed the bogus Matador Islands (inhabited by a race of shy albino lepers, according to their British discoverer) just north of the equator, and even the National Geographic Society's 1982 world map depicted these imaginary islands as a cluster of unnamed dots. In his book *Uninhabited and Deserted Islands*, Jon Fisher has proposed sinking oil tankers in shallow lagoons, then spreading soil on their decks and planting salt-resistant vegetation in order to create more islands.

There is more to the obsession with islands than a lighthearted yearning for sand, sea, and dark-skinned women, more than the carefree life of *Swiss Family Robinson* and *Gilligan's Island*. Islomania has coughed up such anti-Crusoes as Samuel Comstock, a slight blond Quaker boy who became so consumed by his dream of becoming king of a tropical island that at fifteen he signed on as a crewman of a whaling ship and begged its captain to set him ashore whenever it passed an island. When he was twenty-two, he and several fellow crewmen murdered their officers and sailed to an atoll in the Marshall Islands, where his attempt to become the monarch of its natives ended in more bloodshed. Another anti-Crusoe, the Jesuit priest Father Honoré Laval, terrorized and enslaved the inhabitants of the Polynesian island of Mangareva for thirty-seven years, destroying the statues of their gods and forcing them to build a twelve-hundred-seat, gleaming white coral and mother-of-pearl cathedral. By the time French authorities removed him to Tahiti, tried him for murder, and declared him insane, his megalomania had reduced Mangareva's population from nine thousand to five hundred, and had stripped its sick and starving survivors of their customs and beliefs.

Ask the medical community to explain the "undefined and mysterious charm" of islands and you may hear about the soothing effects of wind and wave, the seductive aroma of a beach, sunlight and the ions in sea air triggering a natural high, and watery sounds reminding us of the womb. Ask yachtsmen, and you may hear islands described in the heroic terms mountaineers reserve for the Himalayas. Ask someone vacationing on an island, and you may hear about escape, sensuality, and romance, or about an island being knowable because it has natural limits.

But I thought there had to be more to account for a passion for islands that transcends cultures and centuries, and to explain why islands have been central to the myths and religions of so many peoples—why Chinese mythology places heaven on an archipelago of rocky islands, Greek and Roman heroes inhabit the Islands of the Blessed, Christians built some of their holiest churches and monasteries on islands, and the reedy islets of Lake Titicaca were sacred to the Incas and are still revered by their descendants.

There is a certain urgency to solving the mystery of islomania because islands, like tropical rain forests, are an endangered geographic feature. Global warming threatens to submerge low-lying ones, while the Global Village threatens to overwhelm the culture and individuality of popular ones. The longer I waited to discover why islands are so intoxicating, the greater the chance that their undefined and mysterious charms might vanish.

This has already happened to Key West, now a pale shadow of its once-bewitching self. I spent three summers there in the 1970s, when it remained remote despite a series of bridges and causeways connecting it to mainland Florida. It was North America's answer to the Foreign Legion, a decaying little tropical city where you could live like a hermit or assemble a circle of friends in a snap. Every day I worked in the morning and spent the afternoon at the Sands Beach Club, a fancy name for a postage-stamp-sized patch of sand where you could hang out for the price of a beer. Then I drifted down to a pier at Mallory Square for the daily sunset celebration. As the sun disappeared into the Gulf of Mexico the hippies put down their guitars, the Hare Krishnas stopped chanting, and a hush fell over the crowd. Afterwards I stopped at the Half Shell Raw Bar, where on full-moon nights women in leotards danced on the pier to juke box blues, silhouetted against the shrimp boats.

I returned to Key West in 1991 after a fifteen-year absence and found that a small increase in the diameter of the pipe bringing water from the mainland had also brought chain hotels and cruise liners. A high-rise resort had replaced the Sands and the Half Shell had quadrupled to accommodate college kids who had made Key West a binge-drinking destination. Many native "Conchs" had moved to

Ocala ("Key West in exile"), and Mallory Square had become a honky-tonk of T-shirt shops and touts hawking time shares and excursions to a dying reef.

Key West was not yet the full disaster. Old-timers held out in their backyard gardens. George Murphy, an editor and radio host who lived on a houseboat, told me he hung on because Key West still satisfied his most important ideal, "May you live in the most interesting of places." When I spoke to him six years later, however, he sounded discouraged. Key West now had a Gap, Banana Republic, Planet Hollywood, and Hard Rock Café, with more mass-market emporia promised, including a Hooters, with its franchised big-bosomed waitresses in orange bikinis. "Imagine," Murphy boomed, "a Hooters, in Key West!"

It was easier to imagine a Hooters than the beaches closing, which is what happened next. Key West's antique sewer lines, unable to handle the rise in population and flood of day-trippers, began leaking raw sewage into the shallow waters surrounding the island. When I read that state health officials had closed all the beaches I was reminded of *Crusoe*, a short story by the English writer Victor Sage. In it, Sage's Crusoe builds ingenious appliances that he powers with a generator running on gases produced by his own excrement. As the temperature rises in the summer months, he finds he needs more and more fuel to keep his refrigerator humming and is soon spending his waking hours eating and crapping until finally, because of his determination to preserve his deluxe lifestyle, he has turned his island into a pile of shit.

But a Hooters and *E. coli* bacteria in Key West were not that surprising, given that I was suddenly hearing and reading about islands everywhere being bridged, blasted, swamped by mass tourism, turned into dumps, and transformed by disturbances and events that on any continent would cause less stir than the breeze from a hummingbird's wings.

A California biotechnology company produced genetically engineered vanilla and the Comoros, where vanilla accounted for two-thirds of exports, faced catastrophe. Britain's Royal Mail decided to tie packets of letters in synthetic string and devastated the hemp-based economy of St. Helena. Father Laval's Mangareva was being terrorized again, this time by nuclear testing, its lagoon poisoned by radioactive waste washed into it during the 1970s from the decks of French warships. Coral bleaching threatened reefs in the Caribbean, and mangroves had been cleared for destination resorts in Fiji. Skye in Scotland, Hirta in Norway, and Canada's Prince Edward Island had committed islacide by building bridges or tunnels to the mainland. Some islands faced cultural annexation. The best hotel on the tiny Caribbean island of Anguilla resembled a Moroccan village and offered California cuisine; tour operators were demanding that the Greek island of Rhodes offer German road signs and television channels; and David Guterson, who set his novel *Snow Falling on Cedars* on Washington's Bainbridge Island, told an interviewer that during his thirteen years there he had watched it being transformed into "a neurotic place like anywhere else in the world."

When I began talking about solving the mystery of islomania before it was too late, everyone assumed I needed help choosing my islands, and so I heard about the charms of Maui and St. Bart's, and barebones Greek islands where I could camp on any beach—at least I could have in 1968. I was told not to miss Laucala, the Fijian island then owned by the Forbes family, where you flew in by chartered plane and paid a thousand dollars a day, or a certain Filipino resort island where you stayed in air-conditioned casitas, soaked in sunken tubs, and, if you got lucky, rubbed shoulders with Ferdinand Marcos Jr.

I added these to a growing list of islands to be avoided at all costs. Island-hopping may sound carefree, but every remote island is a potential Alcatraz. Passenger boats are rare, planes infrequent, and hurricanes can strand you for days. I once spent five days on Majuro, the main atoll of the Marshall Islands, waiting for a delayed plane to Tarawa. Robert Louis Stevenson had called it "the Pearl of the

Pacific," and I had seen a photograph of a gorgeous oval lagoon surrounded by a ribbon of narrow islands thick with palms. Majuro still looked good from the air, but after forty years of American trusteeship it had become a Pacific Appalachia of rusty pickups, plywood shacks, and outhouses built over the lagoon. I did not need to return to see if it had become any worse, or to go back to Maui to sit in more rental car traffic jams. And what was the point of visiting Ibiza, Rhodes, or Tahiti when you and I know what I would find?

I eliminated islands like Hilton Head and Daufuskie, whose native people and culture had been clear-cut for retiree golfers, and Caribbean islands that had become glorified cruise-liner docks. I decided against islands failing to meet the Viking requirement that a ship with a rudder can pass between it and the mainland, miniature continents like Madagascar, Greenland, Sumatra, and New Guinea, and uninhabited specks too small to be considered an island under terms of an 1861 Scottish census defining islands as areas of land surrounded by water and inhabited by man, and where at least one sheep can graze. I wanted islands where the population was more than ten but less than ten thousand. I wanted a mix of low atolls and volcanic beauties, temperate and tropical islands, ones more remote than Catalina but more accessible than Tristan da Cunha.

After rejecting the too large and too small, the obvious horrors and remote curiosities, I was left with islands that fell into three categories: islands I could group into types, such as holy islands, private islands, scary islands, prison islands, and utopian islands; islands I already knew; and famous islands that have sparked our love affair with islands. From these, I picked one holy, one prison, one scary, one private, and one utopian island to represent the others. Then I selected the five islands that have provided my most vivid memories. Finally, I chose Bali-ha'i, Atlantis, the Spice Islands, and Isla Robinson Crusoe as the famous islands that, real or not, and whether we know it or not, accompany us to every new island, and persuade us it will be paradise.

7 FAMOUS ISLANDS

1

CRUSOE'S ISLAND — MÁS A TIERRA

The modern obsession with islands starts with Robinson Crusoe, so I started with his island, Más a Tierra, the Pacific Island four hundred miles off the coast of Chile in the Juan Fernández archipelago, where a Scottish seaman named Alexander Selkirk was marooned for four and a half years between 1704 and 1709. After his rescue by the privateer Captain Woodes Rogers, Selkirk recounted his story to the journalist Richard Steele. It is believed that Daniel Defoe read both Steele's resulting article and Woodes Rogers's book, *A Cruising Voyage round the World*, and incorporated Selkirk's experiences into his novel *Robinson Crusoe*. Some scholars suspect Defoe met and interviewed Selkirk, and when a Selkirk descendant recently sold his birthplace to settle inheritance taxes, she lambasted Defoe as "a man of no scruples" who had stolen and distorted her ancestor's story.

I first encountered Más a Tierra in *Two Years Before the Mast*, Richard Henry Dana's account of his 1834 voyage from Boston to California. Dana called it a classic island, the most romantic on earth, and praised its rushing streams, lofty mountains, rich soil, plentiful fruit, and aromatic trees. It had a "peculiar charm," he wrote, perhaps because of its solitary position in the vast expanse of the South Pacific, and "the associations which everyone has connected with it in

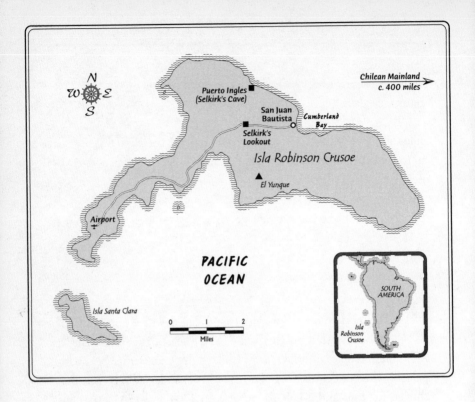

their childhood from reading Robinson Crusoe," ones that gave it "the sacredness of an early home."

To reach this sacred home, which Chile has renamed Isla Robinson Crusoe, I traveled to Santiago, telephoned the offices of Transportes Aereos Robinson Crusoe (TARC), and was instructed to be in my hotel lobby at 3:00 P.M. with $420 in cash. The TARC agent was a stone-faced lady in rhinestone glasses who counted my money twice before parting with a ticket. After snapping her purse shut on my dollars she warned that the rains had started early this year and we had already entered the season of autumn storms, when flights could be delayed for days or weeks. But I was just happy to be buying a plane ticket to Isla Crusoe. An island of two hundred people four hundred miles from the Chilean mainland would not have had air service at all without the highly prized lobsters that were shipped to Santiago on return flights.

TARC was one of several small companies using the antique Cerillos airport. When I arrived at midmorning, the tarmac was shrouded in fog and the terminal deserted. A little girl unlocked a kiosk selling newspapers and snacks, then curled up on the counter and fell asleep. An old crone cleaned the bathrooms, then locked them. A pay telephone rang and rang, echoing through the empty hall.

There were three other passengers. Carlos was a burly young man with a face lost in whiskers and the loping gait of a yeti. He said he had taken a leave of absence from the school where he taught and was going to Isla Crusoe for a week "to forget certain things." But he carried a polar anorak, his luggage exceeded the ten-kilogram allowance, and I suspected he had suffered some crushing tragedy and planned on marooning himself for much longer.

Irene was a parakeet-sized woman in her sixties who had brought along a friend, the plump and timid Alicia, as her silent caboose. Thirty years in the Atacama Desert had sun-blasted her face into a dalmatian pattern and left her straw-colored hair brittle and spontaneous-combustion dry. She made a theatrical meal of every sentence and introduced herself by excoriating everything that had ruined Chile: the corrupt politicians, the McDonald's hamburgers, and owning more things instead of touching more people. Whenever her family or the Atacama became too much, she said, "I threaten to move to this marvelous island and always I imagine living there alone." Her sons had finally given her a ticket and said, "All right, then, go!"

She wore a thin sweater and admitted having left behind her windbreaker. She had it ready to pack, she said, "But then I asked myself, 'Why do I need *that* thing in paradise?' " She stared at the peeling ceiling and shut her eyes. "It will be how everyone should live. No noise or contamination. The islanders will be gentle people who know how to enjoy life. I may stay forever."

I began describing Selkirk's despair upon first wading ashore. She looked appalled and threw up a hand. "Stop! Oh, please stop, dear man. Don't say anything more! If this island is not paradise, I don't wish to know."

The four of us stood alone in the middle of the empty terminal as speakers played, "Put your hand in the hand of the man. . . ." I remembered the Agatha Christie mystery *And Then There Were None*, in which a mysterious host invites ten strangers to a private island off the south coast of England, then murders them one by one.

TARC's Santiago manager appeared. He swooped his arms and delivered a lecture about the complexities of landing on Isla Crusoe. The dirt runway was eight hundred meters long and curved upward, like a ski jump. Beyond it was a cliff. Strong winds were blowing across the airport today, making landing treacherous. We would wait another two hours, until the telephone in the hall rang with the next weather report from Isla Crusoe.

The delay stretched to two days and when we reassembled we had gained another passenger, a young Chilean named Luz with the high cheekbones of an Indian princess. She had graduated from college in the United States and was flying out to visit her mother, a recent divorcée who had moved to Isla Crusoe on an impulse and was supporting herself by teaching the children of the lobster fishermen to speak English. Cerillos airport remained forlorn and foggy. As we climbed aboard, our pilot, a baldy wearing thick spectacles and a filthy cardigan, was kicking the tires. The manager and his wife handed out homemade sandwiches and waved handkerchiefs. I fell asleep and woke two hours later as we descended toward a rugged green island waving a tentacle of brown desert into the ocean. The contrast was stark: a tangle of craggy, thickly forested peaks shooting from a boiling sea to the north, an arid red plateau of rock and dust to the south: King Kong's island married to a finger of Lawrence of Arabia desert.

We landed in the desert and taxied past a smashed Cessna to a shack. The wind had blown out every window and piles of scrap metal kept its tin roof from taking flight. A mestizo with shock-treatment eyes pumped our hands as we descended the stairs. "Marcel is our fireman and weatherman," the pilot said. "He tells us if it's safe to land."

Irene pirouetted. "It's wonderful, wonderful!" she shouted. "I'm always saying I'll move here, and now . . ." She took in the peeling shack and the dust devils dancing across the runway. "And now . . . I guess we'll see."

Marcel roped our luggage onto a Land Rover and we lurched down a crumbling track cut into the caldera of an extinct volcano. A fishing boat waited at the jetty below. We boarded it and spent almost two hours plowing through a roller-coaster sea, past skyscraper cliffs ending in ridges sharp enough to slice an onion.

The crewmen were mahogany-tanned and loquacious. They said they used these razorback ridges to mark their lobster traps and pointed out a jagged pile of rocks nicknamed, for obvious reasons, "the Widow-Maker." They claimed it was not really that windy (in New England, gale force flags would have been flying) and called this cauldron of whitecaps a gentle sea. The new moon often brought a five-day window of calm weather like this. After that, watch out.

They boasted that their island was a United Nations World Biosphere Reserve because it had so many rare plants. Its lobsters were the sweetest in the world because they came from the lobster latitudes of the Southern Hemisphere. Its seals were native only to this archipelago and the most beautiful on earth because of their rare mixture of gray and black hairs. And nowhere else could you find Isla Crusoe's red hummingbirds, or the luma tree, whose hard wood was prized by Chilean policemen for their billy clubs, or the wild cabbage that nourished "Alejandro" Selkirk.

As we rounded the next-to-last headland before the island's only settlement, San Juan Bautista, spotlights of sun fell through the firmament-of-heaven clouds, illuminating a cave with a low stone wall set in its mouth. "Crusoe's cave," the fishermen chorused—the first evidence I had that on this island Selkirk and Crusoe were interchangeable.

An amphitheater of green mountains rose steeply from the shore and surrounded San Juan's ramshackle warehouses and bungalows. The highest mountain, the tombstone-shaped El Yunque, was so rugged that less than a dozen people have reached its summit, and so dark and sinister that an indigenous people would have made it the seat of a fearsome god.

Someone had fastened ten richly illustrated boards with poems about Selkirk and Crusoe to pilings lining the town wharf. Before I could translate them, a jaunty man wearing a country club golf outfit tossed my bag into a wheelbarrow he pushed across the street to his boardinghouse, the Villa Green. "Call me Robinson," he said, explaining it was a popular first name for island boys. There was also a Hosteria Defoe, and a Posada de Robinson, where I drank a beer, alone. I drank a second one, also alone, in a three-table bar where a yellowed clipping recounted how the British navy had sunk the German warship *Dresden* in this harbor during World War I. One survivor had become a castaway, living as a hermit for fifteen years and becoming known as "the German Robinson."

There were more Crusoean echoes in cottages that appeared slapped together from driftwood, backyard greenhouses growing produce to ward off scurvy, and the brave trappings of civilization. Schoolboys wore blazers and ties, like their mainland counterparts, and the bust of the naval hero decorated a plaza where I never saw a single soul walk or sit.

You could hardly blame Isla Crusoe's inhabitants for confusing Crusoe and Selkirk. The government had renamed Más a Tierra for the fictional Crusoe, and visitors came with his name rather than Selkirk's on their lips. When Americans on their way to the California gold fields stopped here in 1849 and 1850, they had been convinced it was the real home of the real Crusoe. One miner called it "the most fascinating spot, to me, on the face of the globe!" He wrote in his diary: "Tomorrow I shall see the enchanted isle! Not the picture of fancy but the real ground . . . perhaps see the cave that Robinson dug, or the ruins of his little hovel." At the Villa Green, I read a 1928 *National Geographic* article titled "A Voyage to the Island Home of Robinson Crusoe," in which the author waited until the penultimate paragraph to point out that Crusoe was not a real sailor who had been shipwrecked on Más a Tierra. When excursion steamers from Valparaiso called during the first half of the century, a man dressed as Crusoe, complete with parrot, umbrella, and peaked goatskin hat, and accompanied by a redheaded Friday, had poled out on a raft to meet them. Even in Largo, Selkirk's Scottish hometown, there was a Crusoe Hotel with a Juan Fernández Bar and Castaway restaurant, but nothing named after Selkirk.

I soon adopted the local habit of confusing the two men. When puzzled stares met my request for directions to Selkirk's lookout, I asked for Crusoe's lookout. I began calling the cave where Selkirk stored his supplies "Robinson's cave," and caught myself wondering if any of the Spanish cannons lying in the grass or mounted along the waterfront dated from Crusoe's time. But I remembered Selkirk when my ankles were brushed by the descendants of the feral cats he had trained to lie at his feet and ward off rats.

San Juan had no venerable government buildings, historic churches, or large buildings. Everyone looked to the sea for their living, depending on the lobsters that could bring twenty dollars in a Santiago restaurant. A century before, the islanders had simply tossed chunks of goat meat along the shore and attracted swarms of lobsters. The lobsters had since become more scarce and it was agreed that if they ever disappeared, so would San Juan. Meanwhile, it was as silent and lonely as a community of six hundred people could be. Lights twinkled at dusk, but the only people about were children gathered in a bar to watch the owner burn warts off his daughter's knee, and a half dozen adults enjoying a favorite evening ritual, watching the red hummingbirds drink nectar from bell-shaped yellow flowers. When night fell, the streets emptied, except for a boy kicking a soccer ball through the supports of a gong, the island's only fire alarm.

I ate cold lobster, alone, in the Villa Green, surrounded by polished wooden sideboards and wall calendars, and listening to the click of a pendulum clock. I read in the hotel guest book about "lifelong ambitions fulfilled," bird-watchers who had "come for the hummingbirds but found so much more," and the joy of the world's most traveled disabled person to find himself, at last, on "the famous island of Robinson Crusoe."

I returned to the wharf with a flashlight to read the poems. One spoke of Selkirk sleeping with Odysseus, another of Crusoe's "island of silence." On my way back to the hotel I bumped into Irene, who was staying at a neighboring boardinghouse. She said, "You know, it is *very* quiet on this island."

■

It was once believed that the silence and solitude of an uninhabited island would drive a marooned seaman insane. A captain leaving behind a loaded revolver was considered a humanitarian, and such acts of charity explain why skeletons clutching rusted revolvers often greeted early visitors to islands like Más a Tierra. The fact that Selkirk, who had a musket, powder, and bullets, survived four years without committing suicide made him a successful castaway.

I had planned on making a solitary pilgrimage to his cave at Puerto Inglés so I could stare at the horizon and wonder if I would have done as well, or become a skeleton clutching a revolver. But Robinson Green had warned against walking there over the sharp ridge separating it from San Juan. Last month, this ridge had defeated a party of Germans who had come from weeks of hiking the Andes. It was most likely the same one Selkirk tumbled down while chasing a goat, escaping death only because he grabbed the animal and cushioned his fall. The Villa Green's proprietor recommended traveling around the headland by boat, so I joined Irene, Alicia, and Luz, who had hired a fisherman named Daniel to take them in his skiff.

The rocky shoreline and rough sea made it impossible to land at Puerto Inglés. Daniel jumped onto a rock with the bowline, shouting, "Have faith in the fishermen of Juan Fernández." We disembarked one by one, grabbing his hand as waves hurled the boat toward the rocks. Irene almost skidded into the sea, and she staggered ashore shivering and frightened.

We stumbled down the beach over polished rocks the size of a baby's head while Daniel rattled off a potted history of Selkirk's experiences. Then we climbed to a bluff overlooking a broad, well-watered valley where he pointed out the remains of a house built fifty years before by an optimistic German farmer who had imported the amaryllis growing wild among the ruined walls. There was water in a creek; there were rabbits, wild oregano, and enough wood for years of cooking and signal fires. An army ranger could have lived off this land for months, but he would always have known that he was on a training course, and that a boat would one day round the headland to fetch him.

I slipped into Selkirk's cave while the others beachcombed. Its walls bore the scars of centuries of graffiti artists and souvenir hunters. Forty-niners heading to the California gold fields had caused some of the worst damage. When their ships stopped to reprovision, they headed to Crusoe's cave to mine for souvenirs they could sell in San Francisco. J. Ross Brown, a passenger on a California-bound packet who wrote a book about his voyage, *Crusoe's Island*, had found twenty prospectors at Selkirk's cave. "They had battered away at the sides, top, and bottom of the cave in their eager search for relics till they had left scarcely a dozen square feet of the original surface," he reported. "Every man had literally his pocket full of rocks."

When Brown left, they were proposing to search for gold in what they called "Crusoe's Valley," and to annex Juan Fernández to the United States.

The mouth of the cave faced the same beach where Selkirk first came ashore. Nowadays, we would call the impulsive and bad-tempered Selkirk a punk, and his family of notorious brawlers and malcontents dysfunctional. He had been rebuked for behaving indecently in church, he fought constantly with his family, and after one nasty punch-up he went to sea with the notorious privateer William Dampier. Within a few years, he was master of the *Cinque Ports*, a ship commanded by the equally hot-tempered Captain Strandling. As the *Cinque Ports* neared Juan Fernández, he and Strandling quarreled over its condition. Selkirk declared its recent repairs so slipshod that he would prefer being marooned on Más a Tierra to facing certain disaster at sea. To his surprise, Strandling ordered him put ashore.

Selkirk had counted on other crewmen joining him. After the ship's boat landed him alone at Puerto Inglés he must have taken stock of the towering mountains and empty valley, weighing the prospect of starving or dying of exposure here against perishing in Strandling's unseaworthy ship, the horror of unending solitude against the pleasure of becoming king of Más a Tierra. As the *Cinque Ports*'s crewmen pushed the skiff back into the surf, he probably experienced some of the conflicting emotions I sometimes feel upon arriving on a remote island: an excitement at having at last reached such a silent, lonely place, and a sudden impulse to escape it—to reboard whatever boat or plane has brought me there, and go home.

According to Woodes Rogers, Selkirk jumped into the water at the last minute and began swimming after the skiff, screaming that he had changed his mind and begging to return to the ship.

Captain Strandling, so the story goes, replied, "Well, I have not changed mine! Stay where you are and may you starve!"

According to Selkirk's testimony to Richard Steele, he was miserable for his first eighteen months on Más a Tierra and "grew dejected, languid, and melancholy, scarcely able to refrain from doing himself Violence." One Defoe biographer, Thomas Wright, depicted Selkirk as eating raw shellfish and seal, afraid to go inland and contemplating suicide. "Voices spoke to him both in the howlings of the sea in front and in the murmur of the woods behind," Wright wrote. "The shore was creatured with phantoms. Then—cooling his fevered brain—came sweet visions of his childhood, the home at Largo, his mother, the fields he had rambled in, the words he had heard in the old kirk, thoughts of God."

Selkirk told Steele he had cried, wandered aimlessly, refused to eat, and remained at the shoreline, seldom lifting his eyes from the horizon. Defoe's Crusoe was similarly distraught during his early days, beginning his journal: "I, poor miserable Robinson Crusoe, being shipwrecked, during a dreadful storm . . . came ashore on this dismal, unfortunate island, which I called the Island of Despair."

After overcoming his depression, Selkirk transformed this valley into the kind of self-sufficient estate Defoe's Crusoe would build. He gathered wild fruits and vegetables and trained himself to outrun and tackle the goats that privateers had released to provide fresh meat when they reprovisioned. He turned the chase into a game, notching the ears of the goats he released and keeping score of those he ate. He dueled with the sea lions like a matador, clubbing them before they could smash him with their tails or grab him in their jaws. He flavored his goat stews with wild turnips, parsnips, and parsley; boiled his lobsters with a native pepper berry; gorged on black plums; sewed together a goatskin cap and coat, using a nail as a needle; and discovered that pimento wood made a clear-burning and fragrant fuel, good for light, heat, and flavoring barbecued goat. He entertained himself by carving his name into trees and by singing and dancing with his cats and kid goats. His life was less luxurious than Crusoe's—no dairy, bakery, or three plantations—but Defoe had given his Crusoe a more forgiving Caribbean climate and allowed him to salvage tools, food, and ammunition from his ship. Selkirk started with clothes and bedding, a gun and ammunition, a knife, a kettle, and a Bible. Like Crusoe, he found solace in religion, scheduling daily services and reading the Scriptures out loud to preserve his ability to speak. Captain Woodes Rogers praised him for being "a better Christian in his Solitude than ever he was before."

Steele reported that Selkirk's manner of life was "exquisitely pleasant" and "he never had a Moment heavy on his hands." His nights were "untroubled," his days "joyous" because of his "Practice of Temperance and Exercise." His life became "one continual Feast." (Woodes Rogers's account of Selkirk's rescue somewhat undermines the "joyous" business: Selkirk burst from the bushes, "a Man cloth'd in Goat-Skins, who look'd wilder than the first Owners of them," bellowing in an indecipherable tongue. Only when he screamed, "I believe in God the Father Almighty, Maker of Heaven and Earth . . ." did the sailors realize he was human.)

Crusoe was literature's first self-made man, not its first conspicuous consumer. He created a comfortable life, but no more. He set aside time for reading, writing, and worship, and celebrated his island for removing him "from all the wickedness of the world." He concluded that "all our discontents" sprang "from the want of thankfulness for what we have." Selkirk made a similar point upon returning to Scotland, insisting he had never been so happy as when he was a castaway on Más a Tierra and "not worth a farthing," leading Steele to conclude, "he is happiest who confines his wants to natural necessities."

Before Selkirk marooned himself and Defoe marooned his fictional Crusoe, tropical islands had been considered fearful places where sailors risked the lonely death of a castaway or the spears of hostile natives. After Selkirk and Crusoe, they were seen as places of redemption and improvement, where you could escape the wickedness of the world, build Utopia, and find God.

For almost two centuries, visitors to Isla Crusoe have described its inhabitants as contented with their simple life and lacking ambition. Richard Henry Dana called them "the laziest people on the face of the earth" and said they passed the time taking long paseos and re-placing the boughs the wind blew from their roofs. They were even "too lazy to speak fast." In 1992, an American couple, James and Mayme Bruce, made almost identical observations in *The Explorer's Journal*, complaining that the people were idle, showed "no curiosity or interest" in visitors, and moved "at an agonizingly slow pace." In 1895, the celebrated yachtsman Joshua Slocum stopped at the is-land for several weeks during his single-handed circumnavigation of the globe. He supported himself by making fresh doughnuts, which the islanders bought with "ancient and curious coins" salvaged from the wreck of a Spanish galleon. He noted that the adults were all healthy and the children all beautiful, and reported: "There was not a lawyer or police officer among them" and "The domestic economy of the island was simplicity itself. The fashions of Paris did not affect the inhabitants; each dressed according to his taste." He departed think-ing, "Blessed island of Juan Fernández! Why Alexander Selkirk ever left you was more than I could make out."

Selkirk had prayed that a British ship would appear on the hori-zon, but Daniel, the fisherman taking me to Puerto Inglés, worried about cruise liners appearing and disgorging hundreds of tourists who would travel by foot, donkey, and all-terrain vehicle to Selkirk's lookout. They might eat a few lobster empanadas, and buy the wallets San Juan's women stitched from fish skins, but they would also tram-ple the lichen, pick the rare cinnamon, spook the hummingbirds, and ruin the simple life of an island where it is still remembered that pas-sengers off excursion boats once stripped bark from the chonta tree, threatening it with extinction.

◾

I met people on Isla Crusoe who had come to live a simple life re-moved from the wickedness of the mainland. They praised the island for offering clean air and water, plentiful food, and physical security, all the "natural necessities." They liked it that no one was rich or poor, and most transactions involved barter and credit. (Banknotes were so scarce my smallest bills sent shopkeepers rummaging through drawers for change, and one man had to shake coins from a piggy bank.) They feared development more than solitude, exile to the mainland more than isolation, and I heard several times how a teenager recently banished for theft had been prostrate with grief, sobbing uncontrollably as he boarded the steamer for Valparaiso.

I met the hawk-featured Marietta in the offices of the agency charged with managing Chile's national parks, where she worked surrounded by samples of the island's endemic species. She had come a few years before with her two boys for a five-day holiday and had never left. Sure, she sometimes missed *la vida intelectual*—the theaters, bookstores, and museums—but there was no crime or pollution here, and plenty of food, if you liked lobster. Her sons loved Isla Crusoe and identified with the children in *Swiss Family Robinson*. "Here, I have time to think, to listen to what is in here," she said, touching her chest.

She led me outside to a bluff overlooking the harbor and pointed to the mist-shrouded mountains. Up there, in an inaccessible valley ringed by sheer walls of rock, the single known wild specimen of a tree growing only on Isla Crusoe clung to life. Several endemic plant species were represented by only a few surviving specimens because the descendants of Selkirk's goats had devoured the rest. This island still had the greatest number of endemic species per square mile of anywhere on earth, 124 on its thirty-six square miles. They made it unique and special, and made Marietta feel special for living on it. As she spoke, I noticed her disconcerting habit, one I noticed among other islanders, of shooting her eyes to the ocean, as if checking for ... well, for what? A steamer on the horizon? A longboat heading for the beach?

She put a finger to her lips. "Shhh . . . listen, and you will hear the birds, and the ocean, and, finally, yourself." Her eyes jumped back to the horizon and she said something I would hear elsewhere, that on a "real" island you could see yourself surrounded by water. She often climbed to Selkirk's lookout because from there, she explained, "I cannot see any people or buildings, just water, everywhere, surrounding me."

Several people insisted that Marcel, the airport manager, was the island's truest reincarnation of Crusoe, or Selkirk. He had come to escape some "problem," perhaps a crime of passion, an unhappy marriage, or debts. He could be temperamental and prickly, or a jolly eccentric. He decided if planes should land by checking the clouds and listening to hear how hard the wind rattled his roof, and he announced the arrival of every flight over the shortwave as if it were a football match, crying "Goal!" after a safe landing.

The most genuine Crusoe/Selkirk, judging by his appearance, was a Frenchman I will call Jean-Paul and whom the islanders nicknamed "El Pescador Furioso" because he fished for hours every day from the wharf. When he first arrived, he had paid for a room at the Villa Green but lived in a pup tent pitched in the plaza. He had since built an A-frame near the shoreline but preferred sleeping in its garden. Woodes Rogers had described Selkirk as "a man cloth'd in goat skins who looked wilder than the first owner of them." Jean-Paul's daily costume was a soiled yellow bathing suit, ripped T-shirt, and silk camouflage scarf draped over an army cap so it covered his face like a veil. His teeth resembled Indian corn, and his sun-ravaged face a peeled tomato. His breath was appalling. He removed his cap and flies circled his pate, but they seldom alighted for long once they smelled what lay below.

His Spanish was more rudimentary than mine and he was pleased to be able to converse in French, so I invited myself to a midmorning beer in his reeking parlor. He started by producing an embossed business card announcing he was a recipient of the Legion of Honor.

Then he marched me through a life history whose high points included incarceration in a North Vietnamese POW camp in 1954, a wound received during the Algerian War, a rewarding friendship with President Omar Bongo of Gabon, and service in several African wars alongside mercenary chieftain Bob Denard. Hanging behind his desk was a glossy photograph of a young paratrooper with the wavy hair and the smooth looks of a matinee idol. It was—*Mon Dieu!*—Jean-Paul, in 1960.

How had that man become this one? And ended up here? Why was a former mercenary hiding out on Crusoe's island? I imagined a tragic love affair, a conscience so guilty it could only find peace four hundred miles off the coast of a country thousands of miles from France, an obsession with islands to match Eric Bailey's. Instead, he was a mama's boy thrown for a loop by his mother's death, someone who had come to an island to recover from a great sadness. While mourning her he came across an article about Isla Crusoe. He reread Defoe's book, flew down from France, bought this waterfront plot, and became a commuting Crusoe, summering here during the French winter, then summering again in France.

I asked why he kept returning, hoping for some soulful meditation on his past as a dog of war.

He shrugged. "It's warm and I like to fish." There it was, the rationale of your average Florida retiree.

I found Irene at the Bahia restaurant. She was sitting on the terrace with her back to the water, drumming her fingers. "You know what I'm thinking now?" she asked. "I'm thinking that maybe this island is *too* quiet for me." (It was a good thing she had not been one of those sailors marooned with a loaded revolver.)

"The quieter the better!" thundered Jorge, the Bahia's legless owner. He had come on his honeymoon in 1962 and been seduced by a place where people nursed sick neighbors and helped raise one another's children. He spat out the word "change" like a piece of bad meat. Like many islanders, he wanted everything, EVERYTHING, to remain the same. He complained about the telephones, not the service but their existence. Like the televisions, they kept people at home, imposing more social isolation on a people who he thought were already isolated enough.

I was thinking maybe Isla Crusoe was too quiet for me, too. One reason for the silence was that every child over the age of twelve left at the end of the Southern Hemisphere summer to spend nine months at a mainland school. This annual trauma, marked by tears and a mournful blast of the steamer's horn, stripped the island of its liveliest members. Another reason was that winter rains closed the airport for several months every year, leaving a monthly supply ship as Isla Crusoe's only link to the mainland, and leaving its people well and truly marooned.

Perhaps Crusoe's shadow fell too darkly on his namesake island. It was a strangely claustrophobic place, empty in the interior but with everyone squeezed into San Juan. I had never been anywhere where people lived so lightly on the land and took up so little psychological space. They were not unfriendly, just living so deeply within themselves that every conversation felt like an interruption, and even when I was among them, I felt alone.

This might have been fine if I had come to Isla Crusoe, like Jean-Paul and the others, to escape some tragedy, or reversal of fortune, or complicated past. If I had needed a dose of mind-numbing sunlight and grief-scouring wind, an island silence capable of smothering memory, a population of natural solitaries, and nothing to remind me of the mainland or my past.

Islands are so self-contained, and even ones within sight of one another so different, they demand comparison. When I land on a new one I weigh it against others I know, asking what it would take to send me seeking refuge on it. Would I make it my home if I had lost everyone I loved? Wanted to escape a loveless marriage, hateful children, an oppressive job? An insoluble moral dilemma, an unforgivable crime? Barren Greek islands are for minor romantic setbacks

and midlife crises. Tropical South Pacific islands are for longer so-
journs and larger calamities: a bankruptcy ruining your closest
friends, a wife falling in love with your brother, a traffic accident
killing a child. But Isla Crusoe was an island where you could disappear forever, one to reserve for the most shattering catastrophe.

■

"Valeria and I are modern Selkirks!" José Maria Gutiérrez announced when I met them on one of my last evenings on the island.
He was a Barbara Cartland hero, with liquid eyes and chiseled features. Valeria had the dark and dangerous beauty of a gypsy queen.
They had arrived five years before, fleeing their upper-middle-class
Buenos Aires roots. He had written the brooding poems about Crusoe and Selkirk I had read on the dock, and she had illustrated them.

Luz's mother, the woman who had come to teach English to the
lobstermen's children, had invited us all to dinner. She lived in one
of the last houses on a steep track leading up from the wharf. Its
exterior looked hammered together by an amateur carpenter. Inside,
some carefully chosen compact discs and paperback editions of great
works filled several bookshelves, proving that this middle-aged divorcée had carefully planned her castaway life. She fetched, cooked, and
provoked conversation with aperçus about literature and music. José
Maria spoke in epigrams, as if casting out lines from his poems. I had
landed in San Juan's literary salon.

I asked him how he had discovered Isla Crusoe.

"First we dreamed it," he said, "then we found it. It's the only
sensible way to find an island, don't you think?"

"It was love at first sight," Valeria added. "We landed at the airport and fell in love." She met my gaze defiantly, challenging me to
point out that the airport occupied the most barren and dispiriting
corner of this island.

Their first job had been managing the airport. For four months
they slept in a tent near the landing strip without running water or

electricity, an existence in some respects harsher than Selkirk had endured in lush and well-watered Puerto Inglés. Her parents assumed they were crazy and hired psychologists and handwriting experts to scrutinize her letters. Her father flew into Isla Crusoe and shared their tent for two days. He went into shock, refused to visit the rest of the island, and was sobbing as he boarded the plane.

She believed they had found Utopia. Everyone was equal and all gave one another whatever was needed. The landscape was pure, "not vandalized," and the waters contained the vidriola, a beautiful fish weighing fifty kilos that swam as gracefully as a shark.

José Maria said, "This island slowly takes over the conscious mind, burying it in its soil." He grinned, daring me to ask for an explanation.

Perhaps he meant that anyone who ever lived here never escaped it. That had certainly happened to Selkirk. Steele reported he "frequently bewailed his return to the world, which could not, he said, with all its enjoyments, restore him to the tranquility of his solitude," and described him as possessing "a certain disregard to the ordinary things about him, as if he had been sunk in thought." Scotland, not Más a Tierra, was the dreamworld for Selkirk, and he dug a cave in his parents' garden, seeking "repose in solitude." In a Borges poem José paraphrased, Selkirk dreamed of the sea and complained about God returning him to "the world of man, mirrors, doors, and names."

José and Valeria agreed that when they went to Buenos Aires to visit their families only their bodies made the journey. Their minds stayed here, "buried in this soil," he said. Isla Crusoe was their reality.

José had been promoted to managing the TARC office in San Juan, a position that made him an expert on the reactions of visitors marooned on Isla Crusoe. Last year a Japanese couple had flown in for a whirlwind day of sightseeing and lobster feasting only to be stranded for two weeks by a series of storms. They had the clothes on their backs, no books, and did not speak a word of Spanish. They became so accustomed to the incessant wind they were soon insisting it had slackened, and demanding to know why the plane was not flying. Even locals became twitchy when the air service was temporarily disrupted, José said. They liked the island's solitude, but liked knowing they could escape it if they wanted. Most of the marooned passengers went through a predictable emotional trajectory. They were furious, then resigned. Finally they relaxed, and "allowed the island to redirect their emotions."

José told them, "You came here to admire nature, and these storms are nature." If that had no effect he added, "Remember that on an island everyone waits for something: for mail, passengers, love . . . and the wisest, they wait for death."

He considered this advice reassuring, but it so unsettled me that when I woke one morning to rattling shutters and reports of a front sweeping north from Patagonia, I set off for Selkirk's lookout, hoping to beat the storm.

The lookout sat in a saddle between the island's wet and dry sides, and Selkirk had climbed to it more than a thousand times, no doubt praying each would be his last. The trail was steep, rising more than fifteen hundred feet in two miles. It wound through tangles of blackberries, dived into tunnels of giant ferns, and switchbacked across a barren slope. I was squishing through bogs one minute, almost blown backwards by wind the next. I hung my boots around my neck and tried walking barefoot, as Selkirk had, but quickly sank into the swampy ground and almost sprained an ankle.

I looked for the one-of-a-kind trees Marietta had promised, but aside from the ferns I saw mostly blackberries and more blackberries and, hopping through them, rabbits and more rabbits. These scourges, introduced by Spanish sailors and mainland colonists centuries before, continued to crowd out native species, condemning more to extinction every year.

Selkirk's lookout was the island's Empire State Building. The views from it were grand and sweeping, perfectly captured by William

Cowper's 1782 poem, "Verses Supposed to Be Written by Alexander Selkirk, During His Solitary Abode in the Island of Juan Fernández":

> *I am monarch of all I survey,*
> *My right there is none to dispute;*
> *From the centre all around to the sea,*
> *I am lord of the fowl and the brute.*

I was monarch of rocky shoreline and jagged mountains, an ocean empty all the way to Australia, and a desert that encouraged the modern castaway nightmare: an astronaut stranded on the moon.

When French novelist Michael Tournier retold the Crusoe story in *Friday*, he called silence the "enforced handmaiden of solitude." Like an Inuit distinguishing between different types of ice, his Crusoe was a "specialist in silence," capable of distinguishing between swampy, airy, and scented silences, and those hard as ebony. The silence of Selkirk's lookout was wind-haunted and lunar, the kind of frightening silence I can imagine enveloping an astronaut whose lifeline has snapped while he is walking in space and who is suddenly sent drifting, the kind I remembered from traveling with Tuareg nomads in the Sahara.

The views from this lookout underlined why an island wilderness is different and more perfect than a continental one. No matter which direction I walked from here, back to San Juan, along the ridge to Puerto Inglés, or down a narrow trail to the airport, I would arrive at the border of another wilderness, the savage sea surrounding Isla Crusoe. In the Sahara, I had known that if I traveled south I would reach the cities in Niger, Benin, and Nigeria. To the north lay Algeria and the Mediterranean; to the west, the Atlantic; to the east, Egypt. Like any continental wilderness, the Sahara was bounded by the civilized world. But this view revealed an island wilderness to be a double one of wild land surrounded by a wild ocean, and I think this, more than anything else, accounts for the combination of despair and exhilaration I feel on wild and remote islands.

I ate a lobster sandwich and decided that for the first time in my life I was sick of lobster. The officers of HMS *Topaz* had erected a plaque in 1868 to honor Selkirk, although he was just the kind of seaman they would have thrown into the brig. Nearby, a certain Gonzalo Morales had carved into a rock: "Thank God for to be here. This place is the Eden." The freshest graffiti celebrated Pearl Jam and Nirvana, proving the Global Village had reached even this end of the earth.

I was told that some islanders believe Selkirk haunts this lookout. Perhaps they were spooked by the wind whistling through the grass, the same sound that had convinced Selkirk monsters inhabited Más a Tierra's interior. For me, it was more haunted by the people who had come searching for his spirit, and particularly by Richard Halliburton, who had climbed here every day for a month hoping to commune with his ghost.

Halliburton was an adventurer and household name of the 1920s whose stunts made him the hero of millions of adolescent boys and the heartthrob of millions of flappers, who never suspected that the man they called "Handsome Halliburton" was a closeted homosexual. He had swum the length of the Panama Canal, flown across the Sahara in a biplane, plunged seventy feet into the Well of Death at Chichén Itzá, and spent two weeks on Tobago, where he grew a beard, wore britches sewed from goatskins, and recruited a native he dubbed "Toosday" to play Friday. He stayed on Más a Tierra for a month, but it merited only five sour pages in his book and he left grousing about "the overvaluation of solitude." He was obviously a poor candidate for Isla Crusoe and islands like it, uncomfortable in his own skin, uninterested in listening to himself or allowing the island to redirect his emotions, and no doubt spooked by this silence.

It was as impossible to visit Selkirk's lookout without wondering what kind of castaway you would have been as to stand on the bluffs overlooking Omaha Beach without wondering if you were brave enough to have scaled them. I decided I could have met the physical challenges of clubbing seals, chasing goats, hiking this trail, and lighting signal fires. But could I have made myself climb here every day, and hope?

How could I, how could anyone, know? Being marooned on an uninhabited and unvisited island outside the polar circles, and remaining undetected and unrescued for Crusoe's twenty-eight years, or Selkirk's four, is no longer possible. Castaway records are not like four-minute miles, records begging to be broken, and islands like this one have become places where people come to find, or lose, themselves.

■

When I stopped in the TARC office on my return to San Juan, José Maria said the weather forecast was bad and only one seat remained on tomorrow's flight. After that, it could be days before there was another plane.

Irene sat on the porch of her guest house, staring at the horizon. "I guess this island is okay for a few days," she said. "But that's all. My children, my nieces, nephews, they are what really matters. Even if this island *was* paradise I could never live on it."

But what gave her the idea it *would* be paradise? Perhaps she had arrived on the island carrying *two* Crusoes on her back: the original one, and a modern Crusoe that reflects our own times more than Defoe's creation. In the eighteenth and early nineteenth centuries, this changeable Crusoe had been an imperial adventurer, converting Friday and bringing civilization to the tropics. In the late nineteenth century, he had become the Industrial Revolution's self-made man, marking his progress by what he manufactured from nature's ingredients. In the late twentieth century, this self-reliant Crusoe fell from favor. When I ran an Internet search for Robinson Crusoe, most of the hits were for resorts and hotels. In Tortola, the Long Bay Beach Resort's air-conditioned, cable TV–equipped cabanas were said to appeal to "the Robinson Crusoe instinct," and a Grand Turk hotel offered a special Robinson Crusoe Day, including a parasol, a deluxe hamper of food, and "oodles of clean towels." Irene had come expecting the island of the sybaritic late-twentieth-century Crusoe, not a seventeenth-century castaway island where you confined your wants to the natural necessities and heard yourself instead of the hum of an air conditioner.

Had I been escaping a tragedy or searching for solitude, I might have considered Isla Crusoe paradise, and buried my conscious mind on it. It was comforting to know that it was as Dana and Slocum described it, an island refuge that was "simplicity itself." It would probably stay that way. It was too remote for an artists' colony, too hilly for a golf course, too wild and beach-poor for a resort.

Dana had believed Más a Tierra's "particular charm" came from its geographic isolation and associations with the Crusoe story, but I liked it that Island Zero, the island more responsible than any other for launching islomania, might be the last one where, after the others were submerged, bridged, or turned into resorts, you could still listen to yourself and enjoy a life almost as solitary and silent as Crusoe's, surrounded by a people caring so little for the mainland that the thought of it drove them to tears. But when I imagined staying on the island much longer, I saw the wind-buffeted Japanese in their flimsy raincoats, and myself dining alone in the Villa Green on lobster and more lobster, pacing the plaza, rationing myself to fifty pages a day of my dwindling supply of books, sharing midmorning beers with Jean-Paul, and initiating conversations with people who would rather avoid them. After considering what I would miss, a journey to Chiloé, an island on the edge of Patagonia, and my daughters' school holidays, I booked the last seat on the next day's flight.

The trip to the airport was funereal. The other passengers were locals morose at the prospect of being marooned on the mainland. Three lobstermen played with hand-held video games as their catch beat against the sides of cardboard boxes. A pregnant teenager flying to Santiago to give birth wept, vomited, and clutched at her husband.

As we climbed into the plane, Marcel shook our hands and shouted, "Bon voyage!" As the plane took off, the prospective father ran alongside, waving his arms and weeping. The lobstermen fell silent and craned their necks for a last glimpse of home. One man cried.

Back in Santiago I experienced the same tenderness and inability to decide which was the dream, the island or the mainland, that follows my departure from remote islands. But my Isla Crusoe culture lag was milder and shorter than usual. José and Valeria had found their soul-mate island, so their trip to Buenos Aires had been the dream. I did not need an island as remote and silent as Isla Crusoe, not yet, so it became the dream, and Santiago's world of "man, mirrors, doors, and names" the reality.

2

SPICE ISLAND — BANDA NEIRA

When I saw the Bandas of eastern Indonesia I understood what José Maria meant about dreaming an island first. Isla Crusoe had a nightmare landscape of razorback ridges, jagged rocks, and black mountains. The Bandas were fragments of lush and extravagant island dreams: palms growing close as a hedge, a Mount Fuji–shaped volcano, a town of crumbling Portuguese forts and Dutch mansions with verandas shaded so deeply they seemed underwater. The colors were so brilliant my eyes ached, the lagoon so smooth I could imagine skating across it, the forests dense enough to hide tigers.

The Bandas appear to be the archetypal island paradise because that is what they are: the Spice islands that sent Columbus sailing west and Magellan circling the globe, the first tropical islands to mesmerize Europe. We expect tropical islands to be mountainous, perfumed, and fertile and to have smoking volcanoes, reefs teeming with rainbow fish, and Garden of Eden foliage because that is what European explorers found in the Bandas and other islands in the Moluccas, and described in their diaries, depicted in their sketches, and buried in our dreams.

The nine Bandas are so small most world maps show their name but not their shape. But they were once the most valuable islands on earth because of a black seed at the heart of a lemon-colored fruit growing on a feathery-leafed tree found nowhere else. This seed, nutmeg, has not always been a minor ingredient in pumpkin pie, Vicks VapoRub, and aftershave. During the Middle Ages it was a hallucinogen, aphrodisiac, cure for dysentery, and sleeping potion (Bandanese still rub it on their eyelids), and more useful and valuable than gold. Like cocaine, it provided stupendous profits for its middlemen, selling in Europe in the fifteenth century for as much as sixty thousand times its cost in the Bandas. It was one of the spices luring Portuguese navigators to sail around Africa. In 1512, a Portuguese captain, Antonio de Abreu, became the first European to visit the Bandas. The spice trade that sprang up following his arrival is credited with launching the modern banking system, plantation-style colonialism, and the multinational corporation. It can also be argued that without the profits from Bandanese nutmeg, and cloves and cinnamon from nearby Ternate and Tidore, there would have been no European Renaissance, and no Rembrandt.

Of all the Spice islands I chose the Bandas after reading about Des Alwi, a Bandanese from one of these islands' Arab trading families. I was intrigued by Alwi's devotion to the Bandas and suspected he was another man intoxicated by islands. In 1930, the Dutch authorities in Batavia (now Jakarta) had banished two prominent nationalists, Mohammad Hatta and Sutan Sjarhir, to Banda Neira, where they became mentors and tutors to Alwi and the other grandchildren of Said Abdullah Baadilla, patriarch of the Arab community. On January 31, 1942, hours before Japanese forces were to occupy the Bandas, a U.S. Navy seaplane evacuated Hatta and Sjarhir because the Dutch authorities hoped they would persuade the Javanese to resist a Japanese invasion. Six months later, Alwi hitchhiked to Batavia on a freighter, joining Hatta and Sjarhir as an aide and confidant. After the war he became a freedom fighter, filmmaker, and member of Indonesia's political, business, and cultural elite. He returned to the Bandas for the first time in 1967 and immediately

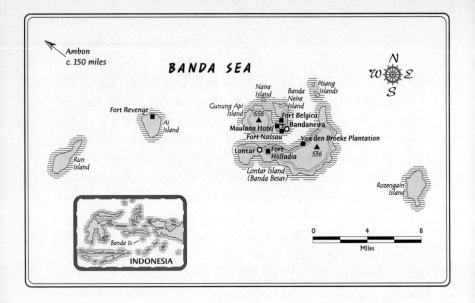

launched a campaign to revive their culture and economy, becoming the kind of Big Man who often dominates a small island and is known as its "king," "emperor," or, in Alwi's case, "rajah."

The moment I landed on Banda Neira, the principal island of the chain, I could see that its charms were unlike those of Isla Crusoe. It had a lively little town whose chatty people would never let a newcomer vanish, and it was a place for embracing life rather than escaping it. Neira was no longer the grand stage it had once been, but its hulking forts and planters' mansions gave it the faded glory of a European spa and provided the illusion that it was still an island worth possessing.

I stayed at the Maulana, a sprawling two-story pink-and-cream stucco hotel with high ceilings and gardens that Des Alwi had designed and built. It had a lovely situation, facing the harbor and Gunung Api, a volcano floating on its own island across a strait. With its Moorish arches, tiled patios, chattering parrots, and Portuguese cannon it could have been the residence of a Dutch governor general, or the palace of a rajah.

Des Alwi, I learned, would arrive from Jakarta a week later than planned. I spent the next week living in his shadow. Every day, I passed several hours listening to the ferociously bright Tamalia Alisjahbana explaining in her Oxbridge-accented English how "Uncle Des," the father of one of her close friends, had restored the mansions of the "perkeniers," or Dutch planters, and was replanting nutmeg on the islands' abandoned plantations. He had persuaded the government to inaugurate a regular ferry service, extend the airstrip, and assign a full-time physician to the islands. He had revived the traditional Korakora canoe races and Cakalele dances, attracted Jacques Cousteau, Sarah Ferguson, the duchess of York, and Mick Jagger to his hotel, calmed rioters marching on the police station, and discovered a coral, which was named *Acrapora des alwi* in his honor.

Tamalia was a graduate of Cambridge, secretary of the Oxford-Cambridge Society of Indonesia, and a publisher of English-language books in Jakarta. Her late father, a philosopher and linguist, had invented the modern Indonesian language and had been an islomane who liked touring islands near Jakarta with his children on weekends, all the while searching for the perfect one. She had inherited his love of islands. She kept a jar of Bandanese soil on her Jakarta mantelpiece and spent several months every year on Banda Neira, collecting material for a book she was writing about the Bandas and renovating a perkenier mansion.

She showed me this mansion at twilight. It had a walled garden, strangler figs, and a veranda facing the street. Bats screeched and fluttered through its vast rooms. She was staying at the Maulana for now, she said, but had installed new windows and doors and would soon be buying a bed so she could sleep in one of these vaultlike chambers. "No one really wants to be alone, Thurston," she whispered, reading my mind. "But this island and this house . . . they are my dream. My brothers and sisters are strong personalities, and a friend told me I could only escape them and be free if I found my own island, and now I've discovered that's true."

Her BBC diction, huge eyes, and Audrey Hepburn cheekbones,

along with her interest in art, botany, history, and archeology, made it easier to see her impressing the smart set in a London drawing room than renovating a bat-plagued mansion on Banda Neira. But here she was, setting out every morning in a flowery garden-party dress, shielding her delicate features from the sun with a purple umbrella, and returning with plant cuttings, blossoms, Dutch musket balls, and shards of nineteenth-century bottles, which she arranged into a still life and sketched. Matriarchs brought recipes for her Bandanese cookbook and wheezy old men shuffled to her table so she could mine their memories for stories. She told me that research for her book had taken her to American libraries, where the pages of eighteenth-century Dutch histories of the Bandas remained uncut, and to The Hague, where elderly Dutch widows also kept jars of Bandanese soil on their mantelpieces. They ground nutmeg onto their Brussels sprouts and teared at the smell of jasmine because when they had been little girls—"little princesses"—their Bandanese maids folded its fragrant flowers into their laundry.

After a week on the Bandas, I understood why memories of them could elicit tears.

Evil seemed to have been tapped and drained from these islands. They had no polluting refineries, poisonous snakes, or kamikaze cab-drivers, no Jet Skis buzzing across their harbors or chain saws echoing through their interiors, no brutal-looking soldiers or Tonton Macoute policemen, at least that I saw. A few satellite dishes rose over the low skyline, but in contrast to Isla Crusoe, most people spent the evenings outside, singing, gossiping, and playing games.

Because there were fewer than a dozen cars you heard the tinkle of trishaw bells instead of horns and dragging mufflers. No Bandanese worked more than a few hours a day, but considerable effort went into gossip, relationships, and keeping the streets clean. Children, uninterested in competitive sports, launched paper kites from overgrown soccer fields. The only criminals lived in a whitewashed prison twinkling with fairy lights that was the dream destination of every Indonesian convict. Its inmates had become *ex officio* members of the community, permitted to lounge on the grass outside, smoking and exchanging pleasantries with passersby.

The word "timeless" (much as I dislike it) reappeared in my notebooks and thoughts. The dreamy Bandanese really did live in an open-air museum of nineteenth-century mansions and seventeenth-century forts. Dutch cannon lay along roadsides and served as bollards on the piers. The ruins of Fort Nassau had become a popular shortcut, playground, and venue for drying laundry. At the mouth of the harbor was the Knorpel Cliff, called that because "knorpel" is the Dutch word for "club" and Dutch soldiers participating in a 1621 massacre had swung clubs to drive the Bandanese off its edge. The most widely available map of the islands was a nineteenth-century one showing the names and boundaries of long-vanished Dutch plantations. A World War II bombardment had frozen the clock on the steeple of the Dutch church. Inside, nine clocks from different centuries offered different versions of the hour and a deacon with parchment skin showed me a 1635 chalice and records of the congregation in 1691, then sold me a commemorative T-shirt that misspelled "church" as "ghurch." At Fort Hollandia, a boy laid down his guitar to offer me a 1729 coin he had found on the grounds. At Fort Revenge, Tamalia's umbrella tip unearthed a shard of china she dismissed as "only nineteenth century." Her favorite scavenging ground, the beach in front of the former Dutch governor's mansion, yielded guilders and musket balls. One of the windowpanes of this mansion carried a suicide note a Dutch civil servant had scratched with his ring stone in 1831. It read: "When will my happiness return? When will the bells toll the hour of my return, to the shores of my country, and the heart of my family, whom I love and bless?" He had fixed a flourishing signature to this and hanged himself. This story, of a man too homesick to bear living on such a beautiful island, remained so well known on Banda Neira that people debated if he was still wriggling when they cut him down.

The Bandanese were great preservers of their relics. In 1935, a local foundation collected enough money to pay for either Banda Neira's electrification or the reconstruction of Fort Belgica. The islanders voted for the fort. After dark, men strummed guitars and sang slushy love songs influenced by the fados of sixteenth-century Portuguese sailors. Some Cakalele dancers wore helmets belonging to the original Portuguese garrison, while others waved bamboo poles flying white rags symbolizing the strips of cloth Japanese mercenaries tied to the necks of Bandanese leaders before beheading them during the 1621 massacre. Until 1900, the dancers had waved the original bloodstained cloths.

This famous massacre was evidence that island histories have their own peculiar rhythms. On continents, economic and political changes evolve over decades; on islands, a ship appears on the horizon, a seaplane lands in a harbor, a European explorer arrives, and a single day changes everything forever.

The Bandas have experienced at least two such days. One occurred on February 7, 1796, when the Dutch garrison surrendered to a British naval force during the Napoleonic Wars and British agents began shipping nutmeg seedlings to Ceylon, Malaya, the West Indies, and Singapore, shattering the Bandanese monopoly and turning the most valuable islands on earth into backwaters.

The other date was February 27, 1621, when the great empire builder of the Dutch East Indies Company, Jan Pieterszoon Coen, sailed into Banda Neira's harbor with the largest fleet of warships yet assembled in Asian waters.

I had heard about Coen during a college course in Southeast Asian history taught by Professor Harry Benda, whose precise, scholarly descriptions of Dutch barbarities had considerable moral weight because he himself had spent three years in a Japanese prison camp in Indonesia. At the end of term, he invited us to choose the most brutal colonial power and we voted overwhelmingly for the Dutch, whose atrocities were so appalling because, like King Leopold's in the

Congo, they had been prompted by commercial calculations. Millions of Indonesians perished due to the nineteenth-century Dutch "culture system" that transformed the island of Java into a gigantic slave plantation producing export crops. But for a single example of genocide in the service of commerce, Coen's reign of terror in the Bandas remains unequaled.

In 1602, a Dutch admiral had bamboozled the Bandanese into signing a treaty giving the Dutch East Indies Company (known by its Dutch acronym, VOC) a monopoly on the purchase of nutmeg. The Bandanese quickly came to detest the Dutch, who offered poor-quality trade goods and nonnegotiable prices. The Dutch considered the Bandanese lazy savages. Coen arrived nearly two decades later, determined to make the Dutch stranglehold on nutmeg more profitable by eliminating the difficult Bandanese. When a lamp crashed to the ground in a mosque where Dutch officers were billeted, he claimed it had been a signal to stage a revolt and ordered his troops to arrest the Bandanese leaders, raze native villages, and drive their inhabitants into the bush or ship them to Java as slaves. Thousands of Bandanese died of starvation or leaped from cliffs to avoid capture. On May 8, 1621, Coen's soldiers herded the most prominent captives into a bamboo enclosure outside Fort Nassau, where Japanese mercenaries beheaded them. The Bandanese died silently, except for one man who said in Dutch, "Sirs, have you then no mercy?" A Dutch officer witnessing the massacre was so appalled he circulated a letter of protest in the Netherlands.

One of the frightening aspects of Coen's campaign was how easily it was accomplished. The same features that make small islands so appealing, their size and isolation, also make them excellent killing grounds. The targets of an island pogrom cannot escape to a neutral Switzerland or hide out in mountains. This is why President Francisco Macías Nguema of the West African nation of Equatorial Guinea could murder or exile roughly half the population of the island of Fernando Po during the 1970s and why Coen halved the

Bandas' population to 7,500 in a few weeks, leaving only women and children, and the inhabitants of the tiny British-held island of Run.

As a result of Coen's "ethnic cleansing," the Bandas became one of the most polyglot islands on earth, inhabited by the descendants of Dutch planters, Papuan and Timorese slaves, Javanese convicts, Chinese coolies, Bandanese survivors, and Arab merchant families like the Baadillas. No one I met better symbolized this heterogeneous population than "Benny" van den Broeke, the last of the Dutch planters.

I hear "planter" and think of men in topees and high leather boots living in sprawling wooden houses far up a river or in a jungle clearing, surrounded by rubber trees and restless coolies. But the nineteenth-century perkeniers of the Bandas were an urbane and pampered lot who preferred gin at the club to the solitude of the bush. They or their ancestors had been VOC managers who wrested ownership of the plantations from the company in the early decades of the seventeenth century, borrowed against their land at usurious rates, and built mansions in Neira town, where they competed to mount the most elaborate family crest over their doors, acquire the best crystal, marble, and European furniture, and feast at the longest tables. They bought carriages to carry them a few hundred yards to church, ate gargantuan midday meals, and spent the afternoon dozing and rocking on verandas, smoking pipes, drinking Bols, and perspiring into powdered wigs, while on Banda Besar slaves and contract laborers picked nutmeg. The planters seldom spent a night on their plantations, where they risked being murdered in their sleep by resentful slaves, and by the end of the century three out of four had lost their plantations to Chinese creditors, proving how tricky and dangerous it can be to import mainland fashions and dreams to a remote island.

The van den Broekes, however, held on until Indonesia's independence in 1949, when the Sukarno regime nationalized nutmeg and delivered the Bandanese groves into the hands of government agencies whose corruption, indifference, and misguided policies have led to the abandonment of thousands of acres of trees once heavy with what Des Alwi called "the Queen of Fruits."

Benny van den Broeke and Des Alwi had been boyhood friends; they now enjoyed a somewhat complicated relationship. Alwi had pulled strings in Jakarta so the van den Broekes could reclaim a twelve-and-a-half-acre rump of their former plantation, and he continued supporting them with gifts and loans. Tamalia said Alwi liked having a descendant of a perkenier family whose holdings dated from 1623 living on Besar for the same reason he had revived the Cakalele dances and Korakora canoe races: because he loved Bandanese history and wanted to preserve it.

After hearing repeatedly how Benny van den Broeke was "our last Dutchman" and "last perkenier," I crossed the strait separating Neira from Banda Besar expecting an elderly white in a rumpled white suit. Instead, the final product of five centuries of Dutch atrocities and nutmeg-grabbing was a creaky, nut-brown old man with long cannibal teeth and a thick mustache, a mummified Nasser. When I arrived, he was puttering around his garden in a filthy bathing suit and Wellingtons, complaining about how squatters from Ambon were poaching his nutmeg out of season. They damaged the trees and left them oozing a red sap resembling blood, he said. This never would have happened under the Dutch, who had sentenced the poachers to a day in jail for every premature nutmeg. "These squatters are Javanese and not high class," he sniffed. "They resent me for still being here, and owning this plantation."

It was not much of a plantation. A parlor wall had collapsed, so I could look out to a Dutch cannon, the van den Broekes' backyard graves, and some tangled and wild rose bushes brought from Holland centuries before.

This word, "before," a favorite one of Europeans or Eurasians who have stayed on, punctuated his sentences. "Before," his family had employed hundreds of laborers, owned two plantations, and built a mansion in Neira. "Before," their plantation had produced more nutmeg than any other. "Before," its nutmeg had been the best because they dried it over fires rather than laying it in the sun.

We sat at a table covered by a faded cloth patterned with Dutch windmills, drinking lime juice and water from cups with plastic lids to repel the flies and eating squares of stale chocolate sent from the Netherlands by a distant relation. Chickens wandered through the room as I leafed through a guest book filled with perkenier descendants who had come searching for their roots, and listened as van den Broeke struggled to find similarities between a visit from Prince Bernhard of the Netherlands in 1991 and the seventeenth-century exploits of Pieter van den Broeke. He had hung reproductions of a famous painting of this ancestor in his parlor and bedroom, presumably so he could eat and sleep under the gaze of a man he called "the Noted Merchant-Adventurer." Pieter van den Broeke had a satyr's leer and mussed-up hair, as if a courtesan had just run her fingers through it after an encounter that would result in the darkening of the family skin. I wondered what his expression would have been if he could have seen his descendant, dark as a slave, wearing a Swiss-cheese T-shirt, and dependent on the charity of an Arab trader.

Benny van den Broeke had the Eurasian's customary obsession with race. Did I know, he whispered, that Suharto was Chinese, Sukarno had Dutch blood, and Tamalia was part German? His visitors often remarked on his Flemish features and if I moved a little closer, and looked a little harder . . . why, I would see Antwerp in his face. He was proud his father was the only Bandanese perkenier to take Indonesian citizenship. Not that it mattered. Sukarno confiscated their plantation anyway, and their name made them a target. His current holdings were too small to provide a living, so he depended on his children, and Des Alwi.

I bought a bag of nutmeg for forty cents, the only charity he tolerated from visitors. His last words were, "Tell Des Alwi I am waiting for him."

My excursions with Tamalia had a dated atmosphere of leisure and privilege. We frequently took the Maulana launch to an outer island where Tamalia read under an umbrella while I snorkeled in the blueberry water. (Elsewhere in Southeast Asia, souvenir hunters, divers, and fishermen have damaged the reefs with dynamite and cyanide, but the Bandanese understood the dangers of overfishing. Des Alwi, who monopolized the dive business, enforced stringent regulations to protect the waters surrounding these islands, and marine biologists have pronounced the Bandanese reefs healthier than Australia's Great Barrier Reef.) At noon, the boatman spread cloths and set up folding chairs on the sand and we ate rice and curried snapper with mustard greens and green bananas, served on good china. Children sat around us in circles and men from nearby villages opened coconuts.

On Run, an island the Dutch traded to the British for Manhattan at the 1667 Treaty of Breda, I asked everyone if they would rather be living in Manhattan. Run was tidy and prosperous, with wood-and-coral houses surrounded by picket fences, flowers, and satellite dishes sometimes pulling in images of Manhattan. Its wealth was based on trade instead of nutmeg, although some women dried small quantities of nutmeg and sold them for pin money. Everyone considered the Run-for-Manhattan trade a hoot and no one wanted to live in Manhattan (although I bet some Manhattanites would happily move to Run).

Everywhere we went Tamalia introduced me to people grateful for what Des Alwi had done, and praying he would do more. We drank coconut milk with a widow who boasted her husband had once given him piggyback rides, and who put her hand to her heart whenever his name was mentioned. We walked across Neira to Mang Koba, a village where people lived in the barracks of an abandoned plantation. In a room lined with mirrored Dutch cabinets a monkey-sized man blamed the decline of nutmeg on Japanese occupiers who refused to pay for the nuts. This had forced people to clear nutmeg and plant cassava root to eat. There had never been a "good time" in Mang Koba during his lifetime, he said, but that might change when Des Alwi revived its nutmeg groves.

"When is Des Alwi coming?" he asked.

"Be patient," Tamalia replied. "He is coming by boat and he'll arrive on Thursday."

As we left, she whispered, "Poor Uncle Des, he can only do so much. These islands are a black hole for his money. Sometimes I wonder why he does it."

■

By 10:00 A.M. the traditional headmen, or "rajahs," of the Bandas started gathering on the waterfront patio of the Maulana Hotel to welcome home Des Alwi. By noon they were fingering worry beads and allowing their cigarettes to burn to ash unsmoked as they fastened their eyes on the harbor's opening, where the launch bringing Alwi to Banda Neira should have appeared. The barman and desk clerk paced the second floor balcony, past the Spartan rooms where Mick Jagger and the Duchess of York had sat knees to chin in the half-sized tubs, douching themselves with lukewarm water. The kitchen ladies, usually as playful and noisy as parrots, huddled on the sea wall, hugging themselves and rubbing away imaginary goosebumps, chilled by what it might mean for them, this hotel, and these islands if Alwi was lost at sea.

Everyone knew he had flown into Ambon at 2:00 A.M., and that Maulana's Dutch diving instructor had met him with the hotel launch. The 125-mile journey across the Banda Sea should have taken six hours, but a freak storm had raged all night, carpeting the ground with blossoms and palm fronds and stirring the most protected harbor in the East Indies into a cauldron of whitecaps. Last year, a similar boat had disappeared with all hands. If Alwi did not arrive by dark, he would run out of gas and drift.

At 2:00 P.M. a rescue boat, low in the water with too many people, set off for an uninhabited island where someone would climb a communications tower and scan the ocean with binoculars. At 3:00 P.M. Tamalia said, "It would be terrible for the Bandas if anything happened to Uncle Des," and disappeared into the office to call the governor and military commander at Ambon and demand they mount a search.

In town, young men watched the harbor from the crenellations of the Portuguese fort. Even the market ladies had turned from their piles of fish so they could face the water. The hush was the historic, holding-your-breath kind I imagine preceding the arrival of Allied troops in Paris.

A faint internal voice suggested that if Alwi *was* lost at sea, I would be left with the easier job of writing a hagiography rather than searching for the hubris, power-hunger, and *folie de grandeur* characteristic of the Big Man on the Small Island. But just as the sun was poised for its guillotine-speed equatorial descent, two boats appeared. Binoculars moved from hand to hand and a cheer rose from the patio. The crewmen of the rescue boat pumped their fists in the air. Des Alwi sat erect on a wicker chair in the second launch, acknowledging the applause with an exhausted wave.

I recognized the hooded eyes, mocha skin, and leonine head from his photograph. But I had not expected such a youthful seventy-year-old. Gray had barely flecked his shoulder-length hair, and he had the ripe, heavyweight good looks of Elvis in his middle years.

He stumbled up the stairs from the dock carrying a liter of Campari and two spiky durian fruits tied in blue ribbon. "Waves like mountains!" he shouted. "It was terrifying! Terrifying!"

He had suffered thirteen hours in an open boat, sleepless, wet, and seasick, but each embrace revived him. "Look what we caught!" he cried. Behind him two men were struggling a huge wahoo into the kitchen. He clapped his hands. "It's worth enough to pay for the whole trip. Sashimi for everyone!"

He showered, drained a whisky, read a fistful of faxes, listened to supplicants, and devoured a mound of raw wahoo. Then he slapped a thick Dutch history of the Bandas onto the table and read me an excerpt from the 1512 diary of a Portuguese navigator that went, "We arrived at the beautiful paradise of spices after two months and to my surprise the Moors had gotten here first."

He exclaimed, "Those Moors were my ancestors!" and led me through a family history filled with Javanese princesses, Japanese samurai, Chinese officers staying behind after the Ming dynasty attacked Batavia, and a grandfather who traded in mother-of-pearl, traveled to Europe on the Trans-Siberian Railway, and entertained the famed naturalist Alfred Russel Wallace in the Baadilla family museum—which, by the way, Alwi himself was restoring to its former glory.

On paper, Des Alwi can sound like a monster of ego.

During our first evening he boasted of being Indonesia's first documentary filmmaker, delivered a monologue on his role in the independence movement, and raised a pant leg to reveal the scar of a shrapnel wound he had received during the Battle of Surabaya. He described the perkenier mansions he had restored, the ceremonies surrounding the naming of the *Acrapora des alwi*, and his search for Bandanese who remembered the traditional songs sung at the Korakora races. When he had returned in the 1960s, houses in the Bandas were collapsing, its culture was dying, and its young people were leaving, he said. There was no airstrip or ferry. You could not find a single plate or glass on Banda Besar, so people drank from coconut shells. "Imagine!" He leaned across the table, a man imparting a secret. "Had I not returned, there would be nothing here. Nothing!"

He asked if I wanted to know the secret of his success. It was money—"My money! Because I refuse to depend on anyone else."

Was there anything else?

"Power! I have too much of it . . . luckily!"

But listen to Alwi deliver these words with his effortless charm and self-deprecating humor, and listen to him while sitting on the patio of his hotel, with its Arabian Nights arches and thick pink walls, parrots swinging on perches, Portuguese cannons pointed seaward, palms reaching to the second floor, and views of Gunung Api's volcano, and you, too, would be seduced before you chopsticked up the last slice of his wahoo.

He even succeeded in breaking the first rule of charm: that whoever thinks he has it usually does not. "Want to hear how I'm the first guy on the Bandas to use charm to get the Dutch to surrender?" he asked. During a visit from Prince Bernhard of the Netherlands, he had arranged for a traditional healer to cure the Prince's nagging backache. When Bernhard insisted on giving him a present in return, he asked for the flag from his yacht. Bernhard protested that this was a traditional signal of capitulation, but just before departing, he pressed a parcel into Alwi's hands. Inside was the flag of the House of Orange.

One guidebook to Indonesia referred to Alwi as "the self-crowned king of the Bandas" and accused him of trying to corner its minuscule tourist business. I had seen evidence of this when I tried to engage the owner of a neighboring inn as a guide. The man had shook his head and stepped back as if I were offering a poisoned apple. He insisted I hire someone recommended by the Maulana, explaining that Des Alwi disliked his guests taking meals or hiring guides elsewhere, and had once suspended his diving privileges, a harsh penalty on an island where Alwi owned the only dive shop.

I came down to breakfast determined to resist his charm and find proof that it is unhealthy for one man to hold such sway over a small island. But I was immediately disarmed to learn that he had slept in the smallest and darkest ground-floor room of his own hotel, and had dressed in tie-dyed blue jeans and a faded pink T-shirt, like an old hippie on the skids.

He looked up from his breakfast to see a party of Frenchmen unloading spear guns at a nearby pier. He leaped up, and moments later the Maulana's diving instructor was standing over them, explaining that Des Alwi prohibited spearfishing and would refuse to fill their tanks unless they kept their guns in storage. It was another example of how he fortunately had too much power.

Alwi interrupted his breakfast again to distribute medicine from Jakarta, give an interview to a radio station over a portable phone, and arrange a meeting with the island rajahs to plan next week's Korakora races. A fax arrived confirming a deal he had been negotiating for months with the government for the nutmeg groves. It provided that the state government would split the profits between a farmers' cooperative and a charitable foundation controlled by Alwi.

I asked him about tourism, expecting some master plan for turning the Bandas into one of those places that after a flash of jet-set popularity become an assembly-line resort rewarding the Mr. Big who has engineered their discovery and cornered their choicest real estate. But instead of rolling out blueprints for pedalo docks he spoke of restoring the former Dutch governor's mansion and turning it into a museum, and providing favorable leases to anyone willing to repair one of his wounded perkenier mansions. He had commissioned a study that concluded that the islands' ecosystem and culture could sustain only 250 hotel rooms. "I already have eighty," he announced. "Enough. No more rooms for Des Alwi."

He opposed any scheduled jet service because he feared it would encourage the Bali-type beach hotels and backpacker flophouses that would destroy the Bandas' culture and environment. He kept some of the best stretches of reef a secret, even from his guests. "My philosophy," he said, "is, 'Better to let people work hard to get to the Bandas.' "

When I first heard of Alwi's efforts to revive the Cakalele dances and Korakora races I suspected him of wanting to use them simply to fill his hotel rooms. But it turned out he was so determined that the revival of Bandanese culture be genuine that he had mounted a worldwide search for elderly men who recalled the Kabata, traditional war songs sung by the crews of canoes at various sacred sites as they traveled to Neira town for the competition. There was an urgency to his search because the songs and races had been outlawed by the Japanese, and had not been resumed after the war. If Alwi failed to revive the tradition before the prewar generation died, it might be lost forever. He had finally tracked down a man in the Netherlands who knew the song of a small village on Banda Besar, and only then, for the first time in fifty years, could its people enter a canoe.

After breakfast, we piled into his Land Cruiser for a stately ten-mile-an-hour tour of his perkenier mansions. I was in the Big Man's entourage. People waved and clapped. Children shouted, "Des Alwi!" He took notes, made promises, and worked the crowds.

He insisted that Neira had the finest stock of colonial mansions in the East Indies and was "a potential Williamsburg of the tropics." On Caribbean islands, houses like these had become small inns and restaurants; here, government functionaries from other islands had stripped them, selling their furnishings and fixtures. The Banda Culture and Heritage Foundation, of which he was president and chief contributor, had bought and repaired twenty-two mansions. He offered twenty-eight years rent free to anyone willing to renovate one, and he was operating several as holiday rentals, "so the Dutch can return and feel like colonial masters," he said.

We drove past a splendid mansion that a Krupp from the German industrialist family had leased, then past others where mango and banana trees grew through ruined ceilings. We walked through one where his workers were replastering walls, installing ceilings of woven mats, and clearing the garden. For the sake of history, Alwi said, he would preserve the pink flowers because they were the last wild spawn of a perkenier tulip bed.

I admired his renovations, but I found Banda Neira's mansions cold and severe—and, let's face it, very Dutch. I was happier to be at the airy Maulana, instead of being a vacationing Krupp padding through these echoing rooms and reclining under mango trees heavy with bats, encircled by high walls meant to discourage murderous slaves.

Alwi was proudest of his museums. He had installed chandeliers and a tile floor in the former governor's mansion, now a museum of Bandanese history. He had filled his great-grandfather's house with family heirlooms and sepia photographs of generations of Baadillas. Another Alwi museum was devoted solely to the British occupation of the islands during the Napoleonic wars. We lingered the longest in a house next to the prison where his mentors, Mohammad Hatta and Sutan Sjarhir, once lived in exile. It was his most successful museum and contained the desk on which Hatta had signed Indonesia's declaration of independence, the suit he wore to a roundtable conference with the Dutch, his typewriter, and numerous personal effects. A photograph showed Hatta and Alwi together in 1980, when Hatta had returned for the last time. A 1936 photograph showed them together when Alwi was nine and came here for lessons after attending the Dutch school. He and Sjarhir and Hatta's other young protégés had also slept in the compound, and these rooms, too, were part of his museum.

Alwi took a seat behind his boyhood desk and ran his fingers over its surface. He could remember where Hatta had stood and the political meetings he began attending at age ten, "as if it was yesterday."

We ate lunch back at the Maulana. As platters of fried taro sticks and curried fish with a kanari nut sauce appeared, Alwi clapped his hands and boomed, "Everything, everything is local!"

Afterwards, he drove me to Banda Besar island in his speedboat so I could admire his nutmeg groves. If I had thought about nutmeg at all before the Bandas, it was as a garnish for rum punch or the secret ingredient in my mother's tuna salad. (Try it, it's good.) It seemed incredible that these brown nuts had been valuable enough to send Columbus sailing west and to persuade the Dutch to trade Manhattan for an island smaller than Central Park, that something once so prized could become so cheap. At independence, the Bandas had 500,000 productive nutmeg trees. After a half century of government ownership, only 60,000 remained. The national government owned the land and the provincial government, based in Ambon, owned the trees. Both had abandoned the groves to freelance pickers and squatters who cut down nutmegs and planted subsistence crops. Alwi said only six old men knew how to cultivate seedlings, and unless his plan to plant new groves succeeded, nutmeg might someday vanish from these islands.

On Besar, we tramped up steep hillsides and into groves where the spongy earth and dense air reminded me of California's redwood groves. An umbrella of giant kanari trees filtered the light, giving it a grainy texture. The trees had fan-shaped bases and gnarled white trunks, like trees in a Disney cartoon that have faces and break into song. The nutmegs were symmetrical, Garden of Eden trees. Nutmeg pigeons, lovely gray-headed birds with incandescent blue feathers, broke the churchly silence with guttural cries.

Alwi ripped away strangler figs and swung a machete, clearing a path so I could see what he considered to be his most beautiful trees. He cracked open a fruit and I smelled rum punch. A delicate scarlet lace, the mace, surrounded the seed. "Have you ever seen anything so lovely?" he asked. Afterwards, we stumbled onto a squatter's cassava patch and he thundered, "Look! They're cutting down the Queen of Fruits for tapioca!"

Alwi said he loved nutmeg because he loved Bandanese history, and the two were as intertwined as the mace and the nut. He would settle for nothing less than nutmeg's complete and glorious revival. He would rebuild the salt breaks that had protected the groves and divide the orchards among Bandanese whose families had picked nutmeg for generations. He would resettle the squatters and send everyone a letter urging them to eat sweet potatoes instead of the nutmeg-threatening tapioca. He would compete, somehow, with the lower production and shipping costs of Caribbean nutmeg. He would plant 200,000 seedlings and rebuild the van den Broeke plantation. The Bandanese would tend these groves and share in the profits. That would be his legacy.

Earlier in the day, he had told me some waterfront houses on Banda Neira would have to go because they blocked the view of the water and sat illegally on a greenbelt. Now on Banda Besar he gestured to the squatters' substantial concrete homes, saying they, too, would have to be torn down. It was the fault of the village headman, who had given these people permission to build here and sold them bogus licenses to cultivate manioc. The headman frequently accused Alwi of returning the island to its colonial days. "He'll have to move, too," Alwi said with satisfaction.

Just when I was feeling uncomfortable with this Big Man talk of tearing down houses and changing diets we stopped in a village where everyone turned out to watch us sit in a circle of chairs and drink coconut milk. Alwi knew whose son had married whose daughter, and whose grandfather had died in the war of independence. He held up his coconut for a toast and praised our hosts extravagantly. Then he whispered, "A little rum would do the trick here," and won me back.

■

The term "rock fever" originated among servicemen stationed in Hawaii during World War II. It means a sudden and desperate need to escape to the mainland. I sometimes get it after a few days on a small island, but I was so reluctant to leave the Bandas I kept postponing my departure. I had not slept so well in years; perhaps the nutmeg in Des Alwi's recipes *was* a soporific. Except for the storm, the weather had been perfect, hot and still days followed by blazing sunsets and cool evenings. There were less than a dozen foreign visitors, the locals were dreamy and gentle, the nutmeg groves cool and beautiful, the food delicious, and with Des Alwi in residence, the

Maulana felt like a jolly house party. Had I not had a family at home, I would happily have stayed on for weeks or months, or longer.

On my last afternoon, Alwi took me to Banda Neira's most beautiful beach, an empty, palm-fringed crescent accessible only by water, then to a reef where fish swarmed like piranha and he had once counted 350 species. As we docked at the Maulana he clapped his hands and shouted, "Let's dance." Two hours later a postman, plumber, and teacher were playing an electric organ, keyboard, and drums on the patio. Alwi wore an aloha shirt and plucked a ukulele while crooning Hawaiian love songs and Portuguese ballads in a gravelly voice he called "something like Louis Armstrong." He shut his eyes and sang, "It's so sad to be alone. . . . Please help me make it through the night."

Tamalia's eyes watered. "Oh, I love him for his romantic spirit," she said in a soft voice. "Anyway, Thurston, who but a romantic would pour money into these islands?"

Romantics have always loved islands, but was that enough to explain why Alwi had invested so much money and energy in hotels that were seldom more than half full, mansions that mostly stood empty, and saplings that would not bear fruit and swell the worldwide nutmeg glut until he turned eighty?

Tamalia believed he was fulfilling a boyhood pledge to Hatta, who often took the Baadilla children to an outer island where they could sing nationalist anthems away from Dutch ears. During one such excursion he had asked Alwi and the others to swear they would use their education to help the Bandas.

I later called Alwi's daughter Mira at her home in Bali. She sounded as voluble and likeable as her father and grilled me for news of Banda Neira. She believed her father was not interested in a financial killing and would rather lose money than encourage mass tourism. He was devoted to the Bandas because of their family history. The Bandas were simply in his blood. "You know, those islands are lost in time," she said wistfully. "People are relaxed. You wait for dinner, and wait, and find everyone from the kitchen is in the street playing guitars. Whenever I return to Bali [an island many people would consider paradise] I get a bad case of culture shock."

I left Alwi's dance for a last walk through town. The moon was a perfect crescent and the loudest noises came from the click of bicycle pedals and the slap of dominoes. I needed a flashlight because every street lamp had been vandalized. The government had installed these lights as part of a beautification project. To pay for their nightly illumination a surcharge was added to every electricity bill, and it had not taken long for a people who once chose a renovated fort over electrification to eliminate its source. I saw the busted lights and thought: Better Des Alwi with his anti-tapioca decrees and bullying of rivals and squatters than the functionaries who installed these ridiculous things, allowed the nutmeg orchards to fall into ruin, and stripped Neira's mansions. Better his resistance to expanding the runway to accommodate jets than perkenier mansions crammed with backpackers and streets busy with mega-resort mountebanks. Perhaps some islands could avoid the extremes of depopulation or becoming tourist resorts only if they became appealing charity cases, and seduced a Big Man willing to save them.

A shaft of light fell across the street from one of Alwi's museums. Inside, a rickety man was dusting the cane chairs, mother-of-pearl tables, Portuguese helmets, and photographs of perkeniers. A huge oil painting of the May 8, 1621, massacre by a local artist left nothing to the imagination. One Japanese executioner had decapitated a man, another was thrusting a sword into a writhing body. A woman knelt by her blood-spattered child. Intestines littered the ground. A nearby portrait of Jan Pieterszoon Coen gave him yellow skin and pitiless blue eyes. His satanic face ended in a sword-tip goatee and the curtain behind him was hellfire red.

Coen's name is a household word in the Netherlands, at least in former colonial circles, and schoolchildren know him as a ruthless but effective empire builder. But in the Bandas he enjoys the eerie immortality islands confer on Big Men, even on horrors like him. Dances and songs recount his atrocities, and the descendants of Javanese slaves and Chinese coolies know he planted their family trees here. The killing ground at Fort Nassau, the Knorpel Cliff, and the Well of Chains where his men tossed Bandanese body parts all keep his name on Bandanese lips, and his memory fresh.

Des Alwi's reward, I realized, would be a similar immortality. He had offered his "love of history" as an explanation for his projects, but I suspected he also planned to become part of that history. Because one forceful individual can change the course of history on a small island to an extent impossible on a larger one or on the mainland, and because Alwi "luckily" had too much power, the Bandas would inevitably bestow on him the immortality that is the reward, and sometimes the motivation, for the Big Man on the Small Island. In four hundred years, no one in Jakarta will remember his name, but he will be a legend on Banda Neira, better known than Coen and celebrated whenever the Cakalele is danced, the Korakora raced, or nutmeg harvested. Circe warned Odysseus that whoever drew too close to the island of the Sirens and heard their thrilling and seductive song would go ashore and stay forever. The siren song of a remote island is the promise Banda Neira extended to Des Alwi, that on this small and human-sized stage your life will count for more and your accomplishments will be remembered.

By the time I returned to the Maulana the band had left and Tamalia had retired. Alwi sat at the keyboard, serenading an empty patio. "This is the moment of sweet aloha," he sang when he saw me. "I will love you ever, promise me you'll leave me never, blue sky, and a Banda smile."

There was nothing, nothing, to dislike about this Big Man. I threw up my hands and went to bed.

3

BALI-HA'I AND THE OCTAGON HOUSE—
ESPÍRITU SANTO

A couple I know who attended the 1949 Broadway premiere of the Rodgers and Hammerstein musical *South Pacific* remember an eerie silence following the final curtain. It lasted several beats before the audience rose as one, shouting and cheering. Tears streamed down cheeks and waves of applause shook the Majestic Theatre. The show ran for five years, launching more than a hundred touring companies and reaching more than twenty million people. The 1958 Hollywood film made mai tais, rattan furniture, backyard luaus, hula lessons, and tropical islands popular and turned the mythical island of Bali-ha'i into a household word synonymous with paradise. Both the theatrical and cinematic versions of *South Pacific* were based on "Fo' Dolla' " and "Our Heroine," two short stories in *Tales of the South Pacific*, James A. Michener's Pulitzer Prize–winning work about rear-echelon American servicemen in the Pacific during World War II. It is a book whose simplicity and passion will surprise a reader familiar only with Michener's sprawling epics, and one that has had such a powerful impact on islomania it could be called the *Robinson Crusoe* of the postwar years.

Michener died in Austin, Texas, on the same day I left for Espíritu Santo, the island inspiring "Fo' Dolla' " and "Our Heroine." It is so isolated that when I arrived three days later neither its

Melanesian natives nor its European expatriates had heard of his death. Because Michener is remembered and celebrated on Santo, everyone was shocked when I told them he had died, and several people asked me for the addresses of his relatives so that they could write letters of condolence. No one had read *Tales of the South Pacific* but many had seen the movie, either at the cinema or on video-cassette, and it was widely believed the story had unfolded on Santo. Within hours of my arrival I was told that if I walked a few blocks from my hotel and knocked on the door of the Teddy Bear Boxing Club, a former tavern and house of ill repute, I would meet the real Bloody Mary.

This was just what I had come to Santo hoping to hear. Bloody Mary was more than the Tonkinese wheeler-dealer and curio mer-chant in "Fo' Dolla'" who stage-managed the affair between her daughter Liat and Navy lieutenant Joe Cable that unfolded on the distant island of Bali-ha'i. She was also an expert on the obsession with islands, who believed that everyone was searching for the "right" island, that every island had a distinct personality, and that there was a right one for each of us, if only we could find it. In the film, she stood against the background of a Bali-ha'i wreathed in clouds and mist and sang, "Most people live on a lonely island. . . . Most people long for another island," and told Joe Cable, "Bali-ha'i mean I am your special island."

The Bali-ha'i of Michener's story is the gorgeous island everyone hopes to find in the tropics, small enough to be seen "in one loving glance," and blessed with a curvy feminine landscape, twin volcanoes swaddled in flaming clouds, and giant ferns of a "wondrous and youthful green." On it, adolescent girls "abound in unbelievable pro-fusion . . . like the fruits of the jungle," and its mysterious wartime family of women includes native girls with conical breasts, "awaiting the immortalizing brush of Gauguin." Every want—from shrunken heads to sex—is satisfied, and when Cable and Liat consummate their love they experience "a passion that few couples on this earth are privileged to share," ending with "speckled moonlight falling upon their intermingled brown bodies" and Cable acknowledging Bali-ha'i to be his true home.

Michener's Bali-ha'i was already so sensual and lush that the film's director, Joshua Logan, merely added outrigger canoes, tiki torches, and thatched huts. In spirit, his Bali-ha'i remained close to Michener's: a refuge from the war, and an island outside time and reality promising freedom and love.

"Our Heroine," the second of the two Michener stories from *Tales of the South Pacific* that provided a basis for the film, is an account of a romance between a French planter, Emile de Becque, and American nurse Nellie Forbush on an unnamed Pacific island larger than Bali-ha'i with a large American military base. Its magical place is not Bali-ha'i but de Becque's house, described by Michener as a one-story octagonal villa with a deep veranda that looks across "the vast Pacific" to the volcanoes of distant Vanicoro and is surrounded by gardens bursting with azaleas, hibiscus, flamboyants, and frangipani, whose "odor of the jungle" has a "slightly aphrodisiac quality."

For the film, Logan turned de Becque's house into a rectangle and gave it a vast terrace with a reflecting pool, wind-bent palms, and sweeping views of a horseshoe-shaped beach, a wall of green mountains, and plantations worked by cheerful Tonkinese. De Becque's terrace is a guilty pleasure, a colonial fantasy of smiling servants on cat's feet bringing bowls of curries and fruit. On it de Becque (Rossano Brazzi) and Forbush (Mitzi Gaynor) fall in love and sing, respectively, "Some Enchanted Evening" and "I'm in Love with a Wonderful Guy."

In the book, musical, and film, de Becque is presented as a man who has been ennobled by his island exile. He has fled France to escape prosecution for murder, though we learn that his victim was the town bully and cheat. Like Valeria and José Maria dreaming of Isla Crusoe before finding it, he first dreams of this island, and he travels to it only after hearing a sailor in Marseilles describe its fertile soil, naked women, and magical views of a distant island with twin volcanoes.

In Michener's story, de Becque enjoys a simple life enriched by books, a radio, an old gramophone, and friendships with a kind and generous people. He tells the American doctors whom he invites to dine at the Octagon House that "hard work and temperate living" are responsible for his success and good health. They marvel at his plantation and praise the dinner—local foods that include grilled shrimp, lobster, endive, and hearts of palm. He is the kind of urbane island exile we would all like to be: amusing, self-sufficient, and racially tolerant; a loving father who is kind to the Javanese, Polynesian, and Tonkinese women who have borne him eight daughters; a man whose determination, energy, and self-sufficiency invite comparisons with Crusoe and who, like him, confines his wants to the "natural necessities" and lives comfortably and joyfully in his self-made paradise, the Octagon House.

I met James Michener in 1991 while we were staying at the same Honolulu hotel during ceremonies marking the fiftieth anniversary of the Japanese attack on Pearl Harbor. I had recently read *Tales of the South Pacific* and was curious to learn whether he had known anyone like Bloody Mary or Emile de Becque, and whether there was an island in the Pacific like that "jewel of the vast ocean," Bali-ha'i, or a building like the Octagon House.

We spent a pleasant half hour chatting about Hawaii, where he had lived during the 1950s. But when I asked about his wartime experiences he so expertly jujitsued the conversation that I realized afterwards he had learned plenty about me while revealing little about himself. Later, in a biography by John P. Hayes, I found a reference to a letter Michener had written his editor at *The Saturday Evening Post* in which he admitted that *Tales of the South Pacific* was "a memorial to the bull sessions at the Hotel De Gink in Guadalcanal," and that "nothing in the manuscript is entirely fictitious." Hayes added that characters like Bloody Mary and Emile De Becque may not have been actual people, but probably resembled ones Michener had known.

The origin of the name "Bali-ha'i" is no mystery. Michener himself explained its derivation in his autobiography, *The World Is My Home*. While searching for Japanese stragglers on Mono Island in the Solomons he entered a pitiful village with scrawny residents and one pig. A cardboard sign nailed to a tree said "Bali-ha'i." He jotted it down because it struck him as beautiful and musical.

I believed that if I could find the island that had inspired Bali-ha'i I would find one of the most beautiful and sensual islands in the Pacific, and if I could find the Octagon House and Bloody Mary, I would find the most beautiful island house on earth, and one of the world's great experts on islomania.

My search was complicated because scores of tropical islands have a Bali-ha'i something—"Bali-ha'i suites," "Bali-ha'i views," or "Bali-ha'i atmosphere." Some even claim to be the "real" Bali-ha'i. Kauai's promoters say Kauai is Bali-ha'i because *South Pacific* was filmed on its north coast. Fiji is Bali-ha'i because its scenery appears in the film's location shots. Bora-Bora is Bali-ha'i because Michener called it "the most beautiful island in the world . . . as close to paradise as men in this world ever get."

In *Tales of the South Pacific* Michener described Bali-ha'i as curving itself into the rough shadows formed by the volcanoes on the greater island of Vanicoro. He placed Vanicoro sixteen miles east of the larger and more populated island that was home to de Becque and Bloody Mary. I reasoned that this unnamed larger island could only be Espíritu Santo in the New Hebrides (now Vanuatu) because it was the only Pacific island that had had Tonkinese laborers, French planters, *and* a huge rear-echelon American military base. Furthermore, Michener himself had been stationed on Santo and spent many afternoons sitting under a gnarled tree in a cacao plantation facing the water, writing notes and outlines for his stories. After the war, he declared that of all the islands in the Pacific, Santo had made the most profound impression on him.

The only place matching Michener's description of Vanicoro was Ambae, a volcanic island twenty-five miles east of Espíritu Santo. When it was not shrouded in mist, it was the only large island visible from Michener's cacao plantation on Santo's east coast. If Bali-ha'i was real, it would have to be a small island curving itself into Ambae's shadow, and if de Becque's Octagon House and the beach where Bloody Mary sold curios existed, they would be on Santo's east coast. If I could find them, I might come closer to understanding the epidemic of islomania that *South Pacific* had launched.

The nearest literary equivalent to Michener's Bali-ha'i is the valley on the Marquesas island of Nuku Hiva, where Herman Melville and a shipmate spent a month with a tribe of hospitable cannibals called the Typee. In his roman à clef, *Typee: A Peep at Polynesian Life,* which I read between my trips to Banda Neira and Espíritu Santo, Melville described a love affair between Fayaway, the beautiful daughter of the chief of the Typee, and an American sailor who, like him, had jumped ship. Not only did the Typee's valley offer a young white man refuge and a sensual love affair, as Bali-ha'i had Joe Cable, it even sounded like Bali-ha'i. It was "a glimpse of the gardens of Paradise," Melville wrote, with "palmetto-thatched houses," and "grassy cliffs and precipices hundreds of feet in height over which flowed numberless small cascades."

Robert Scuggs, an American anthropologist working on Nuku Hiva in the 1950s, heard stories of an American whaler the islanders called "Merivi." He had married Pe'ue, the daughter of a chief, and the Typee considered him a minor god. Scuggs concluded that Merivi had to be Melville, and that according to Melville's orthography Pe'ue was Fayaway. The details of their relationship, remembered for a century by a people without a written history, bore astonishing similarities to the one in *Typee.* Merivi and Melville both had fair skin and reddish hair and had been carried everywhere in a litter. Each had escaped into the longboat of a visiting whaling ship because he feared the Typee's excessive hospitality was the prologue to a cannibal feast.

Scuggs's conclusions were more evidence of the siren song of a remote island, and of its knack for preserving history and conferring immortality. If this oral history could survive six generations on Nuku Hiva, at a time when colonialism and missionary conversions had demoralized the Typee and diseases had almost exterminated them, then it seemed only reasonable to expect Espíritu Santo's inhabitants to remember Bloody Mary and Emile de Becque, and to be familiar with Bali-ha'i and the Octagon House.

■

These expectations seemed even less fantastic when I arrived on Santo and saw how much of the American wartime presence had survived.

I landed on the former Bomber Two, the second airstrip the Seabees (the construction battalions of the U.S. Navy's Civil Engineer Corps) had hacked from the jungle in twenty days, and I drove over Seabee roads and bridges into Luganville, where the Seabees had laid out a main street wider than Park Avenue so tanks could make U-turns. I showered in water pumped from the old American waterworks and drank an Australian beer that had been unloaded onto the former U.S. Navy pier. After driving past houses fashioned from former American ammunition storehouses, American Quonset huts that had withstood fifty years of hurricanes and rust, patchwork shanties of American corrugated tin, and ranches fenced with steel land mats from American airfields, I had tea with Tommy Wells. I stirred my tea with a spoon stamped "U.S. Navy" while he asked if there was any chance, any at all, of another war bringing back his beloved Americans.

I had found Wells through John Noel, a taxi driver I chose at the airport because his Black Panther looks promised some colorful observations about the white man on Santo. Instead, I found he was a mild-mannered politician belonging to the executive body of the Union of Moderates who was proud to be sleeping in a bed left behind by the Americans. As we drove to meet Tommy Wells, Noel delivered a lamentation on the American neglect of Santo, punctuated by triumphant cries of "America!" whenever we passed a bunker, a collapsing Quonset hut, or—the highlight of our journey—an American bulldozer tipped onto its back like a dying turtle.

The road to Wells's compound ran along the same east coast where Michener had been stationed, through cattle ranches and neglected coconut plantations whose palms had buckled at the knees or fallen on their faces, victims of the heart-healthy, coconut oil–free diets of the bourgeoisie in countries whose life expectancy far exceeds the fifty-eight years of the average ni-Vanuatu (inhabitant of Vanuatu). Noel was horrified that Japanese interests had leased these former French plantations, stocking them with Charolais cows that grazed under palms, fattening themselves on coconut meat before landing on the hibachis of Tokyo. "Japanese here! Japanese there!" he shouted. "They lost, but they *have*! You Americans should own these plantations."

He asked for my business card, promising to call the moment a plantation became available. We would combine my money and his political contacts and build a luxury hotel.

Tommy Wells lived with his extended family in a thatched house near the road. We sat on stumps, drinking tea and surrounded by his grandchildren and daughters-in-law. For a ni-Vanuatu to reach eighty-two was a small miracle, and Wells was one of the few people I found with adult memories of the Americans.

Had he liked them? I asked.

"I didn't *like* the Americans, I *loved* them."

He loved them for their generosity. Before, people dressed in grass and leaves, but the Americans handed out clothes, and Wells still had the khaki uniform he wore while guiding American patrols

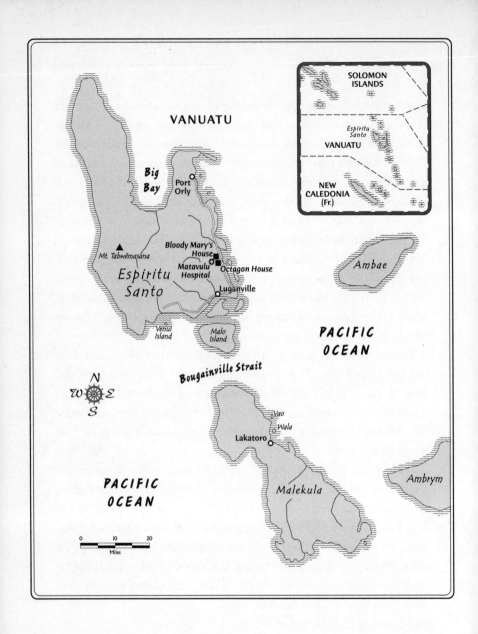

through the interior to search for downed Japanese pilots and infiltrators. The English and French planters and administrators had ignored the ni-Vanuatu, but the Americans treated them like brothers (even if they did call everyone "Bob"), teaching them football, eating local food the planters dismissed as revolting, inviting them into their mess and saying, "Help yourself, we're on the same side!" At last, Tommy Wells ate next to a white man.

His way of repaying them was to remember them. He insisted I write down that his best friend had been Corporal Cooper, and his boss was Captain Burke, a man fond of saying, "I let my revolver do the talking." When Wells told me his last contact with these men had been a letter from Cooper saying Burke had died at Guadalcanal, his eyes teared, and I wondered where else the memory of this hard and silent man was fresh enough to evoke tears. Probably nowhere. Wells had also told his children and grandchildren about Burke, so it is possible that a century from now his descendants will still discuss him, just as the Typee have remembered Merivi, and the Bandanese will speak of Des Alwi.

Wells apologized for not knowing Bloody Mary, de Becque, or Michener, and he had never heard of the Octagon House, which I described as the "funny-looking" house of a French planter. If only Michener had served in the Twenty-fifth Reconnaissance Unit, then he could have told me everything. He had never heard of Bali-ha'i, and the only European planter he had known was his father, an Englishman who gave him his name but nothing else. "He refused to recognize me because of this," he said, pinching the black skin on his forearm, "and because my mother took me off to live with the missionaries." After his father died in Australia, Wells discovered he had a half brother. They met and became lifelong friends and business partners. Their father had been a notorious womanizer, and they often wondered if they had other half brothers or sisters on Santo, and I wondered if Michener had known Wells's father, and if the father had been the model for Emile de Becque, who had sired eight daughters by Tonkinese, Polynesian, and Javanese wives, even though Wells's father was English and had lived in a rectangular house.

■

John Noel produced a steady stream of ni-Vanuatu who had known Americans during the war. I met them in their homes and in cafés, and some showed up at my hotel unannounced, asking only for my address and a promise of correspondence in return for their stories.

Alfred Lecile had been ten when the first American seaplane landed in the channel below the terrace where we sat talking. His friends had panicked and fled to the bush, thinking it was the start of a Japanese invasion. But Lecile saw the star on the wings and stuck around to shake hands with the pilot, Bill Schmidt. Within days he had seen his first crane, forklift, and aircraft carrier. When some sailors drove an amphibious truck into the water, he thought they were committing suicide. The speed of the transformation was dizzying. One week, he was eating food from the forest, the next he was opening a tin of Spam. In July of 1942, there had been no roads into the bush, and everyone traveled by boat; a month later, truck convoys rumbled over washboard roads. Before the Americans, newspapers and mail came every five weeks and the only radio on Santo belonged to the government; afterwards, planes and ships arrived daily with sacks of mail, and ni-Vanuatu and Americans sat together in Quonset hut movie theaters. When Lecile watched his first movie, he believed John Wayne had really shot the villain. He saw Dorothy Lamour, Bing Crosby, and Bob Hope on the screen and, a few months later, Bob Hope in person!

I had hoped that some of the 500,000 Americans who had passed through wartime Luganville might have returned, like the elderly English veterans who live in French villages, or the Americans who had retired to Saigon, and that they would remember Michener, Bloody Mary, and de Becque. But Lecile believed the only American who came back had been a sailor named Ray Jenkins, the projectionist at the movie theater where Lecile himself worked after the war. Since then, videos had killed the theater and Jenkins had died, as had the theater's owner, a colorful Australian trader named Tom Harris who had been one of Michener's buddies. Lecile had screened *South Pa-*

cific countless times at this cinema. He believed the real Bloody Mary was a Frenchwoman who ran a waterfront bar on the east coast at Surrunda Bay, near the American seaplane base and hospital, but he had never heard of a planter with a strangely shaped house. Like many people on Santo, he thought Ambae was Bali-ha'i because it was the correct distance to the east and was often wreathed in cloud or obscured by mist. When seen from Santo at sunset it even resembled the Hollywood Bali-ha'i.

John Noel was beaming when he showed up at my hotel with Chris Vanohulu. He was a celebrity, the Man Who Burned American Uniforms. "They were nice clothes, too," Vanohulu said, plucking at his own shabby shirt. "Better than anything I've worn since." He had offered to wash the Seabees' soiled work clothes, but because the clothes already filled several warehouses the Americans insisted that burning them was quicker. When he reported to work wearing a penis sheath, they told him he had to wear clothes in order to burn them. After that, nothing the Americans did ever surprised him.

■

I sometimes found it disorienting to be in a third-world country where Americans remained so popular, although I soon suspected that whenever a ni-Vanuatu of a certain age saw me, he saw cargo.

The Melanesian cargo cults have been a staple of "Believe It or Not" Sunday supplement articles whose accounts of natives wearing tattered American uniforms, hacking out landing strips from the jungle, and scanning the sky with binoculars while hoping for the return of World War II–vintage planes stuffed with Spam, radios, and long trousers have always had a cruel, mocking edge. But on Santo, where the cargo had come and gone so suddenly, it seemed only logical it might happen again. After all, in a few months the Americans had turned a mangrove swamp into the largest forward base in the Pacific, with five airstrips, three seaplane bases, four hospitals, ten tent cities, twenty-six miles of roads, forty-three cinemas, seven telephone exchanges, an optical laboratory, a Masonic temple, a mess hall feeding a thousand men every hour, and more consumer goods than you could find in the typical small American city. Then, four years later, in the blink of an eye, the Americans threw much of it into the Pacific. So which was more fantastic: the sudden arrival of so much cargo, or its sudden disappearance? That Americans owned so much, or could abandon so much? That they had so many clothes, or that they burned them?

An event the ni-Vanuatu call "the biggest pig-sticking of all time" occurred on a point of land near the entrance to the Segord Channel that gained the nickname "Million Dollar Point" because that was the local estimate of the value of what was dumped there, although it was undoubtedly much more.

When the war ended the U.S. military began burying surplus tires, tools, and jeeps in huge coral pits near Million Dollar Point. But the quantity of the matériel, combined with the eagerness of the servicemen to return home, required more radical measures. The Seabees built a ramp running into the sea and every day Americans drove trucks, jeeps, ambulances, bulldozers, and tractors into the channel, locking the wheels and jumping free at the last second. Engine blocks cracked and hissed. Some Seabees wept. Ni-Vanuatu witnessing the destruction of wealth their island would never see again, at least in their lifetimes, thought the Americans had gone mad. When Michener returned in 1950, a British planter told him, "Not even the Americans could explain what they were doing. One day, they oiled the engines carefully. The next, they threw them into the sea."

I was told Million Dollar Point happened because American manufacturers insisted that their equipment must never return to the mainland as surplus, or because the War Department wanted to protect the future market for U.S. goods in the Pacific. The most popular explanation is that the military wanted to punish the French planters, who had refused to buy the vehicles for eight cents on the dollar because they believed when the Americans left they would drive them away for free.

After the Americans departed, ni-Vanuatu wandered through Luganville, searching for the waterworks, generators, and goods surviving the Million Dollar Point massacre. Tonkinese copra cutters raised jeeps and turned them into taxis. Australian salvage firms hauled off the bulldozers. During the 1950s, a second wave of scavengers shipped tons of Million Dollar Point scrap to Japanese steel mills. The only Pacific power not benefiting from it was the United States.

By the time I walked through Million Dollar Point, anything worth a sou had been salvaged and the most valuable relics were hundreds of sturdy green Coke bottles stamped "Oakland 1942." The busted gears, treads, engine parts, and axles tinging the sand brown with their rust reminded me of the flotsam I had seen on American invasion beaches on Tarawa. Then, I had thought it scandalous that the United States could spend millions to reconstruct the shattered cities and economies of its former enemies, but had not bothered to clean up a small island that had been a neglected British colony. But at least Tarawa's burned-out landing craft and underwater gardens of jagged metal were the detritus of a fierce battle. The matériel at Million Dollar Point was pure waste, a preview of the postwar culture of surplus and disposability. It also underlined two universal rules of island life: that once large manufactured goods arrive on an island they seldom leave, and that continental powers have always considered islands convenient places to test what they fear, or dump their trash.

I had already seen an eerie counterpart to Million Dollar Point on Christmas Island. After arms talks with the Soviet Union collapsed in 1962 and President Kennedy ordered the resumption of nuclear tests, Great Britain offered Christmas Island, then part of its Gilbert Islands, as a site. An American general named Starbird rebuilt the former British nuclear test facilities in four months, transforming the island into a gigantic outdoor nuclear laboratory. After the high-altitude tests finished, the islanders returned to their homes and General Starbird left behind a vast junkyard. Twenty-five years later, crabs scuttled through pancaked Quonsets, falling coconuts had shattered the windshields of jeeps parked in neat rows, and observation towers lay on their sides, like dead elephants. Nothing was radioactive, but it was there for eternity, and like the poisoned landscape of Million Dollar Point, it spoke volumes about the contempt continental powers have for remote islands.

■

I discovered that the biggest obstacle to finding Bloody Mary or the Octagon House was a 1980 rebellion that had concluded with most of Santo's French planters being deported in chains and handcuffs to French New Caledonia. Their ill-advised support for the separatist revolt against the newly independent government in Port-Vila on the island of Efate had been the final, bitter fruit of the bizarre Anglo-French Condominium. This gimcrack arrangement had governed the New Hebrides since 1906, producing the "zany life" of these islands that so appealed to Michener, and a rivalry between Francophone and Anglophone natives that is still in evidence.

Anglophones continue living in the south of the island, near what had been the compound of the British Resident, the senior British official on Santo. Francophones dominate the north. In Luganville, alternate streets carry the names of British and French heroes, so there is a Winston Churchill Street followed by an Avenue Fevrier Despoints, and so on. Cyriaque Melep, Santo's customs inspector, complained to me that because of their different educational systems, British- and French-influenced ni-Vanuatu had different ways of thinking and processing information. This was why Anglophones blamed the death of Lady Diana on a plot by the French intelligence services while Francophones spoke of an assassination ordered by the Royal Family.

The Condominium (more commonly known to Europeans as the

"Pandemonium" and to ni-Vanuatu as "the Snake with Three Heads") had been a desperate solution to the fact that although neither Britain nor France wanted to rule these islands' cannibal tribes and feuding traders, neither wanted the other to rule them, either. The result was a double lashing of colonialism: separate French and British administrators, police forces, schools, post offices, hospitals, prisons, and courts. Villages with Catholic churches and mission stations fell into the French sphere of influence, while villages converted by Protestants fell into the British one. A third government, the Condominium, included members of the British and French administrations and was supposed to coordinate the chaos. A court with one British and one French judge, along with a president appointed by the king of Spain, settled disagreements, although with some difficulty since for many years the Condominium's president was an elderly man who spoke neither English nor Bislama (Biche-le-mer, the Melanesian pidgin) and only a smattering of French, and was stone deaf.

Typical of the Condominium's achievements was an agreement that the Union Jack and the tricolor should be raised simultaneously in front of government offices, and that when one side flew its flag at half staff in mourning, the other would do the same so that neither national symbol would ever fly above the other. Typical of its failures was a lack of initial agreement on whether cars should drive on the right, as in France, or left, as in Britain, with the result that for many years people chose whichever side pleased them, and ni-Vanuatu still trade stories of young men refused a motor vehicle license by one police force who immediately obtained one from the other.

The Condominium ended in appropriate comic opera fashion. In the mid-1970s a right-wing American organization, the Phoenix Foundation, purchased land on Santo and received the friendly and naïve welcome its inhabitants reserve for Americans suspected of bringing cargo. The foundation's leaders, who had spent years searching for a remote island to transform into a libertarian, tax-free Utopia, formed an alliance with Jimmy Stevens, a flamboyant local personality with twenty-five wives and forty-eight children. Stevens had already launched a nativist movement urging a return to traditional customs. In May 1980, two months before Britain and France were scheduled to grant independence to the New Hebrides, he proclaimed his own independent state of Venarama on Espíritu Santo and occupied Luganville with a force of bow-and-arrow-armed warriors. After independence, the new national government at Port Vila called in troops from Papua New Guinea. The rebellion was crushed, Stevens taken prisoner, and many of his French sympathizers, who were the kind of longtime residents who might have remembered the Octagon House and Bloody Mary, were deported to New Caledonia.

■

I was born in the first year of the postwar baby boom, and like many people my age have lived in the shadow of that war ever since. After watching all those black-and-white war documentaries, reading those fat wartime histories, and comparing my own restless generation with the one preceding it, I often feel a secondhand nostalgia for a time I never knew and a war I never fought. On Santo I felt closer to this war than ever before, although its wartime ghosts were the jolly, rear-echelon ones of mischievous nurses and sly natives, suave planters and wheeler-dealer Seabees. There were no fields of white gravestones or burned-out tanks, and the horrors had happened offscreen and outside the narrative.

A Peace Corps volunteer named Eric Kvick also saw the ghosts. He was a Vietnam veteran who had joined the Peace Corps for the usual Foreign Legion reasons, boredom and a busted marriage, and was amazed to find himself assigned to the same island to which his father had been evacuated three times from Guadalcanal, for treatment of wounds, malaria, and shell shock. "He was ecstatic to be alive," Kvick told me, "and I grew up hearing Santo was paradise."

It had been paradise for him, too, the dream island of every divorced, middle-aged man. He lived in a bamboo shack with ocean views, had started a furniture business that provided good jobs for ni-Vanuatu, and fallen in love with a visiting American woman. For him, Santo really *was* Bali-ha'i.

Whenever he rode his bicycle he wore his father's World War II topee and imagined the old man sitting behind him. He knew he was seeing many of the same things his father had: the airstrips where he had landed, the Quonset huts where he had eaten and watched movies, even the Coke bottles he might have pressed to his lips. He felt his presence strongest at the site of the Matavulu military hospital, where his father had recuperated. A hurricane had swept away the wards and administrative buildings, but Kvick cried when he walked over their foundations. More than the city where his father had lived, or the cemetery where he was buried, this island felt like his true home, "and that's why I'm going to leave his topee and dog tags here," Kvick said. He rubbed his arms. "Look, just thinking about him here gives me goosebumps."

I felt brushed by the wartime ghosts when I saw the jungle-clutched wreck of a B-17 so intact I expected corpses in the cockpit; when a Frenchman spoke about sailors playing saxophones, jazz floating on the evening breeze, and how American pilots had dropped miniature parachutes holding hard candies onto school yards; and when I leafed through photographs of Santo's happy-go-lucky war that a Chinese trader kept in scrapbooks and saw Eleanor Roosevelt in a nurse's uniform and a sign, BACHELOR'S CLUB GIRLS WANTED APPLY INSIDE, that could have been painted by *South Pacific*'s slap-happy sailors.

The World War II ghosts hovered over Unity Park, where I could see pilings from the dock where future president John F. Kennedy's PT boat may have landed, and over the concrete foundations of the nearby Nambagura Hotel, where he may have gone drinking and whoring and met a woman who might or might not have been Bloody Mary.

PT 109, an account of Kennedy's wartime exploits written by

Robert J. Donovan, claims he "went ashore" at Espíritu Santo before proceeding to Guadalcanal, but while I was in Luganville I heard he had never set foot here, or had spent a single night, or had stayed for weeks and frequented the Nambagura Hotel.

I heard that Bloody Mary had been a famous Parisian beauty and Santo's most sought-after courtesan; that she had been a frightening witch who patrolled the halls of the Nambagura Hotel with a riding crop and whipped unruly customers; that she was a Tonkinese woman, like Michener's Bloody Mary, who returned to Vietnam after the war; that she was a mestiza known as "Bamboo Annie"; that she was a Corsican named Françoise Gardel; and that she was a former Miss Paris named Carmen who lived with her dogs and goats on the ruins of her former establishment, the Teddy Bear Boxing Club, a plywood-and-tin shanty closed by the authorities after a celebrated 1962 murder. A man once renting a room from her reported being dazzled by old photographs showing her porcelain skin and emerald eyes. When a French film crew begged her to speak on camera, she slammed the door in their faces.

Faded drawings of bears in boxing gloves still covered the Teddy Bear's façade. An hour after I staked it out, a stooped woman scuttled through the front gate, shouting "Snoopy!" and chasing after a mutt. She had the curved spine and milky eyes of the indoor elderly. Her feet were swollen and coal black, her teeth Stone Age stumps. She had dyed her hair black, a touching vanity, but missed a small skunk-stripe surrounding a bald spot. She looked about the right age to have made love to JFK in 1942.

She said she trusted me because I was American, but I thought she was hoping for cargo. "I am *desperate* to go to Nouméa," she whispered. "But first, I need to sell this property." It stretched to the water and was, she said, an ideal site for a *"hôtel grande luxe."* She grabbed my arm. "Perhaps *you* could buy it?"

"Are you Bloody Mary?" I asked.

She turned and ran inside.

The following day, Yvan Charles persuaded me that Carmen had arrived after the war, and that Françoise Gardel had been the model for Bloody Mary. She had lived at the same plantation where Michener was stationed, and when the two met again in 1984 they embraced and wept. Gardel had passed away last year at the age of 102, while living at the Little Sisters of the Poor home in New Caledonia.

Yvan Charles and his wife, Elaine, owned the Bougainvillea, a bungalow hotel occupying a bluff overlooking the channel where American ships were once so thick that as a boy he imagined walking across them to the opposite shore. He had emigrated to Australia as a young man but had returned to Santo years later on a vacation and become, like Des Alwi, so bewitched by the island of his youth that he had also built a hotel, in his case on the grounds of his father's former cacao and vanilla plantation. Despite his many years in Australia, he had the formality of the French hotelier, choosing his words carefully and calling me "Monsieur." He told me people who saw *South Pacific* suspected that his father, who had a famously sharp eye for women, had been the model for Michener's de Becque. Françoise Gardel had been "a woman with a heart of gold, Monsieur, a hard worker who stood for righteousness." He lowered his voice. "Well, okay, she ran a bit of a brothel, but she insisted on good manners." After the war, she had to take in washing to keep her restaurant going. "Well, a heart of gold, but maybe a tough nut, too," he conceded, perfectly summarizing the Bloody Mary of *South Pacific*.

The next day, Peter Morris, an English-speaking planter who still lived on Santo, told me Gardel's coffee and french fries had been the best on the island. She had been a "hard lady" and such a fine horsewoman people suspected Arab blood. When Michener returned in 1984, Morris said, he was devastated to find everyone he had known except her had died. They embraced under the same nambagura tree where he had written notes for *South Pacific*, crying like babies. Michener was so appalled by her poverty and elephantiasis he paid to send her to the Little Sisters.

Morris contravened the conventional wisdom that every South Seas expatriate is an eccentric worthy of a short story. He was a matey and straightforward man without sides, despite a background that could have inspired a Somerset Maugham short story. A 1935 photograph showed him cradled in the arms of his father, a tall and distinguished Englishman who was standing outside a thatched cottage in what looked like Devon but was actually the neighboring island of Malekula. After the father's early death, Morris's mother had married a French windjammer captain. She refused to speak his language, and he reciprocated by not learning English. They communicated in Bislama, but sent Peter to a French school. His strangely pleasing French-Australian accent was the result. All in all, he said, a typical Pandemonium story.

Morris himself appeared to be out of a nineteenth-century photograph. Muttonchops set off his long face and he had allowed his white hair to curl at the shoulders. He owned a cattle ranch on the south coast but slept in Luganville with his ni-Vanuatu wife and their young daughter. His brother and sister, his sons by a first marriage, the planters who had known his family, everyone he had grown up with— they had all died or emigrated to Australia, but he had stayed on.

As we drove to his ranch he said, "I have too many memories of growing up here to leave. Every palm grove and curve in this road means something to me." He worried that the history of Santo's English planters was being forgotten. Their homes had collapsed, and their children had emigrated to New Caledonia or Australia. Even the famously large and busy bed of Monsieur Laborde had been auctioned, a great loss because he might have been Benoit, the "fat and ugly" French planter in Michener's story who lives in the bush with a retinue of mistresses and claims Liat after Joe Cable refuses to marry her. Like Benoit, Laborde had been obese, and had kept six wives. He also drank champagne and ate chilies in his enormous bed.

Another reason Morris stayed on was that it had always been his dream to own an island, and now he did. And not just any island, either, but Venui, an islet of twelve thickly forested acres that was once home to the British Resident. It lay two hundred yards offshore, far enough to discourage the midnight robberies that terrified the colonial whites, and to make casual visitors think twice before paddling over to disturb the Resident, who enforced a rule that visitors were welcome only when he flew the Union Jack.

Morris walked me over the ruined foundations of the Residency and urged me to peer into cells once holding Anglophone miscreants. This sprawling house had been one of Santo's architectural treasures and he had ambitious plans for reconstructing it. "Santo has many notable buildings," he said. "One of our best is the house of Monsieur My, a French planter and amateur mathematician who believed a structure without right angles could better withstand hurricanes." To prove his theory, My had built a house in the form of an octagon.

■

Santo has miles of palm-fringed beaches, and for years there have been rumors of Club Med resorts and international jetports. Australian developers were always poised to build a six-hundred-bungalow resort, and Japanese interests were always planning to erect high-rise hotels on a bluff overlooking Pali Kula Bay. Foreign investors saw Santo's undeveloped beaches and they imagined package-tour resorts, golf courses, and wealthy retirees. In the 1970s, some Hawaii developers had promised "a retirement paradise . . . in a community like Hawaii was 50 years ago, but with planned modern comforts and conveniences on an island where the cost of living takes you back 30 years." Nothing came of any of these plans because several native families had advanced conflicting claims to the best beachfront property, and the traditional chiefs opposed concrete buildings and preferred bungalows resembling the houses where *they* lived. There were other drawbacks. Luganville's hurricane-pounded Quonset huts and concrete traders' store offered nothing for tourists, and the island's interior was a forbidding jungle of ravines, swamps, and mountains wreathed in cloud, so impenetrable that only half of the sixty American planes that crashed into it during the war have been recovered.

When a trickle of American veterans began returning to Santo fifty years later, a soft-spoken ni-Vanuatu named Glenn Russell traded his farm for a minivan and launched Butterfly Tours. He told me his clients wanted to revisit the airfields where they had been stationed, the hospitals where they had recuperated, and the beaches where they had landed. Some brought wartime snapshots so they could be photographed standing in the same spots.

I asked him to show me what he showed them, then drive me to whatever remained of Françoise Gardel's bar and Monsieur My's Octagon House.

He took me to the Blue Hole, a jungle pool surrounded by banyans dripping with Tarzan vines that was prettier than the one on Bali-ha'i where Joe Cable courted Liat. Every Hollywood star who came to entertain the troops swam and posed for photographers here, and Russell claimed to know exactly where Carole Landis had reclined.

We drove down airfields bordered by the hibiscus that Seabees had planted for camouflage, and paused at the cottony-white beach where Marines stormed ashore expecting Japanese resistance, and where you could still dig up American coins and shell casings. We stopped at the lovely horseshoe-shaped beach at Surrunda Bay, a former seaplane base where veterans and their children came to return cowrie shells collected during the war, an act of closure indicating that they, like Kvick's father (and Joe Cable), considered this island a "true home."

The site of the former Matavulu hospital, where nurses like Nellie Forbush had tended wounded servicemen like Kvick, was the coolest and quietest spot I found on Santo. It had a steady breeze and avenues of palms throwing a blanket of shade over the foundations. From the edge of a bluff I could see for miles up and down the coast. A line of poker-chip-shaped islets floated offshore, creating a procession of lagoons and scalloped bays.

We drove through the copra plantation where Michener had been billeted and stopped at the edge of the water. "This place, this very place is where Bloody Mary sold her grass skirts," Russell announced, stamping on the concrete slab that once anchored Madame Gardel's establishment. He was a large and gentle man, and this was the first time in two days I had seen him so excited. "*This* is where she dyed the skirts yellow with malaria pills, and where the sailors danced with her girls," he said. Hurricane Wendy had flattened the restaurant and what he called "the girls' barracks," leaving only a concrete outhouse.

"Shut your eyes, Thurston," he urged, purring like a hypnotist. "Can you see the Catalina seaplanes offshore? The officers in white uniforms? Michener sitting under this tree? Bloody Mary living over there?" He pointed to an abandoned shack at the edge of the sand. "Believe me, this is the birthplace of Bali-ha'i."

I could see there had been a large building here and I was willing to believe it had been a restaurant. I knew a colorful Frenchwoman named Françoise Gardel had owned it and, although she was not Tonkinese, her character, "a tough nut but a heart of gold," resembled that of Bloody Mary. I knew Michener had written the notes for South Pacific under this tree, and that when he returned forty years later to discover Gardel living in this tin shack they had the kind of emotional reunion you might expect between an author and one of his most memorable characters. So I shut my eyes, willing myself to see them. I opened them and saw Ambae, the island with the "profile of an upturned ship" that Michener called Vanicoro in his book. Bali-ha'i was supposed to lie "in its shadow," but when I had gone to a Luganville travel agency to buy a ticket on the weekly plane I noticed a wall map showing only two small rocks, but no small islands, no potential Bali-ha'i lying anywhere nearby.

The Octagon House was a mile down the coast. Its caretaker was a Mr. Titus Taru, a wheezy old man related by marriage to the New Zealander who had taken a long-term lease on the house but was often away. When Taru learned I was an American he whipped out a photograph of himself at sixteen, bare chested, wearing a white sailor's cap, and opening his mouth for a Navy dentist. Fifty-five years later, this photograph, folded and creased, sat in his front pocket.

He summoned Mr. Rovo Bani, an elderly man with a jack-o'-lantern smile who had worked for the My family. Bani made Monsieur My sound like de Becque, a white man who inspired loyalty, never raised his voice, and was patient with his employees. My's daughters had been beautiful and kind, the family had been happy, and, yes, during the war they often entertained American doctors and nurses from Matavulu.

I asked Bani and Taru about Madame Gardel. They laughed and slapped their thighs. "Yes, yes, yes, Bloody Mary!" they chorused. She came to My's parties with her whip and made the Americans laugh.

In *Tales of the South Pacific*, Emile de Becque asks a young nurse at his dinner party, "Where could I find a lovelier spot than this?" But the real Octagon House had an even lovelier situation and interior than the house Michener had given de Becque. Its parlor rose two stories to a glass ceiling, and twelve-foot-high Art Deco doors opened onto a veranda overlooking a fine beach. Unlike the movie version, there was no vast patio overlooking the water, no panoramic view of Kauai's mountains. This was a smaller-scale paradise of wind-bent palms, white froth marking a reef, and two islets framing distant Ambae, or, if you preferred, Vanicoro.

As the lowering sun turned Ambae a Technicolor red a faint breeze filled the house with the aphrodisiac scent of frangipani. Michener had attended Monsieur My's parties, too, I thought. He had sat on this veranda, stood on this ocean-blue rug, and wandered through these oddly shaped rooms, making mental notes while the nurses and doctors in dress whites sat flirting and gossiping on this sofa with its pink-palm-tree-patterned slipcovers.

"Bali-ha'i mean I am your special island. Mean, here I am,"

Bloody Mary said. Well, here was Espíritu Santo. It was no Bora-Bora, not even a Banda Neira, but it was pretty enough. Its palms lined its ridges like the pillars of a ruined acropolis. Its battered waterfront town was a place I could imagine making friends instead of drinking buddies, and there were not many third-world islands where everyone liked Americans best of all. Like all fertile tropical islands, it offered the security of knowing if the remittances from home ever stopped coming, you could do a Crusoe and live off the land. If Emile de Becque could feed his guests hearts of palm, wild chicken, lobster, and freshwater shrimp, you would never starve on Espíritu Santo.

I could also imagine, to answer de Becque's question, lovelier spots than the Octagon House. The terrace of the Maulana Hotel and the patio of de Becque's house in *South Pacific* had more dramatic situations. But this was a perfect island house, beautiful in its simplicity and design. It was cool without being air-conditioned, and perfumed by the surrounding gardens. Its unusual shape gave it great personality, and it was swaddled in an insular white noise of breaking waves and rustling palms.

I remembered what Des Alwi's daughter Mira had said about Banda Neira being "lost in time." Like Neira's perkenier mansions, the Octagon House was a place where past and present were tightly braided.

■

Several friends were amazed that I had never read the D. H. Lawrence's short story "The Man Who Loved Islands." I finally found a copy and finished it during my journey to Santo. In it, Lawrence writes that islands immerse you in the "dark mystery of time." On them, the past is "vastly alive" and the future "not separated off," perhaps because they float in oceans in the same way as the earth floats in the timeless mystery of space. "Isolate yourself on an island, in a sea of space," he writes, "and the moment begins to heave, ... the solid earth is gone, and your slippery, naked dark soul finds herself out in the timeless world. . . . The souls of all the dead are alive again, and pulsating actively around you. You are out in the other infinity."

The "man" of Lawrence's title searches for the ideal island, one small enough so he can fill it with his personality. First he buys an island off the English coast. It has a farm, three cottages, and four miles of coastline, and he plans to make "a minute world of pure perfection." He peoples it with a butler, housekeeper, mason, carpenter, and farmhands—a community he hopes will become happy and self-sufficient, and honor him as the source of their contentment. Instead, the farm loses money, a storm wrecks his boat, and his carefully chosen inhabitants squabble. Some abandon the island because they fear that its isolation is bad for their children.

His second island is smaller, scarcely more than a hump of rock he shares with his five most faithful employees. After having an unwise affair with the daughter of his widowed housekeeper, he escapes to a third and even smaller island. Here, on a few treeless acres of low rock, he builds a stone shelter where he lives alone, briefly enjoying the autonomy and mastery of the castaway. He exults at having found a damp and sea-washed space where "time had ceased to pass," then succumbs to hallucinations and loses his mind.

It is easier to say islands play tricks with time than to explain how they do it, to say a four-hundred-year-old massacre is remembered on the Bandas as if it happened last year, and Eric Kvick felt his father's presence on Santo as if he were still alive, and leave it at that. These things may happen, as Lawrence said, because an island whose horizon is empty in every direction resembles a self-contained universe, floating in water instead of space and capable of setting its own rules, or because relics like Des Alwi's desk and the Octagon House detach islands from their temporal moorings. But however they do it, some remote islands can provide the ultimate freedom, from time itself.

The Octagon House had so perfectly woven past and present it was several minutes before I noticed the mildew spotting its ceiling, or saw that its rug was unraveling and worn to the matting, or that five decades of harsh sunlight had turned its pink slipcover palm trees beige. I pulled some books from the shelves. Every one was stamped "Department of the Navy" and had been published before 1946. Their backs broke off in my hands and pieces of their yellowed pages fluttered to the floor like confetti. I looked up. Ambae had become a pink smudge on the horizon, so faint that before my eyes it vanished like smoke.

ATLANTIS — THE MALDIVES

Ever since Plato described the brilliant civilization that once flourished on Atlantis, finding that island has obsessed geographers, adventurers, and treasure hunters. The most likely candidate is Thíra (Santorin, or Santorini), an island seventy miles north of Crete that was partially submerged in 1470 B.C. by a volcanic eruption. Thíra's dazzling white houses, perched on a cliff that is part of the caldera, have since become a much-photographed emblem for the Greek islands, and I once spent several days staying in one of them. Although the view was spectacular, the rest of the island was disappointing. The town was crowded and noisy, the food dreary. The beaches were mostly black sand, scorching hot, and lined with concrete villas. I also decided against making Thíra my symbolic Atlantis because although it may have inspired the Atlantis legend, it promised none of its most compelling aspects: that an island's isolation and security can nurture a Utopia, that a civilization can flourish on a remote island while remaining unknown to the rest of the world, and that an entire island can vanish without a trace.

If you believe, as I do, the increasingly credible warnings of global warming, then you must accept the possibility that hundreds of low-lying coral atolls and barrier islands will be submerged or made uninhabitable by rising sea levels, and that there will soon be thousands of little Atlantises, particularly in the Caribbean, the Pacific, and the Indian Ocean. The boom of surf against the reefs of atoll nations like Kiribati, Tuvalu, and the Maldives will become muffled, then vanish. Their palms will yellow, salt water will pollute their water tables, and instead of exporting copra, fish, and cowrie shells, their people will export themselves to high islands and mainlands. For the first time in human history two entire geographic features, the barrier island and the atoll, will become extinct, and if they do islomania will also be diminished because the islands of a coral atoll, more than any other, provide the refuge, stark beauty, and elemental pleasures that make islands appealing.

The most prominent and influential organization to warn about global warming, the United Nations–sponsored Intergovernmental Panel on Climate Change (IPCC), has forecast a sea-level rise of between twenty and eighty-six centimeters by the end of the twenty-first century, with a best estimate of forty-nine centimeters, or eighteen inches. It breaks this rise into incremental advances of eight to twenty-nine centimeters by 2030, with a best estimate of eighteen centimeters, and of twenty-one to seventy-one centimeters by 2070, with a best estimate of forty-four centimeters. Figures like these encourage the misconception that the oceans will rise slowly and uniformly, like water in a bucket under a dripping tap, and suggest that there will be time for orderly evacuations—for uprooting family headstones and pouring native soil into jars. But my correspondence with Terje Dahl, the self-described "Norwegian Robinson Crusoe," suggested that before an island is submerged, warming oceans will hatch monster hurricanes that will destroy its dwellings, salinate its aquifers, and kill its taro, breadfruit, and coconuts, rendering it suddenly uninhabitable. This is what happened to the home of Dahl, who calls himself the world's first "climate-refugee," its first modern Atlantan.

He had sailed to the South Pacific single-handedly on a twenty-two-foot yacht and after wandering for several months married a

Polynesian woman on the remote Tuvaluan atoll of Nukulailai. He and his new wife moved across the lagoon from her home island to an uninhabited one, where they built a house, planted a garden, and crafted a Crusoean life from whatever the island provided, inventing delicacies such as reef shark marinated with basil. Prior to 1990, Tuvalu had suffered only three damaging hurricanes in the entire century. Over the next three years, seven storms battered its atolls. The worst one, Hurricane Nina, sent coconuts falling like bombs on Dahl's compound. The wind peeled off his roof and waves crested over his garden. In the entire country one hundred families were left homeless, a huge number for a nation of only twelve thousand people—the equivalent of ten million Americans losing their houses. Dahl's mother-in-law begged him to take his wife and daughter to safety. They gave away their possessions and moved to Oslo, where he feels guilty about living in a nation made wealthy by the fossil fuels that produce the greenhouse gases he blames for the hurricanes ravaging Nukulailai.

He and his family returned after several years for a visit. The week after they left, another hurricane swept away Nukulailai's livestock and devastated its bananas and breadfruit. Salt water seeped into taro pits, forcing its inhabitants to buy imported rice, and for twenty-eight days his wife's cousin drifted at sea in an open boat. He told me that the storm had left her other relatives "standing in the middle of their islands, up to their knees in water, waiting to die."

Dahl discouraged me from traveling to Nukulailai, saying that a field trip boat called only several times a year, and he had paid a fortune to charter a boat during his previous visit. I chose the Maldives as my global warming Atlantis instead, both because they are easy to reach and because, since 80 percent of the land on these eleven hundred islands is less than one hundred centimeters above sea level, no nation on earth stands to lose more islands to global warming.

When I first read how rising sea levels threatened to submerge the Maldives, my reaction was that it was unfair that a country contributing so few greenhouse gases to global warming—one with no heavy industry and fewer than three thousand carbon-dioxide-emitting vehicles—should be among its earliest victims. A mainland country like Bangladesh, where a third of the population might be drowned or exiled by rising sea levels, faced a much greater magnitude of human suffering, but at least it contained enough high ground to preserve its language and culture. After the Tuvaluans had moved to New Zealand or Australia, their Polynesian culture would survive on high islands like Tahiti, and after Abemama was submerged, its culture would continue on high Micronesian islands like Kosrae. But the Maldivians' culture and language were unique to their atolls, and would disappear if they became uninhabitable. No wonder their president, Maumoon Abdul Gayoom, had become such a global warming Jeremiah, demanding that developed nations reduce their fossil fuel emissions by 20 percent by 2005, and warning that during the next century his country might, like Atlantis, "disappear from the earth."

Unlike Atlantans, however, most Maldivians will survive the catastrophe, and a hundred years from now they will probably gather in the Sri Lankan villages and European guest worker slums where they will then live to fan the embers of their dying culture. They will teach their children to speak their vowel-crammed language and bewitch them with stories of an Atlantis of planetarium skies, blinding beaches, and teardrop islands. They will stand out, a race of Lilliputians smothered by their hand-me-down overcoats, resembling refugee children befriended by soldiers. Like Kurds, Armenians, and Palestinians, they will nurse ferocious grudges. Their Great Satan will be the industrialized West, whose air-conditioned desert cities, energy-hungry industries, and sport utility vehicles have made a disproportionate contribution to the greenhouse gases that warmed the oceans and submerged Maldivian islands inhabited for five thousand years.

Like all refugee peoples, they will be crackerjack historians. The key dates in their tragic past will be twenty-first-century ones, but they may recall two from the previous century: the May 1991 storm

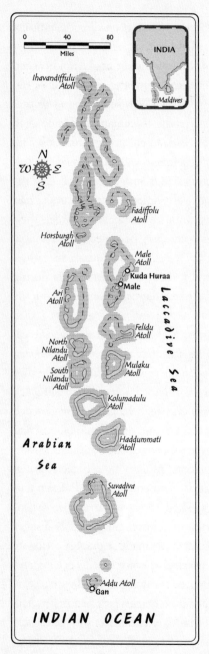

that put the first Maldivian island under water and tossed
coral boulders onto the runway of Hulhule airport, and
the April 1987 storm that sent
waves crashing onto the roof-
tops of the capital island of
Male, nearly washing President
Gayoom and several of his
cabinet members into the Indian Ocean.

A few Maldivian historians
may even argue for a third date,
although at first glance it appears unconnected to their fate.
This is the September day in
1972 when a Sri Lankan air
force plane brought investor
George Corbin and twelve Italian travel writers to the Maldives, ending an isolation that
was positively Atlantan, launching its tourist industry, and
prompting the widespread mining of coral to build resorts,
in the process weakening the
reefs that are an atoll's defense
against hurricanes and rising
sea levels. A few such historians may also come to see
this September 1972 day as
the moment when the Maldives
began becoming a fossil-fuel-

dependent modern nation, and therefore both perpetrator and future victim of Global Warming.

In 1972, the pioneering Italians found a nation that had been utterly ignored, one essentially unchanged from that described by the French adventurer Alan Villiers in a 1959 *National Geographic* article. Villiers had arrived at the Maldivian capital island of Male from Ceylon on a creaky sailing ship that was then its only connection with the world. He found a nation of 83,000 people without a single policeman, telephone, or European—not even a beachcomber, merchant, or honorary consul. Male was a dazzling white city of coral paths and houses smothered in orchids and flowering vines. Its people ate fish, coconuts, and taro and were passionate kite-fliers, like the Bandanese. The sultan owned the only car and his subjects traveled by sailboat and bicycle. In 1959 probably no people on earth committed fewer crimes, had fewer worries, released fewer greenhouse gases per capita into the atmosphere, or lived more lightly on the planet. It was a civilization that was, in its own way, as utopian as Atlantis.

Within a year of the Italians' visit, the first resorts opened on uninhabited Maldivian islands. Scheduled jet service began in 1977, color television came in 1978, and by 1980, 42,000 foreigners a year were visiting the Maldives. In 1997, 350,000 tourists, most of them Europeans on package holidays, landed at Hulhule airport, where a fleet of helicopters and speedboats whisked them away to one of seventy-five self-contained resort islands.

As their plane approached Hulhule's crushed coral airstrip in 1972, the Italian travel writers had the same view I did as my plane descended twenty-six years later: hundreds of thin flat islands circled by white sand and crowned with palms waving like pennants, islands from their childhood picture books and adult castaway fantasies. When they saw these necklaces of islands stretching north and south to the horizon they probably thought: *Robinson Crusoe, Swiss Family Robinson, Bali-ha'i, The Blue Lagoon*—solitude, adventure, romance, and sex. I saw them and wondered if I was looking at geographic dodos,

and if in another fifty years, a traveler would see only their faint underwater outlines.

Describing a new place from an airplane is a cheap trick, like having a character in a novel gaze into a mirror and describe himself. But
the Maldives were best appreciated from above. From sea level, they
were one low flat piece of land after another; from above, they were
as distinctive as snowflakes. There were islands with narrow beaches
and a screen of waterfront palms, sandy circles capped by a tangle of
foliage, sandbar islands and swampy ones, green islands and deserts—
so many beautiful islands so close together I thought of butterflies,
flamingos, and other beautiful things that come in flocks. Some lagoons were boomerang-shaped, others resembled amoebas or balloons. There were shallow turquoise lagoons and deep, royal blue
ones, such a spectrum of blues that as we landed I was thinking, blue
skies, mood indigo, David Hockney, California swimming pools, lapis
lazuli, midnight blue, and peacock blue, and wondering if atolls are
so appealing simply because people love blue.

Male was across the lagoon from the island sacrificed for the airport. It did not have the skyline of a city expecting to disappear any-
time soon. The low-slung town I had seen in a five-year-old aerial
photograph had become so top-heavy with cranes and high-rise
buildings it looked in danger of capsizing. At every turn, it undermined the David and Goliath fable of Maldivians as noble and help-
less victims of everyone else's profligate energy consumption. If
President Gayoom believed his own warnings, why build a new four-
story presidential office complex on waterfront land that might be
flooded in a generation? Why waste a grant from Pakistan to build a
new parliament, when it could be used to gather a people scattered
over 199 inhabited islands onto larger ones where they might be
saved by seawalls? Why did a country without a single policeman in
1959 need a new headquarters for its National Security Service when
the organization already occupied a large white fortress? (An at-

tempted coup supported by Tamil mercenaries from Sri Lanka had almost toppled Gayoom in 1988, but it was the only way he could have been removed, since the Maldives lacked any democratic mechanisms for doing the job.) And what about the atrium of offices and stores? The six-story building with the exterior elevator sliding up and down in its glass tube? The new smoked glass headquarters of the Maldivian coast guard? The D day–sized flotilla of freighters in the harbor waiting to offload their Evian water and Carrier air conditioners? Should the international conscience of global warming permit the construction of air-conditioned buildings guaranteeing decades of fossil fuel consumption? Why should anyone else take global warming seriously, if even the Maldivians did not?

The most palatable explanation for the construction boom was that thanks to the tourist boom, health care had improved, Maldivian life expectancy had risen, and the population had almost doubled, so this dense city had run out of room. A more disturbing explanation was that the Maldivian elite believed that the new seven-foot-high, Japanese-financed seawall would protect them long after other islands were submerged or abandoned, allowing them to live on, alone, and enjoy their modern city. More likely, like almost everyone else on earth, the Maldivians believed in global warming in their minds but not in their hearts, talked about the death of their nation but acted as if it was inconceivable.

I asked people if they really thought their country might one day vanish into the Indian Ocean. The captains of the airport shuttle boats and the T-shirt vendors smiled and shrugged. The government functionaries I ambushed as they were climbing onto their bicycles were more concerned. They agreed it must be serious because the President himself had spoken of it.

I had never been in a country where striking up a conversation was more difficult or less rewarding. I had imagined the European package tourists would have accustomed the Maldivians to visitors, but even when I found someone who spoke English, and such people were rare, long spells of silence punctuated our exchange. Most people were small and delicate, the right size for their small islands and coral houses. They seemed flummoxed by the tall buildings and European tourists, and perpetually dazed and confused, like time travelers rubbing their eyes after being hurled into the future.

Despite all the feverish construction, Male lacked almost everything that makes an island appealing, even to an undemanding visitor. Imagine an island of 65,000 people jammed into a square mile, where waves crash against barriers resembling saw-toothed concrete tank traps, where there is no open space and you can never escape the sound of farting motorbikes, and you have Male. There was not a single sidewalk café or beach. Alcoholic beverages were prohibited, curio stores sold shabby souvenirs from Southeast Asia, and the population was shy and uncommunicative. The modern buildings were ugly, the public park was open only for a few hours on Friday afternoons, and the interior of the seventeenth-century Friday Mosque, the most noteworthy attraction, could only be viewed by infidels who obtained a permit from the Department of Religious Affairs. Male's principal charms were a ratio of bicycles to people that must be the highest of any national capital, so that during the afternoon rush hour it turned into a tropical Amsterdam, and the fanatical cleanliness of its inhabitants, although I am not sure how charming that is.

An English visitor in 1934 reported never having seen "any place kept cleaner," and despite its growth and overcrowding, Male remained spectacularly, even oppressively, clean, largely because of an army of elderly men who swept up every paper or dead leaf moments after it hit the ground. My favorite hangout was the waterfront market, where men gathered in sociable circles to comment on fish so fresh they were still gasping. Next door was the cleanest public toilet on earth, whose fanatical attendants hosed down the floor and scrubbed the commode after each patron.

I visited the National Museum to see the cultural riches threatened by global warming. The principal displays consisted of tattered furnishings from the demolished palace of the sultan and knickknack gifts from the British governors of Ceylon. (The Maldives had been a British protectorate until 1965.) Crammed onto a small veranda were the only pre-Islamic holdings: a lovely white limestone Buddha discovered on a remote southern atoll by Thor Heyerdahl, and two statues of five-faced devils, just the kind of strange and wonderful ruins you might imagine for an Atlantis.

To be fair, the threadbare exhibits were an accurate reflection of the Maldives' threadbare history. These islands had never commanded trading routes, grown precious spices, or produced a class of adventuresome seamen and traders. A brief Portuguese occupation in 1573 had ended with the massacre of the garrison. Otherwise, between its inhabitants' twelfth-century conversion to Islam and the arrival of the Italian travel writers in 1972, the only Europeans spending any time among the Maldivians had been castaways, and the world had left them alone to fish, pray, procreate, and pick coconuts. There is a certain undeniable charm and purity to a people who are so utterly self-sufficient and unconcerned with events transpiring outside their reef. Who could blame them for being uninterested in history, theirs or anyone else's? Or for razing the sultan's palace when they became a republic? Or for demolishing the Portuguese fortress after Independence, and using its cannon for landfill?

On the museum's third floor, I found a framed 1866 magazine article by C. W. Rosset, the first European to make a systematic exploration of these islands. He spoke of coconut mat homes and clean streets, and said the peaceful and hospitable islanders were "shy and suspicious of strangers."

My experiences with Ismail Firaq, deputy minister for tourism, confirmed the enduring accuracy of Rosset's observation. Officials at the Maldives Mission to the United States had urged that I begin my enquiries with Mr. Firaq, and whenever I asked desk clerks and assistant hotel managers about global warming and tourism, they said,

"Ask Mr. Firaq!" But he ignored my e-mails and faxes, and was never available when I telephoned. Twice I reached him at home, and twice he made appointments he skipped without apology. When I refused to leave the Ministry of Tourism without seeing someone, a nervous secretary produced the youthful and painfully shy Moosa Zameer Hassan, an environmental analyst who was embarrassed by Firaq's performance but unwilling to speak for him, or for himself for that matter, except to remind me of the government's praiseworthy eco-tourism initiatives and regulations, such as prohibiting construction above the foliage line (except in Male), limiting development to 20 percent of any island's total area (except in Male), and requiring water to be desalinated and waste compacted on islands open to tourists.

Perhaps Mr. Firaq made himself unavailable because he, too, was "shy and suspicious of strangers," or maybe he was putting into practice the policy of his superior, Minister of Tourism Ibrahim Hussain Zaki, who had recently boasted to a Western journalist that because of government regulations, "contact between Maldivians and tourists is very minimal," thereby reducing "any cultural impact on Maldivian society."

The assumption that any impact would be negative, at least for the Maldivians, may be justifiable, considering the assault on island cultures elsewhere by mass tourism. But it has to discourage anyone who struggles to believe travel can sometimes enrich visitor and host. Still, I had to admire Mr. Zaki's honesty. No twaddle for him about tourists charmed by friendly natives, or travel encouraging under-standing. Here at last was someone unafraid to voice the unspoken thoughts of countless West Indians, Balinese, and Hawaiians, namely: Leave your money, and leave us alone. What was more, because of the Maldives' unusual geography, it was possible for this sentiment to become law, and for the government to throw some islands to the wolves while preserving the nation's conservative Moslem religious and cultural practices on the rest.

The first evidence that Mr. Zaki and his ministry considered me a cultural Typhoid Mary had come at the Hulhule arrivals hall when I fed my bags into an X-ray machine so sensitive it could allegedly detect the outline of a cross or a Buddha, or the label on a bottle of gin. The segregation of tourists from Maldivians began outside the terminal, with visitors climbing into the helicopters, seaplanes, or speedboats that would deliver them to a gulag of resort islands that were taboo to Maldivians who were not employees or paying customers. Foreigners, in turn, were forbidden to stay overnight on all the 199 islands inhabited solely by Maldivians except Male and Gan. The practical effect of this policy was to make the off-limits Maldivian islands puritan fortresses where alcohol was prohibited. On them, traditional customs were observed, lives ordered by religious faith, and people quarantined from the pernicious influences of modern culture. The tourist islands were posh little Alcatrazes.

A persistent traveler could theoretically visit a Maldivian island if he persuaded a resident to sponsor his visit, and then obtained a government permit. But this was a hurdle few people had the time or stamina to jump. Most visitors encountered no Maldivians except the cleaners who changed their sheets and the waiters who cleared their plates. Because Maldivians were not permitted to serve alcoholic beverages, and were reluctant to live apart from their families in resort island worker housing, about half of all hotel employees were foreigners, mostly from the subcontinent. This meant that a traveler leaving the country with a notebook filled with the names of Maldivian friends and an understanding of Maldivian culture had probably broken the law, and anyone who believed that one of the charms of an island was its friendly people was out of luck.

I left the airport for the first time on the fuel-hungry speedboat of the Taj Lagoon resort, a place I had chosen because it was relatively inexpensive and catered to several nationalities. (I had read that on islands where everyone was German and Italian you could spend a week eating bratwurst or spaghetti Bolognese.) The boatman said I was the only passenger because I was the hotel's only independent traveler. Everyone else arrived or departed en masse.

The Taj Lagoon was a third of a mile long and less than a hundred feet across at the widest point—so small that solitude was impossible and I could not walk anywhere without seeing another guest. Most of its natural vegetation had been cleared to make room for its concrete bungalows, bar, reception room, and restaurant. Air conditioners rattled and wheezed, a generator thumped, and the lagoon echoed with Jet Skis. The Hulhule flight path lay overhead, providing a steady counterpoint of roaring jets and chop-chopping helicopters advancing the global warming timetable by a few seconds as they carried people to islands beyond speedboat range.

Nothing at the hotel said Maldives (although I am not sure what would have said that since I was prohibited from visiting a Maldivian island). Lunch was a moussaka of cabbage and Velveeta, dinner a buffet of Indian curries accompanied by Austrian zither music blasting from loudspeakers. In the lounge, Maldivians in calypso duds played "Guantanamera" and "Que Sera, Sera" while guests wrote postcards. It was impossible to imagine the submergence of the Taj Lagoon leaving any kind of hole, even a pinhole, in anyone's civilization.

The earnest young Indian manager told me the island was susceptible to flooding because it was saucer-shaped and lay only a meter above sea level. It also faced the ocean on one side. "If the scientists are right," he said, "we'll be under water someday. But we're running at ninety percent of capacity, so we should get our investment back in six or seven years, knock on wood."

■

The most gilded holiday island in the Maldivian gulag is the Kuda Huraa Reef Resort, where I spent several pampered days disturbed only by the death of a coconut rat. It was the Maldives' newest resort, designed to the personal specification of a Singapore multimillionaire and "his favorite plaything," an assistant manager told me. Its sleek, thirty-two-foot speedboat inspired envy from tourists climbing into lesser craft at the airport, where I had to return whenever I wanted to travel between islands. The resort had the customary powdery beach and villas perched on spider legs over the water. From offshore, little distinguished it from the Taj Lagoon and other lesser islands. But once on land I could see no expense had been spared in the effort to create what its literature promised as "the champagne and caviar of all island resorts" and "quite possibly the closest to what we deem as heaven on earth."

I spent most of my first day sleeping and swimming. I soaked in a bath facing a picture-window view of the lagoon, wrapped myself in the terry cloth bathrobe, and fell asleep on the king-sized bed. The villa was all blond wood, wicker, and natural fibers, austere and sepia-toned, with no splashy colors to battle the water's restful blues. I allowed myself to be impressed with details like the flagons of musky Thai herbal shampoo, the hot water shower spray on the deck, and a cap made of natural fibers for the spare roll of toilet paper.

I gorged at the lavish buffet lunch in the oceanfront dining room and swam in the free-form freshwater pool, whose turquoise tiles tinted the water so it matched the lagoon. As I walked back to my room past the health club, I noticed, through its picture windows, three thirty-somethings working out on StairMasters and treadmills, and realized in that instant that the secret to enjoying Kuda Huraa was to forget about global warming. It was better not to ask why people flew thousands of miles to a tropical island for health club machines, or if electric saunas and air conditioning on a desert island did not symbolize the kind of fossil fuel consumption that would one day send these StairMasters to the bottom of the Indian Ocean. Better, instead, to gorge on Scottish smoked salmon, quench your thirst with Evian from France and Tiger beer from Singapore, pile your plate with honeydew melon flown thousands of miles from goodness knows where, swim laps in the freshwater pool, crank up the air conditioner to cool your high-ceilinged villa, and rejoice you did not need to close your mouth in the shower or brush with Perrier because the tap water was desalinated, thanks to the imported fuel powering the desalinization plant.

I tried doing this, and letting myself be impressed with Kuda Huraa's much-trumpeted ecotourism features. Some were government-mandated, like the below-the-palm-tree building height and the prohibition against anchoring dive boats on the reef. But pulping garbage and using effluent from the sewage treatment plant to water plants were Kuda Huraa touches. I could not imagine a better-managed or more ecologically correct resort, or one that would be, once the waves rolled across it, a more exquisite corpse.

Kuda Huraa's literature frequently invoked Crusoe's name, and a brochure published by Mr. Firaq's ministry proclaimed, "Every resort is Robinson Crusoe's island but equipped with modern amenities subtly hidden away." You could quibble with the "subtly hidden away" part, but you had to concede the Maldivian resort islands were in the Crusoean tradition of improving your material surroundings. It could be argued that if Crusoe could have equipped his island with a karaoke machine, relaxed in a Traditional Thai Herbal Aromatic Spa, hidden his valuables from cannibals in an electronic safe, had his faxes delivered in a bamboo canister, or covered his spare roll of toilet paper with a natural fiber cap, he might have done so, although his prayers and journal might have suffered.

One inarguable difference between Crusoe's island and Kuda Huraa was that while Crusoe built everything from native materials and ate native foods, everything here was imported. Another was that he had a large island to himself, while these London high-lifers, picky French, purse-lipped old Germans, and refrigerator-sized Russians were sharing a small island with less space than the average cruise liner. Most of them spent their days thumbing fat novels, rotating on chaise longues like slabs of rotisserie meat, and snubbing one another, perhaps to maintain the fiction that this desert island was supplying space and solitude. I counted it as a good day when I could force a few nods or smiles from people I encountered again and again on the paths or in restaurants.

Had I not been traveling alone, I might have kept the Crusoe-with-all-the-amenities ball in the air longer, and missed the coconut rat (the only mammal besides humans and flying foxes adapted to atoll life) scampering over the feet of two Russian molls at a neighboring table in the open-air dining room. The women jumped and squealed. Their male companions chased the rat outside and stunned it with a kick before stomping it to death. They returned to the table and ordered a bottle of Veuve Clicquot (my wedding champagne) to celebrate, and I remembered my favorite atoll island, Abemama, whose beauty and charm had rested in the simplicity of its ingredients, just sand, water, palm, and sky.

No one on Abemama had minded the coconut rats and everything I ate had been grown on the island or caught from its waters. I compared Abemama and Kuda Huraa and wondered what in God's name we were doing here, crammed onto a fragile 450-foot-by-150-foot island capable of sustaining, at best, a few fishermen and some rats. Both Kuda Huraa and the Taj Resort had been "lost" decades before their actual submersion, subtracted from the inventory of real islands once air-conditioning, saunas, StairMasters, and all the other folderol submerged their genuine insular pleasures of silence, solitude, and simplicity.

I returned to my villa past the health club. Even at 9:00 P.M. it was brightly lit and busy. I realized that if you wanted to design a tourist industry with a maximum fossil fuel emission per visitor you could hardly improve on the Maldivian model in which everyone flew thousands of miles to a remote island, moved around by power boat and helicopter, and stayed at resorts where the food and building materials were imported and generators kept the air conditioners humming and the saunas hot.

Until Kuda Huraa, I had associated conservation with preserving fragments of prairie, stands of old-growth forest, and tracts of desert—continental spaces. When I thought of the extirpation of geographic features I saw deserts flooded, wetlands drained, prairies ploughed, and mountains strip-mined, but not an island losing everything making it an island, except the water surrounding it. I thought about conservation in continental terms because those have been the terms of the most influential American conservationists. Thoreau means Walden Pond and New England. John Muir is Yosemite and the fight against the Hetch Hetchy Dam. Aldo Leopold's *A Sand County Almanac*, the great conservationist work of the last fifty years, is grounded in the prairies, forests, mountains, and deserts Leopold knew as a Forest Service employee and University of Wisconsin professor. Leopold uses these continental spaces to argue for a "land ethic" that gives land the same rights as its inhabitants, and recognizes land "as a community to which we belong." But if despoiling one desert acre and one mile of riverbank contravenes this ethic, then how big is the land crime that bleaches an entire reef, turns an island into a Taj Lagoon or Kuda Huraa, or submerges it?

I stayed up reading the 1996–2005 Tourism Master Plan for the Maldives I had bullied out of Mr. Hassan. It recommended doubling tourist beds from ten thousand to twenty thousand, adding a new runway and apron to the airport, and doubling visitor arrivals. What lesson could be drawn, then, from the fact that the International Conscience on Global Warming, a nation advocating a 20 percent fossil fuel reduction for the developed world, planned on doubling its own fuel-intensive tourist industry? That few officials believed the submersion scenario? Poor countries argue that Western nations that have already profited from the prolific use of fossil fuels should make the greatest sacrifices, but the Maldives were no longer poor. They had added twenty years to life expectancy and raised their literacy rate to 90 percent. They enjoyed the highest per capita income and growth rate in South Asia and the United Nations was proposing to move them from the "poorest" countries list to the "developing" one.

Considering the natural constraints of atoll islands, you could say the Maldivian tourist islands had already met, or exceeded, their sustainable level of development.

Like any cruise liner whose passengers sometimes want to escape the pleasant monotony of shipboard life, Kuda Huraa offered excursions. I chose the one to Buda Huraa, an official Handicraft Island twenty-five yards across a channel. As our group walked through a gauntlet of cinder block buildings leading up from the pier, shutters flew up and merchants beckoned us into one-room stores crammed with Russian dolls, Thai carvings, Filipino T-shirts, and painted fish from Sri Lanka—airport art from other airports.

"Tour now, buy later," snapped our guide, a bored hotel employee named Shafew.

Not only was there nothing to see on Buda Huraa, no one except these merchants wanted to see us. People stared blankly from their hammocks and string chairs. The reception was so chilly I would have welcomed a beggar.

Shafew's tour took twenty minutes. He walked us up a street of coral and cinder block houses so we could admire a school volleyball court. Then we saw the village generator, a graveyard, and a salt pond bordered by stunted banyans. He urged us to peer into holes where, if we got lucky, we might see a coconut crab. (We did not.)

While the others shopped I bullied him into introducing me to the atoll chief, a young man named Abdul Rahem who lived next to his souvenir store. We talked in a parlor where the only furniture was a television that sat on a pedestal like an idol.

"Tell me about your island," I said.

"We are designated shopping island for foreigners. We have one hundred and five households, and forty-five have televisions and VCRs."

"What do your people think of Kuda Huraa?"

"Only twelve of our men have ever been there to work."

"Do more people want to go?"

He shrugged. "Why should they?"

Buda Huraa's people made their living from fishing, he said, although that was becoming more difficult. Before 1972 they had fished from sailboats, and fish filled the surrounding waters. Now they drove diesel boats and there were fewer fish nearby, so they traveled greater distances and used more fuel.

Did he think global warming would submerge Buda Huraa during the lifetime of his children and grandchildren?

He only knew that the weather had changed. Before there had been sunshine, now there was rain. He said, "The best thing we can do is stop building with coral. If we protect our reef, maybe it will protect us."

■

The only place besides Male where I was legally permitted to mingle freely with Maldivians was Adduu atoll. I flew there in a rainstorm and landed at the former Royal Air Force base on Gan island. The British had left this atoll with an educated, Anglophone population, twenty-three miles of roads connecting Gan to the islands of Feydhuu, Maradhuu, and Hithadhuu, and the three causeways that have silted Gan's beaches and left them eroded and weedy. Gan had some former RAF buildings and a former noncommissioned officers' club that had become the Ocean Reef Club, a hotel designated for foreigners.

During the day, Gan filled with elderly Maldivian laborers who, like the retainers of an exiled family keeping the silver polished and the fires lit, trimmed hedges, swept leaves, repainted guard posts, and emptied the RAF's "Keep Gan Tidy" trash cans. Every evening, they returned to one of the other islands, leaving behind Gan's only overnight residents, the guests at the Ocean Reef and several hundred Sri Lankan ladies who lived in RAF barracks and sewed underwear in RAF warehouses converted into factories. (This enterprise was not some brilliant economic development scheme but simply a way for Sri Lankan entrepreneurs to make an end run around U.S. import quotas.) Every morning and evening, I saw the Sri Lankans' stony,

prisoner faces, framed in the windows of the buses shuttling them between barracks and factory. They were locked in a circle of sweatshop
hell lacking even the comfort of returning home at the end of a
shift. When I asked the locals why they did not also work in this factory they said it was not worth it to spend so much time away from
their families, working twelve hours a day for a hundred dollars a
month.

Enjoying a holiday on an island you are sharing with sweatshop
laborers was the least of the challenges facing a guest at the Ocean
Reef. The resort was a package tour of Devil's Island with dark and
shabby bungalows and no beach. A typical meal consisted of beef
stew, soggy chips, watery coleslaw, and, on an atoll famous for fruit,
canned pears. It rained almost all the time while I was there, and had
been raining for a week. Aside from the former RAF pastimes of
billiards, squash, and Ping-Pong, there was nothing to do except
scuba dive and watch the BBC World Service on cable television, all
the while flapping your arms to ward off swarms of flies.

I biked across the causeway to the other islands and asked people
if they believed this atoll would soon be submerged, forcing them to
become refugees in the homeland of the Sri Lankan ladies. The owner
of the Causeway Store said President Gayoom might be worried about
global warming but he was not because Allah would save the Maldives. But Abdullah Saeed, a brisk man wearing a pink Ralph Lauren
shirt who administered the regional hospital in Hithadhuu told me,
"Educated people who can compare the weather with several years
ago believe in global warming. What can we do? We don't have any
industries, we don't emit any of these gases." Then he explained that
his father had been a trader who often sailed to Sri Lanka to buy
goods, and until the late 1970s Maldivian fishermen used boats powered by pandanus leaf sails instead of engines.

Another freak rainstorm was beating down so hard on the roof of
the government offices that Hasid Usaf, chief of Adduu atoll, had to

shout when I asked if it was true that some Americans were investing in a thousand-bed resort on nearby Viligili island.

"It is going through. Definite!" he boomed. "Tourists will fly into Gan on big jets. The papers are being signed in Male, although you are wrong about the beds. There will be fifteen hundred."

Did the investors believe in global warming?

"Global warming is international talk. Our president has raised the issue in those forums, but we haven't had any really bad experiences. . . ." He glanced at the photograph of Gayoom over his desk and added, "It's not that we don't believe him, but there are differences among the scientists."

Would Maldivians become refugees in Sri Lanka?

"No one believes that, do they? You don't think we'll have to leave, do you?"

Back in Male I tracked down the big names in global warming circles. Ibrahim Rashid, a career civil servant who had helped launch VESHI (Volunteers for Environmental and Social Harmony and Improvement), believed a big turning point had come when the storm and floods of 1987 inundated Male neighborhoods recently reclaimed from the ocean. The storm was devastating because the reef protecting the island from previous storms had been extensively mined for coral to fill this reclaimed ground. He worried that the government's new restrictions on mining coral would be ignored on islands where people could not afford imported concrete, and that the Maldives' exploding population would foreclose the possibility of gathering people on a few islands more easily protected by seawalls. There was talk of opening more uninhabited islands to relieve population pressure, talk of more expensive seawalls, and café talk about emigration, or a *Waterworld* solution of living on gigantic boats. "Some believe in global warming and some don't," he mused. "Some think it will take forty years, others centuries. Some hope our coral will grow fast enough to save us. Some wealthy families have purchased land in Sri

Lanka. They claim it is not because of global warming, but *they'll* always have a place to go to."

Abdullah Majeed, the deputy minister of planning, human resources, and environment, was the Maldives' most distinguished meteorologist. He had made a nuisance of himself at all the major environmental conferences of the 1980s and 1990s, and he detested the OPEC bullies and lobbyists for American oil companies. He had walked out of the Nairobi conference when a Saudi Arabian delegate told the representatives of small island states that they were only a few million people who could move elsewhere.

After twenty-six years in the meteorological service he was certain the weather had undergone dramatic changes. The waves crashing into the roofs of Male houses; the one-and-a-half-degree rise in the ocean's temperature; the seven inches of rain that fell in four hours in 1994 and flooded his house; the eight inches falling in two days before my arrival, flooding streets in Male and leaving three feet of water in some areas; the rougher seas; the gale force winds blowing eight months of the year—*some* of these phenomena *must* be caused by global warming.

The government was doing what it could, banning coral mining from inhabited islands and reducing tariffs on imported construction materials. But people still mined reefs on uninhabited islands, and the Maldives' damaged reefs were not keeping up with rising sea levels. With the population growing and Male already overcrowded, the government might have to open uninhabited islands to settlement, and some of their reefs were being mined as we spoke. He had recommended consolidating the populations on the ten or twelve largest islands and protecting them with seawalls higher than Male's. But moving people who had strong attachments to the ground inhabited by their ancestors was ticklish. Even evacuating people from the six most endangered islands had proven difficult. And building seawalls around a dozen large islands required considerable foreign aid.

Theoretically, the whole population could move to India or Australia, and this would solve the problem of their existence, but not of their culture. They would be a small group of conservative Muslims, speaking a foreign tongue, knowing only fishing and seamanship, and scattered like atolls in a sea of Christians or Hindus.

His best hope was that the developed world would reduce its fossil fuel consumption by 20 percent, which was the recommendation of the Alliance of Small Island States. Otherwise, he would have to hope that because no one knew exactly what the regional variations of global warming might be, the Maldives would suffer less than other low-lying atolls. "Maybe we won't be wiped out, maybe only half our atolls will be flooded," he suggested. "Even so, how can we maintain a routine life?"

When I mentioned the Maldivian tourist industry's small yet symbolic contribution to greenhouse gases, I heard more about the government's environmental programs—the ban on mining the reefs of inhabited islands, the ban on shark fishing, the requirement that resorts provide five meters of beachfront per visitor, the marine parks, the planting of a million trees, and so on. Some resorts had installed solar panels, he said. Some crushed cans and burned waste in incinerators. The German airline LTU gave its passengers plastic bags for bringing home dead batteries and empty sunblock bottles.

I liked Mr. Majeed so much I could not bear to remind him that, only months before, President Gayoom had told delegates to an IPCC meeting in Male: "It would make no difference whether environmental damage is caused by a developed country or a poor one, by one far away or nearer home. Those who do not want to be part of the solution will certainly become part of the problem. They will, in fact, hasten an ecological tragedy of worldwide proportions."

Some day, people concerned about global warming may take President Gayoom at his word and demand a real ecotourism free of air-conditioning, motorized transport, and imported food—a Robinson

Crusoe existence *without* the amenities. They may also ask themselves how they can justify traveling ten thousand miles to a desert island to run on a treadmill in an air-conditioned health club, sing karaoke, and buzz around on Jet Skis. The obvious answer is that if this is all they are coming for, they should probably stay home and contribute a few seconds to the life expectancy of a Maldivian island.

2 PERSONAL ISLANDS

5

BELOVED ISLANDS —
FISHERS AND CAMPOBELLO

When I drew up a list of the islands where I had spent at least a night, I was astonished at the sharp and distinct memories they evoked.

There were a dozen Greek islands, many of them bleak and stony, yet each with something—a whitewashed monastery built into a cliff, a forlorn Italianate mansion capping a headland, a Holy Land smell of wild rosemary and thyme—to distinguish it from the rest. There were fourteen Pacific islands. Tarawa was men singing hymns while digging their taro pits by lantern, Aitutaki was the redheaded grandchildren of American airmen punching a volleyball, and Abemama little girls playing jacks on the steps of a church, slapping hands, touching their ears, and crossing themselves twice while the ball was in midair before grabbing a fistful of cowrie shells.

The summer resort islands of the eastern seaboard of North America summoned up particularly compelling memories. "Family," "summer," "island," and "home" are potent words. Combine them in a shingled house with a porch and wicker furniture, a meadow running to the water, a bell for calling children to dinner on summer evenings. Then set it all on a rocky, balsam-scented island to which a family has been returning for generations, and you can encourage a powerful nostalgia in anyone who has spent time as a child on an island off the northeast coast of North America between June and September, and excite powerful longings in anyone who has not.

■

I had not been to Fishers Island since 1965, but I sometimes flew over it on the way back to New York from Europe. It is a distinctive island from the air, long and vaguely fishhook-shaped, with fresh-water ponds that sparkle and flash like mirrors. One look down, and until I landed at Kennedy I was lost in memories wrapped in a dense fog or overlit by a white summer sun. They included the customary sexual fumblings and athletic frustrations of a teenage boy, but lacked the anxieties and insecurities coloring my mainland memories of that period.

In a 1985 article about Fishers Island in *New York* magazine that I clipped and saved, an upper-class matron praised it for offering her children "an affirmation of American values." Another woman said she and her husband, who had both summered there as children, continued to return with their own children because she wanted them to have "real roots." She also liked it that she could "turn them loose" and know nothing bad could happen to them.

My own parents chose Fishers Island for its location. My mother loved islands because of her Nantucket connections, but was reluctant to summer there or in Maine and become a summer widow. But Fishers was in the mouth of Long Island Sound, in New York State and near enough to New York City for my father to join us on weekends. For several years, beginning in 1960, we rented a Victorian house on a street of fishermen and summer people of modest means, at least by Fishers standards. During this time, my father died, my mother remarried, and we moved between several New York apartments. But Fishers remained a constant, where I felt most rooted.

Unlike an East Coast barrier island that is all dunes and grass, or a Maine one that is rock and pine, Fishers had a little of everything. The east end, with its freshwater ponds, pocket forests, and rocky inlets, had the cautious beauty of a nature reserve. Isabella Beach had the kind of towering sand dunes you find on Cape Cod, but without the crowds. The sheltered harbor at the western end could have been in Maine, and the leafy village surrounded a green, like one in the Berkshires. Fishers was more pretty than beautiful, but its geographic variety made it the kind of miniature island world that leaves indelible memories.

The first wealthy white man to visit Fishers was Governor John Winthrop of the Connecticut Colony, who bought it from the Pequot Indians in 1644. His descendants raised livestock on it for two centuries before selling it to the first in a line of industrialist families. The last of these turned it into a summer resort.

On the eastern end, usually capitalized "the East End," the summer homes of the du Ponts, Firestones, Whitneys, Watsons (IBM), and Simmonses (Beautyrest mattresses) lay hidden down sandy driveways and camouflaged by Frederick Law Olmsted landscaping. Members of Fishers' Old Families, as we called them (and as they liked being called), exhausted themselves at sports, entertained modestly, and retired early. They sat on hand-me-down wicker settees, drove old clunkers known as island cars, ate off chipped china, and wore baggy khakis, floppy white hats, and threadbare sweaters in muted heather colors. Three times a week, they paid a quarter to sit on tattered seats in the former Army base cinema and watch third-run movies. When it rained, they pulled out warped jigsaw puzzles. If the shabbiness was bogus, I did not notice it. And so what if it was? Big Money hiding itself is easier to take than big money triumphant. Perhaps this simplicity is what that matron meant by American values.

The Old Families employed several clever tricks to make Fishers so difficult for outsiders to reach or enjoy that it felt more like fifty miles off the coast of Connecticut than five. The most effective was a rule that car reservations for the ferry could only be made in person at the dock on Fishers Island. This guaranteed that outsiders would have difficulty getting their cars onto the ferry at New London on busy weekends, and discouraged them from coming over at all, since they could never be sure of returning when they wanted. The Old Families also made sure there were no taxis and no rental cars or bicycles, so foot passengers had no way to explore the island. Even if visitors overcame these obstacles, there was little to see or do. There were no public tennis courts or golf courses, and the best beaches lay beyond a No Trespassing sign at the entrance to the East End. Social life revolved around the clubs, and anyone not belonging to at least one had a lonely summer, something driven home to me one evening when I passed Richard Nixon walking down Chocomount Beach in his stiff-jointed way, wearing office shoes and a windbreaker. It was the only time I ever felt sorry for him. After losing the California governor's race he had moved his family to New York and rented a house on Fishers only to have the Old Families blackball him from their clubs. They may have been Republicans, but Fishers came first and they feared that if he had a good time he might keep returning and "put Fishers on the map"—an unsettling prospect for people who would rather have airbrushed it from every atlas.

Fishers provided a combination of freedom and security that is an appealing feature of geographically remote islands. When our parents said "Fishers is great for kids," what they really meant was that we could amuse ourselves, leaving them to play golf, sail, and party without worrying about us. They turned us loose, and we enjoyed the adult-free idyll of R. M. Ballantyne's *The Coral Island* and the early chapters of William Golding's *Lord of the Flies*, although unlike Golding's castaways we were a tolerant and gentle bunch, willing to put away the mainland habits of cliques and rivalries for the summer. We understood that it was impossible to escape to another town or find a new circle of friends, and that because no one graduates from an island, we would be returning year after year, perhaps for the rest of our lives.

My summers on Fishers proved what my daughter Edwina said about kids getting to do what they want on islands. My friends and I biked to movies, dances, and beer parties, and hitched rides up and down the island with older kids. We spent our days sailing, playing tennis, body-surfing, water skiing, and loafing, building bonfires and making out. We brushed against our parents at weekly dances at the rickety clubhouse at Hay Harbor, where dads fox-trotted with their daughters and sons taught their mothers the Twist. But most of the time we were shipwrecked children, and our parents were ghosts.

Like any island tribe, we had our customs and rituals. We raced sailboats every Wednesday and Saturday, and on Sunday we gathered at the same beach for lunch. Instead of painting our faces, we painted graffiti on the roads. Once a year, we held a ritualistic party at our sacred spot, a line of empty concrete gun emplacements, or "pits," at Fort Wright, an abandoned army base built during the Spanish-American War to guard the entrance to Long Island Sound.

Many islands have lonely and taboo-protected sacred spots that survive because a dependence on weather and tides encourages nature worship, and because without vast continental spaces to sap their potency or a city's clutter to slow their momentum, island myths gain velocity and power as they move between generations. Abemama has a royal tomb so taboo gulls flying overhead fall to the ground dead. Native Hawaiians leave flowers and cans of Budweiser and Spam on volcano rims for the goddess Pele. During the bittersweet week preceding Labor Day, the summer teenagers of Fishers gathered at Fort Wright for a pit party that combined the secrecy, fire, music, taboos, and sexual frisson common to island sacred places. Our tribal elders, kids over eighteen who could buy beer, announced the party at the last minute to bamboozle the state trooper. We lit a bonfire in a pit and sat above on its concrete apron, playing guitars and singing folk songs. There might be a band from New London, or we would dance to radios. We knit stories of the summer's parties and of the couples who had broken up that we would remember for at least another summer. Cicadas cried and the surf boomed. Sparks flew into the night and huge shadows flickered across concrete walls.

Our tans were mahogany and our hair streaked gold from the sun. An unspoken taboo outlawed fights and I remember it broken only once, when a famous child actor recently married to a summer girl provoked a brawl that ended in tears and bloody noses. That winter he died in a car crash.

I knew some of my former friends continued summering on Fishers Island with their own families, and it reassured me to think that an island with so little development and so much empty land could survive just off the coast of the Washington-to-Boston megalopolis. The summer people of Fishers Island could take care of themselves, but I wished them well anyway, and hoped the next generation was enjoying pit parties, putting down roots, and riding bikes through a landscape where big money still hid itself. I hoped the Fishers of my memory and the present-day island would be much the same. After all, if one of the largest concentrations of wealth on the eastern seaboard could not save the remote soul of one narrow, nine-mile-long island, then who, or what, could?

■

New London's once bustling downtown had become a South Bronx of derelict buildings, empty storefronts, and winos sprawled across benches left over from several failed beautification campaigns. Passengers arriving for the Fishers Island ferry were like actors wandering onto the wrong set, guests at Gatsby's party turning up in an Atlanta burned by Sherman. Many were wearing and driving their money, and from the upper deck I watched the crew back aboard a rich fleet of Saabs, Infinitis, Mercedes, and high-end sport utility vehicles. The same clever car reservations game was in play, and we left some lesser vehicles on the dock.

I was on the Ship of Blonds. Blond ponytails bounced and blond arm hairs glistened in the sun. Towheaded boys swung on their fathers' furry blond legs. Had we been this groomed, this beautiful? Our mothers this nervous and overexercised? Passengers on the ferry had always known each other, but on this crossing everyone was a stranger.

I stayed on the island with a college classmate but spent much of my time riding around on my bike. At first glance, it appeared the Old Families had succeeded in embalming their beloved island. There were none of the huge marinas, shopping centers, and developments that have transformed the coast of southern New England, and the village remained a small town of hedges, front porches, and leafy streets. One bar had burned down, another had expanded. The pharmacy had closed, a new school had opened, and some houses at Fort Wright had been renovated. At Chocomount beach, I found charred driftwood in a spot where we always built fires. At West Harbor, the same class of boats I had sailed, Bulls-Eyes, bobbed on their moorings. My ghost was in the courtyard of the Army base cinema where we had gathered under the naked light bulbs after every movie, on the headland of flat rocks near Hay Harbor where I took girlfriends, and on the porch of our house on Hedge Street where we played bridge and drank beer decanted into Coke cans. Everything looked so unchanged I could have been seeing it with fourteen-year-old eyes.

In a short history of the island I found at the library I read that "no one who ever participated in them will ever forget the 'pit parties' of the 1960s, held in the abandoned gun emplacements of Fort Wright. They included live music, keg beer, and a lot of good fun." But none of the kids I met knew what a pit party was, or had even been to the pits. I biked out and discovered they had become an informal dumping ground, and time and weather had obliterated our initials and arrow-pierced hearts.

I began to suspect that although Fishers had retained the appearance of a remote island, its soul had moved closer to the mainland. The roads were busy with expensive imported cars and sport utility vehicles, and I did not see a single island car. I was told that drivers passed without exchanging waves because so many were nannies

or short-term renters. Before, a small NO TRESPASSING sign had announced the East End. Now the sign was huge, and its message was
reinforced by a guard who stopped me several times because my bike
lacked a resident's sticker. There were fewer children riding bikes,
more being chauffeured by nannies and au pairs, and at the Hay Harbor dance, where we had at least danced with our parents once a
week, the same large tribe of child-minders was teaching its charges
the Macarena. At parties I overheard the following said, without
shame: "He earned four hundred million from that deal when four
hundred million *meant* something." "Their house is a ten-year project, then it'll be ready for *Architectural Digest*." "The only way to get
these island contractors to finish a job is to threaten them."

It was agreed that the Old Families, whose fortunes came from
making things, were slowly being replaced by newcomers whose
wealth came from moving money. (The real island royalty were Old
Family kids who had also made Wall Street killings.) The newcomers,
who had usually attended better colleges and tended to be smarter
than the Old Family children, tended to fuss more over their interior
decorating and landscaping. At a party I met the sister of an old friend,
a spunky tomboy who had never missed a summer on Fishers. She
agreed people were less friendly, and slammed the "big money yuppies" for stripping fine old island houses of their fixtures and furnishings and replacing them with matched sets from New York
department stores. These people were rude to island workmen and—
the most unforgivable sin of all—rude to the help at the clubs. She
had considered leaving, but where could she go? The simple island
life may have ended on Fishers, she admitted, "but at least we're not
as bad as Nantucket."

The new summer people had also disappointed a docent at the
museum who had come in the late 1950s to teach at the school. Unlike the Old Families, few of the newcomers took the trouble to get to
know winter people like her. "They don't come for the whole season," she complained, "and I guess they must be hard up, because if

they can't be in their houses they rent them out, giving us more traffic and people. Sometimes I don't even know everyone who's on this island."

My Fishers Island had a population of fifteen hundred summer people and five hundred year-round residents. But with the closing of the Navy and Coast Guard bases the winter population had plummeted to under three hundred while the summer one had doubled to three thousand. This new ratio of ten to one had changed the island. Many summer people were two-career couples lacking the time and temperament for the long vacations that had nurtured island summer communities. They came for two weeks instead of two months, and some houses were like ski condominiums, occupied every week or two by a new family. This was why members of the dwindling population of townies were treated more like employees of a resort than members of a community, and why the summer children found it more difficult to create the close-knit community that had nurtured my memories. To preserve the illusion of remoteness, the summer people continued to restrict development, opposing bike paths and a larger ferry that would have brought over day-trippers. But their own frequent comings and goings, huge cars, and decorated houses had diminished Fishers's remote soul, leaving it more distant from ruined New London, but closer in spirit to Greenwich, Connecticut, and to Wall Street and the Upper East Side of Manhattan.

On my last afternoon I noticed cars parked at the school and I joined a meeting in the gymnasium, where an educational consultant hired by the Fishers Island Civic Association to study the school was presenting his report to an audience of winter and summer people. He summarized it by saying that this school—with its seventy children, highest per-pupil expenditure in New York State, and student-teacher ratio of five to one—was a happy and exciting place. But this was apparently not what many people wanted to hear, and there was considerable grumbling. Many in the audience had expected him to recommend closing the high school and sending its students to schools in Connecticut. Some summer people complained of high taxes, arguing that it would be cheaper to send island children to boarding schools. Some winter people believed that the high school could not provide enough socialization and stimulation, and that its extracurricular activities were too limited, in part because thirteen of its twenty-one students were magnet students from Connecticut who took the ferry home every afternoon. Perhaps they were the wrong kind of people for an island, or perhaps—and more likely, considering the type of education Americans believe their children need—few families are prepared to endure the educational challenges of living on a remote island.

I went from the school meeting to a party at a faux Norman chateau occupying some high ground in the island's interior that had been empty for several years and fallen into disrepair. A young couple with lucrative Wall Street jobs had recently bought it and were restoring it, and this party was to celebrate the baptism of their infant daughter. The afternoon light seemed filtered through gauze, the kind filmmakers use when characters remember an idyllic childhood. The adults stood on a grand terrace with sweeping island views while barefoot girls in white dresses and yellow ribbons cartwheeled across the lawn. The parents had cautious tans and health club physiques and wore black city clothes. They talked about their jobs and about how, by purchasing this white elephant, our hosts had proven themselves to be incredibly brave.

A patrician woman with a well-bred nose was introduced to me as a doyenne of the summer people. Once I established my credentials as a lapsed old-timer she happily excoriated the Wall Street newcomers surrounding us and I heard, yet again, how they were rude to the townies and failed to grasp that Fishers needed the winter people to support the doctor and the year-round ferry service, to open and close summer houses, and, most important of all, to man the volunteer fire department to prevent houses from burning down over the winter. She had attended the school meeting, too, and was furious at the consultant, believing he should have recommended closing the costly high school and sending the kids to boarding school. After all, tuition at Choate or St. Paul's was half the $50,000 a year it was costing to educate a student here. "Offer a free prep school education and people will be falling over each other to winter here," she said. But it had apparently not occurred to her and the other summer people who advocated this solution that a prospective volunteer fireman might resist sending his children to boarding school, or that wintering on an island without teenagers might be spooky, or that people attracted to Fishers by a free prep school tuition might depart once their children graduated, leaving the winter community as transient as the summer one, or that if the only way to save an island community was to bribe mainlanders to join it, then it might already be doomed.

■

I traveled directly from Fishers to its great bogeyman in Massachusetts, Nantucket, where a couple I know were spending a week in a rented house with the wife's mother and stepfather. I had not been back since 1955, when my family arrived there on a ferry that was so empty my sister and I held races on its pitching deck, and for three days seemed to be alone on a horror-movie set of wet cobblestones, empty moors, banging shutters, and moaning foghorns.

New York Times columnist Russell Baker had been enchanted by Nantucket's solitude and simplicity when he began summering there in the 1950s. During the 1990s he wrote jeremiads excoriating the trophy houses blighting a landscape once notable for its bare oceanic beauty, the elephantine sport utility vehicles jamming its narrow lanes, and the tycoons jockeying for parking spots at its supermarket. He warned that a "quiet, magically preserved piece of the past," an island he made sound as timeless as Banda Neira, was becoming "a vast stage set for flaunting wealth." Around this time, I read in the Times that on one summer Saturday, Nantucket's airport had more takeoffs and landings than Logan Airport in Boston. I also noticed a classified

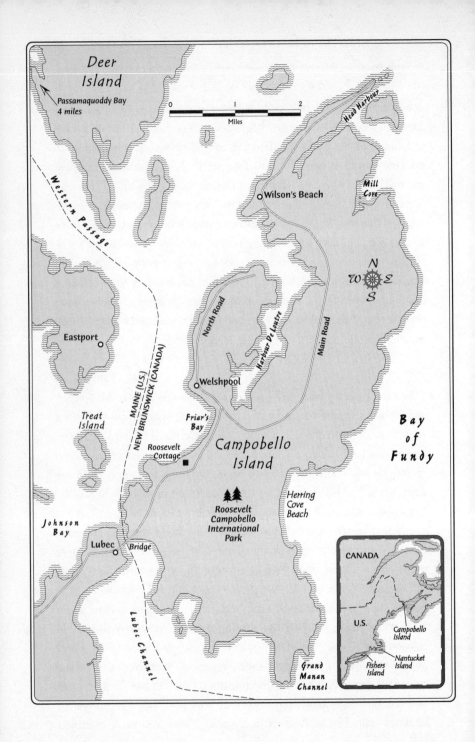

advertisement in my local newspaper announcing, "Framers wanted on Nantucket Island. Must have own hand tools and transportation." So many houses were being thrown up on Nantucket's moors that contractors were reaching hundreds of miles into the Adirondacks for workers.

After I arrived on Nantucket, it took me thirty minutes to rent a bicycle and another thirty to escape a town where traffic jammed the narrow roads to the curb, forcing even bikes to a halt. A line of cars sat idling outside the Stop & Shop, waiting for a parking space; private jets crossed the sky; and an unbroken procession of joggers, Rollerbladers, and cyclists filled the bike path. The restaurants I called for reservations warned of ninety-minute waits for tables. During my stay I rarely purchased anything, even a newspaper, without standing in line. Anything you could buy in a suburban shopping mall, you could buy here, too: chewy bagels, frothy cappuccinos, slick educational toys, whatever. The mainland celebrated gargantuan stores, big salaries, huge portions of food, and jumbo-sized houses with vast kitchens and bathrooms, and so everything on Nantucket that was new was large, too. The airport was being expanded to accommodate larger private jets. Huge homes flew flags the size of spinnakers and houses miles from the harbor still had widow's walks perched on their enormous roofs, like cherries on rich sundaes.

I stayed with my friends in a neglected stucco house on an ocean bluff. Its thin walls and cubbyhole kitchen were throwbacks to an earlier age. One morning, a real estate agent stopped to warn us it could not be rented next summer because he had just sold it for $2.2 million. Perhaps it would be a tear-down.

The development and crowding flabbergasted the stepfather, who was returning for the first time in fifteen years. He muttered how this Nantucket, where the median price of a home was over half a million dollars and it cost a quarter of a million simply to join a golf club, bore no resemblance to what he remembered. "Who would pay to come here?" he kept asking.

I reminded him he had.

"And I'm never coming back."

You often hear about islands being "loved to death." But Nantucket was simply attracting people who loved the *idea* of an island, not the reality, who wanted to live large rather than small, and wanted an island where you could buy anything, except simplicity.

■

I had never been to Campobello, the small Canadian island in Passamoquoddy Bay where President Franklin Delano Roosevelt spent all his boyhood summers, courted his wife, and brought his own children, but for almost four decades it had symbolized the simple island life for me, occupying almost as prominent a place in my memories and dreams as Fishers Island. It first bewitched me in 1960, when I read a biography of Franklin Roosevelt and saw the movie *Sunrise at Campobello*, which was filmed on location at his cottage, in rooms still containing the Roosevelt family furniture. As the movie opens, on August 10, 1921, we see the Roosevelts sailing, swimming, and extinguishing a brushfire, then returning to their three-story, barn-shaped Dutch colonial "cottage." The children roughhouse with their father (played by Ralph Bellamy) and practice for the evening entertainment, a reading of *Julius Caesar*. After Eleanor Roosevelt (Greer Garson) uses a megaphone to summon them to dinner, she and Franklin have a romantic moment as the sun sets over the bay. That night, Franklin experiences the first symptoms of polio, but even as physicians come and go, his family continues its pleasant summer routine of baseball games, picnics, and hayrides.

This close and busy family life is one I suspect I have been trying to emulate ever since, and it may account for our living on a rocky, forested shore of Lake Champlain and filling our summers with sailing, softball, and driftwood bonfires. I know that when I see my daughters run up our meadow from the water in their bathing suits I experience a déjà vu I understood only after I watched *Sunrise at*

Campobello for the first time in almost forty years, and saw the Roosevelt children, also in bathing suits, dashing up their meadow.

I was reminded of the Roosevelts at Campobello when I noticed Des Alwi slowly and thoughtfully running his fingers across the grooves in his boyhood desk, speaking about his youth on Banda Neira as if nothing as important or memorable had happened since, and saying he could remember it all, "as if it was yesterday." During Franklin Roosevelt's last days in the White House, when he was sick and exhausted, he often startled aides and visitors by launching into accounts of long-ago sailing excursions and picnics on Campobello. What made these reminiscences so striking was that since being struck by polio on Campobello he had returned for only two visits that are better measured in hours than days. The reason, according to his sons, was that he could not bear to revisit a place where he had once been so active and happy.

I remembered Roosevelt, Des Alwi, and my own boyhood on Fishers Island when I read *My World Is an Island*, an autobiographical work by Elizabeth Ogilvie, who has set her novels and children's books on the coast of Maine and its islands, and who has lived for most of her adult life on Gay's Island, one so near the mainland you can walk to it at low tide. In her introduction to *My World Is an Island*, Ogilvie recalls a clear and pale insular sunshine, feeling spongy black earth underneath her toes, wild strawberries ripening in the fog, flowers blooming by a seawall, and cuckoos gliding between apple trees. The island is a "spiritual presence" she carries everywhere, she says, as much a part of her as the color of her eyes. But the reader soon discovers that the island of these sharp and indelible memories is not Gay's, but Ragged Island, a place of "wild and astonishing beauty" twenty miles from mainland Maine where her mother summered, and where Ogilvie spent the first four summers of her life and several summers during her teenage years. For her, the "real" Ragged Island is not the geographical one of the present, with its unfamiliar buildings and people, but the one of her youth, where she remembers walking home across a marsh in the moonlight after a square dance and being "so blessedly, eternally young."

I was reminded of Ogilvie when I visited my friend Carolyn Marsh on Narrows Island, a three-acre island in a Maine lake her father purchased in 1956 for reasons that still mystify her. He was an Ohio native who had shown no great interest in islands or water, yet one day, seized by a sudden need to own an island, he bought Narrows. Afterwards, she and her mother and two sisters spent every summer there, living in a rambling wooden cottage with a screen porch, stone fireplace, and dock, and doing without a telephone or electricity. Her father drove twelve hours each way from Connecticut to join them on weekends.

Carolyn and her sisters still summer on Narrows, and because she lives nearby she sometimes goes out in winter, when the lake is frozen and it is the only place she can be sure of not hearing a man-made sound. She is the right person for an island: self-sufficient, frugal, an avid reader, comfortable with solitude, and greedy for small pleasures. When I finally saw Narrows, I realized that forty summers on it had nurtured the traits I find so appealing in her.

It is one of seven islands in a lake with so many twists and bays it is often hard to know whether you are seeing the mainland or another island. There is nothing remarkable about it, no rock shaped like a camel, no hill resembling a nose. It is a quarter mile long and vaguely teardrop-shaped, with beavers and herons, blueberry bushes, and clumps of pink and white lady's slippers. Its pines are straight as telephone poles, and its shoreline is rock and bush. The ground is a plush bed of needles and moss.

For Carolyn, the "real" and the "geographic" Narrows Island— the one of her memory and that of the present—are almost identical. She led me to the flat rock where she washed her hair as a teenager, and said, "The ghost of my old self is here." Then the stories spilled out. Over there was the rock where her father ran aground and kept rowing as his boat spun like a pinwheel, and across the water was the dock where her boyfriend slept after driving all night from Connecticut to surprise her.

We boiled lobsters on the same stove her mother had used, and as Carolyn set out the plates she said, "These have seen forty summers of lobsters." A table in the sitting room was where the family had spread out puzzles, a wicker chair where she read the Hardy Boys mysteries still filling the bookshelves. "This room was Mother's," she said, opening a door. "When I think of her in it, alone during the week, and younger than myself, I feel incredibly close to her."

■

The journey from New York State to Campobello is really no easier or shorter than when the Roosevelt family made it, and it still contributes to the impression that you are traveling to a remote island. The Roosevelts took a train from New York City to Boston, caught an overnight Pullman, transferred to a steam train at a remote Maine junction the next morning, rode it to the end of the line at Eastport, crossed Passamaquoddy Bay on a motorboat, rowed to their dock, and dashed up the meadow to see who could be first into the house. My trip there meant nine hours driving across northern New England on winding secondary roads, an overnight stop in Bangor, three more hours to Lubec, the easternmost town in the United States, then Canadian immigration formalities before crossing to Campobello on the Roosevelt Memorial Bridge. Despite this bridge, built in 1963, the island still feels remote, a dead end beyond the dead end of Lubec, an isolated scrap of a foreign country where the money, time, and flag, even the accent of the fishermen, suddenly change.

Sunrise at Campobello had revealed little of the island's landscape, and I had imagined the stark beauty of a Monhegan, or Mount Desert's rounded hills and deep fjords. But Campobello lacked the fearsome cliffs or craggy mountains that fix an island in your memory. Instead, its beauty was as modest as the Roosevelts' life on it. It was a pretty little scrap of pine, balsam, and rock smelling like Christmas, surrounded by unswimmable cold water, and plagued by the dramatic tides that every day turned its Bay of Fundy beaches into mud flats. As with many islands near a mainland, the views from it were better than those to it, and from the Roosevelt cottage I saw a sweeping panorama of the inlets, islands, and peninsulas that cut Passamaquoddy Bay into the superb sailing ground that delighted generations of Roosevelts.

This sailing and the island's low-key social life are what first attracted prominent East Coast families to Campobello. Roosevelt's father began summering there in 1881, and by 1900 it had several large hotels and a reputation as a resort for patricians wishing to live more simply and cheaply than at Newport or Bar Harbor. Campobello's summer people preferred parlor games to lawn parties, reading to their children to masked balls, and they did not mind that their golf course had only three holes and doubled as pastureland for the islanders' cattle. This low-key summer colony flourished for three decades. But by 1910, when FDR was beginning to teach his children to love the island as he did, it was already in decline, hurt by the passing of two-month-long summer vacations and the arrival of automobiles that enabled people to holiday away from the railway lines. The big hotels closed, but many of the original summer families, reluctant to abandon an island where they had put down roots and made so many memories, hung on through the early decades of the century. Campobello's twelve hundred present-day inhabitants survive on fishing, odd jobs, pensions, and welfare, and are in some respects more isolated than in the time of the Roosevelts. There are fewer than a dozen seasonal residents and only a few dozen guest rooms, and most tourists who come in the summer to tour FDR's cottage leave after a few hours.

An often-reproduced 1913 photograph shows the Roosevelt family enjoying a picnic on the beach at Herring Cove. When I took a sandwich there it was so empty and unchanged they might have packed up their wicker hampers and left moments before. The nearby fern forests and headlands where FDR delighted in laying out paper chases have been preserved as a Provincial Park; Passamaquoddy Bay is as undeveloped as when he sailed it; and, across the water, Eastport has kept its nineteenth-century silhouette of steeples, warehouses, and canneries. Inside the Roosevelt cottage, curators have positioned the family possessions to give the impression that Eleanor has just used the white megaphone in the dining room to summon her children, or FDR has just laid down that Horatio Hornblower novel and wandered outside.

Like me, my daughter Edwina claims Franklin Roosevelt as her favorite president, and I was glad I had brought her along when we met Betty Lank, a striking ninety-three-year-old woman with porcelain skin and a halo of white hair who is the last island resident to have unclouded memories of the Roosevelts, and who speaks as if her father helped carry FDR off the island on a homemade stretcher just last week. She adores children and had devoted her career to nursing sick ones at a Boston hospital before retiring to the same white Victorian house overlooking the harbor where she and her eight brothers and sisters were born and raised.

"I was just your age, dear, when I was friends with Anna Roosevelt," she said, fixing her gaze on Edwina, as if having a ten-year-old in her parlor could return her to 1914.

Perhaps it did, because we heard about Captain Eddy Lank teaching FDR to sail, and FDR's father, "Mr. Roosevelt," landing the swordfish still hanging in the dining room of the lodge where we were staying. Betty Lank remembered riding in a pony cart across unfenced meadows to the Roosevelt cottage, having tea and building sand castles with Anna Roosevelt, and the hush falling over the congregation at St. Anne's Church whenever the handsome Roosevelts marched down the aisle to their pews. No one minded them taking the center pews while the islanders sat on either side. "They were churchgoing people, so we loved having them here," she said firmly.

Everyone was pleased Campobello made them so happy, and impressed that they lived as the islanders did, without electricity, telephone, a doctor, scheduled ferry services, or newspapers less than a week old.

When Lank was a girl she considered the Roosevelt cottage a castle. The shingled Dutch colonial was indeed large, but notable mostly for its gardens, multiple chimneys, and fire engine red paint. The Roosevelts had furnished it to the standard of a comfortable New England inn, with wicker and flower-patterned slip covers.

When I visited the cottage, I saw that Eleanor Roosevelt had slept on the kind of narrow iron bed common to hospital wards, and her children played lotto and stuck stamps into albums in a low-ceilinged playroom with flowered wallpaper. Their rooms were no grander than those of the servants down the hall. As I leaned across a cord to peer into the spartan dining room, a guard remarked, almost apologetically, "The Roosevelts were pretty simple people."

In the late 1950s the Roosevelt cottage was offered for sale for $50,000, including its furnishings. A real estate agent's flyer described them as "homey, well-used possessions which actually took part in the everyday living of the President and his family." But no one wanted to buy a house on distant Campobello, even if it had belonged to a former president. In his 1982 book about the island, Stephen Muskie (son of Edmund Muskie, the late U.S. Senator from Maine) recalled overhearing a visitor to the cottage asking a guide, "How did he ever find his way to this godforsaken hole?" That Campobello could become an unsalable white elephant in the 1950s, and a "hole" in the 1970s, demonstrates how much attitudes toward family vacations, and islands, have changed since the Roosevelt years.

As I walked around this damp, windswept island, I tried to picture any of the presidents who followed Roosevelt vacationing on it. Jimmy Carter might have been content with its simple pleasures, and perhaps John F. Kennedy, whose family compound in Hyannis was a kind of self-contained island where everyone pursued the summer pastimes popular with the Roosevelts, would have liked it. I could see

Harry Truman in this house, although perhaps not on this island. His beloved Key West had been another dead-end island, and his "Winter White House," a former naval officer's house, was so modest that his wife and daughter shared a small bedroom and bath, and visiting Supreme Court justices and cabinet members doubled up in a spare room with two narrow beds. Try to imagine, say, William Rehnquist and Henry Kissinger sleeping two feet apart and listening to each other's snufflings and snorings. Or, for that matter, try imagining Gerald Ford at Campobello instead of Palm Springs or Vail, or the Reagans coming here instead of Pacific Palisades. You cannot, of course, because since Roosevelt and Truman, the governing classes not only expect much more comfort and luxury but are increasingly uncomfortable with silence and solitude.

At the time I visited Campobello, I decided that President Clinton, the most rootless of our modern presidents and a man whose idea of an island is hectic Martha's Vineyard, would be the least likely to summer on Campobello. But shortly after leaving the island I was leafing through a copy of *Arkansas Mischief*, by Jim McDougal, the mountebank who had been Clinton's friend and partner in the notorious Whitewater development, when the word "Campobello" leaped from a page. In 1983, McDougal had spotted an advertisement in *The Wall Street Journal* offering 3,900 acres on the island for the bargain price of $211 an acre. McDougal, also a fan of *Sunrise at Campobello*, had immediately flown up from Arkansas to inspect the property. "Here were thirteen miles of the cheapest ocean frontage to be found on the eastern seaboard," he wrote. He saw it as the biggest venture of his life. Its beachfront had no souvenir shops, motels, or condominiums, so it could theoretically attract the kind of Bostonians and New Yorkers who had made Martha's Vineyard and Nantucket popular. He believed "there was potential here to make twenty to thirty million dollars."

The story followed a predictable trajectory. McDougal discovered that Campobello had no zoning or municipal government and was a tabula rasa, waiting for a Big Man to come along and shape its destiny. He offered Clinton, then governor of Arkansas, as a reference, claimed backing from a consortium of Arkansas businessmen, and took title to a third of the island. In truth, as Federal bank examiners later determined, Madison Guaranty, the Arkansas bank he controlled, had financed the entire $3.7 million deal and stood to bear the entire loss.

McDougal's development company built some rudimentary roads and made some minimal improvements before chopping the land into one-acre lots and selling dozens of the oceanfront ones for $25,000 each. McDougal tried to buy the islanders' friendship by offering every local newlywed couple a free acre. Campobello might have been good enough for the Roosevelts, but it apparently lacked sufficient diversions for the average Arkansas Rotarian, so McDougal and his associates, whom the islanders soon dubbed "the Arkansas Travelers," rolled out goofy schemes for a water-slide park and a ski hill, although Campobello lacked real hills or reliable snow.

Franklin D. Roosevelt Jr., who was born on the island in 1914 and served on the international commission overseeing the Roosevelt cottage, worried that the Arkansas Travelers would "destroy the feeling of the island," since one of its charms was its being "a remote, secluded place where you can enjoy nature, the woods, and the water surrounding it." Linnea Calder, a former Roosevelt housekeeper, declared, "The Roosevelts liked this as a rustic island. I don't think they would have liked this."

McDougal protested that he idolized FDR, pointing out that he used a cigarette holder he cocked at a jaunty Rooseveltian angle, and could even recite the fireside chats in Roosevelt's accent. The Campobello development would be not only "the deal of the century," and the potential "flagship" of his empire, he said, but also a grand tribute to Roosevelt.

Had McDougal succeeded in finding hundreds of island-lovers willing to drive twelve hours from New York or eight from Boston, his flagship might have sailed, and Madison Guaranty might have sur-

vived, since it was Campobello, rather than the smaller Whitewater investment, that brought Madison Guaranty to the attention of bank regulators. There would have been no Whitewater investigation, and Campobello would no longer be remote. The ski hill was nutty, but the water slide was not, nor was an eighteen-hole golf course, the sine qua non of any island development. The Arkansas Travelers would have built themselves wood-and-glass palaces that would have put Roosevelt's cottage to shame, and with the golf course and his friends in place, could Clinton have been far behind, perhaps closing a sweet deal on some waterfront acres? The Roosevelt cottage would have provided an excellent photo-op backdrop, and Campobello would have given him the roots he lacked. In return, he would have put it on the map.

McDougal's flagship began sinking in 1986 when federal bank regulators, concerned about Madison Guaranty's real estate liabilities, replaced its board of directors. The Resolution Trust Corporation, a federal agency, took over 3,400 unsold acres on Campobello. Bank examiners inspecting the property praised its "scenic beauty" but concluded that because of its "damp, cold, and foggy" weather, and the severe tides that left waterfront lots hundreds of yards from the water for much of the day, the island where the Roosevelts enjoyed so many happy summers was "unsuitable" for a resort.

That the Roosevelts loved Campobello is incontestable. In one documentary, Franklin Roosevelt Jr. described it as his father's "island of youth and energy," where the family "spent many happy, wonderful summers." James Roosevelt remembered his mother reading aloud by firelight, community picnics where roaring fires illuminated the sky, and a "marvelous sense of isolation."

Even Eleanor Roosevelt, who was famously unfond of sailing and vigorous sports, adored this island, telling one interviewer: "There was a little coal stove on which you did all your cooking and the lamps sometimes smoked . . . and you went to bed by candlelight. But it had great charm." The endless fogs comforted her, she said, and the howling winds left her feeling serene. Her grandson Christopher

Roosevelt believed she loved Campobello because she could "let her kids run free," and it afforded her more freedom than Hyde Park or Washington, while it gave FDR a "refuge and nourishment," and a "real boyhood."

This same freedom, and the opportunity to put down roots in a community to which a family returns every summer, is available at some mainland resorts. But the "marvelous sense of isolation" is peculiar to islands, and it is this isolation that by limiting distractions and demanding self-sufficiency makes for deeper roots and richer memories. When the fog rolled in, the Roosevelts lit the oil lamps and spent several days reading, conversing, playing games, and amusing themselves, instead of driving into the next town looking for fun.

Would Roosevelt have revisited Campobello in his mind during his last days if the family cottage had been deep in the Maine woods? Would I remember the pit parties whenever I see bonfire embers glowing if Fishers had not been an island? Would Carolyn Marsh see the ghost of her old self so clearly if her house had been on the shoreline of her lake, instead of one of its islands? I suspect not, because islands are better at creating and preserving memories, particularly youthful ones, and the best islands for doing this are simple and uncluttered ones.

During the early years of the Roosevelts' marriage, when the family was moving between Hyde Park, New York City, and Washington, D.C., Campobello remained their constant. Every summer, they returned to where FDR had learned to fish and sail, grown to manhood, and courted his wife. They saw the same views from their porch, found the same books on their shelves, and the same people working in their kitchen. The geographic island of the present and the "real" island of FDR's memories remained identical. On it he remained forever young, and when he reminisced during his final days about those long-ago sailing races and picnics, he spoke in a distinctive accent that although commonly mistaken as acquired during his years at Harvard, bore an uncanny resemblance to that of a Campobello sardine fisherman.

SILENT ISLAND—ISLE OF JURA

In 1968, three years after my last summer on Fishers Island, my London flatmate Jamie Fletcher invited me to spend a week at Ardlussa, his family's estate on the northern end of the Isle of Jura in Scotland's Inner Hebrides. Because the islands I knew best were summer resorts, and because the Inner Hebrides sounded more civilized than the Outer Hebrides and Jura was only sixty-seven crow-flying miles from Glasgow, I imagined a kind of Fishers Island with a Scottish brogue. Instead I landed in a double wilderness of rugged mountains surrounded by treacherous seas.

There was nothing cozy about Craighouse, where the ferry docked in those days, none of the huddling together of an island village in Greece, just a straggle of gray stone cottages facing a rockbound cove. Behind it loomed the Paps of Jura, three breast-shaped peaks that give Jura such character and make it an island impossible to confuse with any other.

The seventeen-mile drive to Ardlussa took, as it still does, fortyfive minutes over a one-lane road that twisted over purplish moors and skirted a Big Sur landscape of headlands crumbling into rocky inlets and fingers of forest running into the sea. Red deer stood on ridges, ears pricked, watching like Indian scouts, and a deep fjord almost cut the island in two. The good road, along with telephone and mail service, ended at Ardlussa. A track wound another seven miles across the moors to Barnhill, the lonely farmhouse where George Orwell lived between 1946 and 1948 while writing *Nineteen Eighty-Four*.

I returned to Ardlussa every year for the next seven, sometimes staying as long as a month. I sheared sheep, ricked hay, played in the annual games, drank in the pub, and danced at the summer ceilidhs. I enjoyed stalking stags more than shooting them, hiking to the hill lochs more than fishing in them, and I liked being on an island dominated by the prehistoric constants of wind, water, and stone, where you could imagine a brontosaurus emerging from a loch and pterodactyls sailing between cliffs. I even liked the fickle, fast-changing weather—the dazzling sunlight, fair-weather clouds racing across the sky like express trains, and squalls that pelted cliffs with tiny fish and carried lime from the beaches, fertilizing bushes bearing raspberries as big as eggs.

Jura was a real insular attic. Standing stones erected before the pyramids remained undisturbed, and the remains of Stone Age forts and burial mounds were a short walk from Ardlussa and Barnhill. On the wild and uninhabited Atlantic coast, a four-hundred-year-old skull sat on a ledge overlooking the rocky beaches of Glengarrisdale Bay. A nineteenth-century crofter had turned it up while plowing a field and a gash on one side suggested a sword wound. A Gaelic inscription carved into the rock identified it as the skull of a Mclaine killed during a 1647 clan battle. Its location was common knowledge and the 1976 Ordnance Survey map of Jura identified "Mclaine's Skull" in the same typeface as any bay, mountain, or natural feature. Anywhere else, it would have been protected by a fence or locked in a display case, but on Jura it lay undisturbed for decades, both proof and symbol of the island's remote soul.

I first realized that islands are natural attics while staying on Aitutaki, an atoll in the Cook Islands where the coconuts bore the teeth marks of rats whose ancestors came as livestock on canoes paddled by its Polynesian discoverers, and mynah birds introduced by Europeans to control pests had become pests themselves. A Mr. S. E.

Christian, the descendant of Bounty mutineer Fletcher Christian, had signed the note in my hotel apologizing for some noisy renovations; the blond girls riding bikes were the grandchildren of the American airmen who had built an airfield during World War II; and an American officer who had married a native lay buried, following island custom, in a raised white tomb in the front yard of his widow, whose nineteenth-century Christianity was another island relic. Aitutaki also taught me that one of the rules of insular life is that once something arrives on an island it can stay for centuries. Large objects are difficult and costly to remove, and islanders are instinctive pack rats, so things that might be lost, junked, plowed under, paved over, or locked behind glass on a mainland are preserved on an island in an amber of water and isolation. But relics like Eleanor Roosevelt's megaphone, the perkeniers' mansions, and the Octagon House are more than quaint curiosities. Like Des Alwi's desk and Carolyn Marsh's lobster plates, they are touchstones for island memories, proof that an island is not a place like anywhere else, and the outward and visible sign of an island's inward and invisible grace, its remote soul.

My yearly visits to Jura ended when I married, wrote books that took me to Africa and the Middle East, and moved to the Champlain Valley, where I live on a peninsula with a narrow neck that would become an island, if the water would only rise a few feet. Following some complicated family maneuvers, Jamie Fletcher took possession of Barnhill in 1990. He and his wife, Damaris, continue to live on their farm on the Scottish mainland, but visit Jura every summer, with Jamie staying on into the fall to take paying guests stalking.

When I heard they were going to the island for a few days to make repairs on the house and open it for the summer, I decided to return for the first time in two decades.

May is usually a good time for the west coast of Scotland. The bracken is low, the midges are unhatched, and the weather is good. It

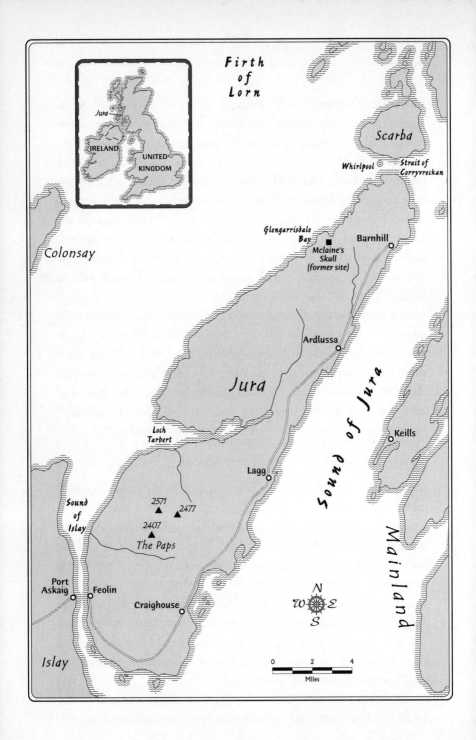

was sunny and warm during my time on Jura, but inside Barnhill, the two-story farmhouse where George Orwell had lived, it remained so damp I could see my breath.

The day I arrived, I huddled around a coal fire in the parlor with Jamie and Damaris, drinking whisky and speculating about what relics remained from Orwell's tenancy. They believed he had planted the yellow azaleas near the front door and used the hay-turner in the front meadow. But a broken motorbike that was probably his had been stolen when a bikers' magazine identified Barnhill as one of the five most inaccessible places in Great Britain, and challenged its readers to be photographed at all five.

Inside the house, the only certain Orwellian relic was the bathtub, a claw-footed and rust-stained Victorian behemoth deep enough for a drowning. I climbed into it every evening and during a lukewarm soak (hot water is scarce at Barnhill) wondered why Jura had changed me from someone vaguely fond of islands into an islomane, and why Orwell had moved from London to a place he praised as "extremely un-get-at-able," and had written his great anti-Utopian novel, one set in a frightening urban landscape, on an island littered with prehistoric standing stones and burial mounds, and in a farmhouse without telephone or electricity whose foundations probably incorporate boulders from Stone Age forts.

Orwell's friends and biographers have struggled to explain his attraction to Jura. It is agreed he chose this particular island because his friend David Astor, who owned the neighboring estate, had persuaded Jamie Fletcher's father to lease Barnhill to him. But why escape to a Hebridean island? And why, after his first summer, did he make Barnhill his permanent residence, abandoning his London flat and country house?

It is said he wanted to escape the London literary treadmill, had complained of being "smothered under journalism," and that living on an island had been a long-standing dream—one reflected by an entry in his wartime diary speaking of "my Hebridean island which I shall now probably never see." It is claimed that he needed a change of scenery after the sudden death of his wife, worried London was vulnerable to nuclear attack, wanted his adopted son to play outside without fear of traffic, loved Jura's stark beauty, and was a man who embraced solitude, and liked living rough.

His own letters called the island "one of the most beautiful parts of the British Isles" and spoke of uninhabited bays with "beautiful white sand and clear water with seals swimming." The essayist and critic V. S. Pritchett, who declined Orwell's invitation to visit Jura, pronounced him "a man who did very badly want to suffer." Inez Holden, a female friend who stayed at Barnhill, referred to his "fantastically silly Robinson Crusoe mind."

Orwell's life on Jura was as Crusoean as his health and situation would permit. He hunted rabbits, planted a garden, butchered venison, trapped lobsters, and rode a farm pony to save petrol, behaving like a man turning his back on a mainland already becoming the anti-Utopia of *Nineteen Eighty-Four*. Despite his professed desire for solitude, many of his letters were invitations to visit Barnhill. So many people accepted that he pitched a tent on the lawn, and at various times his household included his son's nanny, his sister, and other long-term visitors, becoming its own closely knit island community.

In his memoirs, Orwell's friend T. R. Fyvel looked for an explanation for Orwell's decision to remain in Barnhill through the autumn and early winter of 1948, much later than was wise for a man afflicted by tuberculosis. He concluded, "In Orwell's journey to Jura and his decision to stay there to write *Nineteen Eighty-Four*, there remain some questions to which we do not know the answers."

One evening I climbed from Orwell's tub and, still wet, scribbled down "natural beauty," "self-sufficiency," and "escape from mainland distractions," but decided they were not enough to explain Orwell's attraction to Barnhill.

The Barnhill I remembered from the 1970s had been the loneliest house in Britain, a two-story farmhouse adrift in acres of meadow and facing a barren mainland peninsula and the Sound of Jura, where boats are rare even in summer. Whenever I passed it I would cup my hands over my eyes and peer through its windows, trying to imagine Orwell inside. Now I could wander through his bedroom, soak in his tub, and sit in his kitchen, drinking mugs of tea and wondering if the answer to his islomania was trapped inside like some odorless gas, or ghost.

Barnhill had a distinctive voice. Windows rattled, a faucet dripped, and floorboards had their own groans. In the evening, with the wind stilled and the Sound of Jura turned a polished silver, I willed myself to hear the clack of his typewriter keys and his tubercular cough, and to see a gaunt man in baggy flannels with pale eyes lost in sockets deep as Jura's caves.

One night I stayed up late reading. When I finally extinguished the last electric light in the house the hum of the generator abruptly ceased. The ensuing silence was a presence, a silence I could hear, the waterproofed silence of an island wilderness, and the same one known to the prehistoric people who had built forts from these stones. It absorbed the insular white noise of gulls, wind, and surf. It was more secure and absolute than a mainland silence that could always be shattered by the hoot of a train, the grinding gears of a truck, or the ringing telephone Orwell had wanted to escape. Even at San Juan Bautista, on Isla Crusoe, I could never be certain that a television, barking dog, or rattling jeep would not pierce the carapace of silence. At Barnhill the silence was total, wind-haunted, and lunar, like the one at Selkirk's lookout. It was the kind that allows an island to immerse you in D. H. Lawrence's "dark mystery of time" where the future is "not separated off" from the past, a perfect silence for writing a futuristic novel like *Nineteen Eighty-Four*, and one confirming the observation of Orwell's official biographer, Michael Shelden, that here Orwell heard only the sound of the sea in the distance and could work, "as though writing the book on another planet."

The next morning Damaris Fletcher showed me "Pleasure Spots," an Orwell essay that had appeared in the magazine *Tribune* four

months before he first came to Jura. In it, he predicted the Pleasure
Spots of the future would be outfitted with sunlight lamps, pools with
artificial waves, and amplified music, and would follow five principles:

1. One is never alone.
2. One never does anything for oneself.
3. One is never within sight of wild vegetation or natural objects
   of any kind.
4. Light and temperature are always artificially regulated.
5. One is never out of the sound of artificial music.

To this last principle he added, "The function of the music is to prevent thought and conversation, and to shut out any natural sound,
such as the song of the birds or the whistling of the wind, that might
otherwise intrude."

Three things struck me: Orwell's desire to find a natural silence,
his fear that escaping the tyranny of artificial music might become impossible in the future, and that a few months after writing this he
moved to Jura, the antithesis of a Pleasure Spot. His five principles
have also proved a far more accurate prediction of the future than
Nineteen Eighty-Four, foretelling the computer- and media-driven indoor existence that has become common, and summarizing the strategy pursued by Las Vegas, Disney World, cruise ships, and the resorts
that have turned islands that were once as remote and silent as Jura
into Pleasure Spots.

At first glance, Jura appeared to have changed little in twenty years.
Its economy remained dependent on the distillery and six estates and
its population hovered around two hundred. Craighouse still had one
store, one pub, one hotel, one red telephone booth, no petrol station,
and cottages straggling for a mile down the road. Its stone houses
were still the same color as the Paps, its Land Rovers, gum boots, and

anoraks the same dark stalking green of the landscape. It felt like a village that would be happy if no one noticed it.

After reading "Pleasure Spots," I considered Jura again, with a more critical eye, searching for evidence it was losing its remote soul.

A new playground of brightly colored swings had led one islander to grouse to me that children of earlier generations had built dams in the burns and sand castles on the beach. "The real playground is outside everyone's back doors," he muttered.

For years, the islanders had opposed streetlights on the grounds they would ruin their views of the stars. In the mid-1990s, they relented and voted for lights, although only a few were erected before the allocated funds ran out, leaving Craighouse almost as dark as before.

I met Mike and Joan Richardson, who pursued a modified Crusoean lifestyle in a farmhouse north of Barnhill that was Jura's last inhabited place. They kept a foulmouthed parrot and a pack of dogs who used a gutted Land Rover as their kennel, and did everything for themselves—fishing, raising sheep, growing hydroponic vegetables, and collecting antlers for sale to Chinese herbalists, who ground them into sexual stimulants. Joan liked Jura because living there was a challenge. Mike told me its wild and empty land "allowed the brain to expand." They believed the biggest change in twenty years had been the attitude toward Christmas. When they arrived, it had been a simple religious holiday centered around church and family, but television had transformed it into a commercial extravaganza of partying and gift-giving.

Jura's unofficial historian is Gordon Wright, an elderly man whose craggy face perfectly matches the island's landscape. He told me a visit to a neighbor's home once meant tea, scones, whisky, and an exchange of ghost stories. Now you watched your hosts watching television, and he was collecting Jura's folklore before it vanished with this generation of the elderly.

An eccentric couple I can see as clearly as if they had just left the room had previously rented Lealt, a cottage midway between Ard-lussa and Barnhill. He was an intense and twitchy man who spent his summers excavating Stone Age forts and his winters riding ore trains in Mauritania, searching for pockets of slavery to report to the Anti-Slavery Society. His wife spun wool and knitted mud-colored sweaters that never quite lost their animal odor. They lived on bread, blackber-ries, and plants they alone deemed edible. He had died, she had moved away, and Lealt's new tenants were a cheerful and big-hearted English couple anyone would want as neighbors, but whom the pre-vious occupants would have despised. They had remodeled the cot-tage with wall-to-wall carpeting and installed a good sound system.

If you believe, as I do, that the more artifacts and unique customs an island preserves, the less likely it is to become a Pleasure Spot, then one of the more disturbing developments had to be the disap-pearance of Mclaine's skull. It was rumored a party of Boy Scouts had left it on the ground, where famished deer had devoured it, or poach-ers overnighting in a nearby cave had stolen it, or a Mclaine descen-dant had given it a proper burial.

To be honest, none of Jura's changes really amounted to much, or indicated an island becoming another Martha's Vineyard or Mykonos. One nineteenth-century visitor to Jura had observed it was a common sight to see "five or six grown-up naked individuals, half-naked and savage-looking, watching a pot of potatoes (their sole food for nine months of the year) without any idea or wish of changing their manner of life," and you could still find evidence of a resistance to change.

Steve Walton had moved to Jura from Coventry fifteen years be-fore because he believed it offered a safe and friendly environment for his children. He managed the Jura Hotel and told me he was about to forfeit its two-star rating from the RAC (Royal Automobile Club) and AA (Automobile Association) rather than accede to their demands that he equip every room with a telephone and television.

There was also widespread opposition to making Jura less un-get-at-able. A group of businessmen from the mainland and Islay, a more populated and developed neighboring island, had proposed an "Overland Route," a direct ferry service across a narrow point in the sound between Jura and the mainland that would have considerably shortened the journey to Jura and Islay. A trip from Glasgow to Craighouse presently took nearly seven hours and involved a long drive on winding mainland roads, a two-hour voyage to Port Askaig in Islay on a ferry making only eight runs a week in the summer, then another ferry across a choppy strait to Jura. Considering all this, one might have expected the islanders to embrace the Overland Route's hourly service between the mainland and Lagg, a village a few miles north of Craighouse. The company argued its ferry would bring a petrol station, more jobs, and more visitors, increase the population, and facilitate day trips to Glasgow. But Jura's inhabitants, perhaps reasoning that if this ferry would put them within day-tripping distance of Glasgow it would also put 650,000 Glaswegians within day-tripping distance of them, rejected the route in a 1992 referendum, and rejected it again four years later by an even wider margin.

I asked everyone I met why they had opposed the route.

Gordon Wright said he worried it would rob Jura of its freedom, just as television was stealing its oral history. "It's a strange thing to talk about the freedom one enjoys on an island," he added, "because most people imagine finding freedom in large continental spaces, but on Jura we have the freedom to escape."

Bill Jones, a Yorkshireman who worked as a stalker and would not meet me at the pub until 9:00 P.M. because he liked staying outdoors until it was too dark to fish, praised the island for teaching him to be patient and trust people. A successful life on the mainland required the opposite skills. Who cared if a direct ferry meant lower prices and a better selection of soap powders and snack foods in the store? he asked. Jura's greatest pleasures were all free anyway. He flapped his hand dismissively toward the mainland, saying, "People over there assume everything we want is on the mainland, but if we *really* wanted those things, we wouldn't live on an island, would we?"

Jamie Fletcher's younger sister Kate lived in the seaside village of Inverlussa, where the attractions were the typically eccentric ones of a remote island: the grave of Mary MacCrain, who had lived to the age of 128, and a young Yorkshireman known as "Pete the Feet" who, on this boggy, stony, adder-infested island, walked everywhere barefoot. Even as a girl, Kate had been a fierce islomane who would burst into tears when she had to board the ferry at the end of the summer. "And I still cry when I leave this island," she insisted. She had opposed the Overland Route because it would make Jura just that, an overland highway between the mainland and busier Islay. She worried about losing the security of knowing who was on Jura, and believed most mainlanders had forgotten how to back down a road, a crucial skill where deep ditches lined the road. Her parting remark could have come from an Orwell essay. "If people need to get to the mainland that badly," she said, "perhaps they should live on it."

The spires of Glasgow are visible from the Paps on a clear day, but it is still disorienting to have a late lunch at the Jura Hotel, cross to Islay and board the afternoon flight, then land in Glasgow forty-five minutes later. Whenever I returned to the mainland from Jura, I experienced a culture shock that mimicked jet lag. This time I felt particularly tender and disoriented, as if I were sleepwalking through the airport concourse and seeing everything through the wrong end of a telescope.

When I opened the door of my airport hotel room, a computer-activated television played hurdy-gurdy music and flashed a welcoming message. The television came on again by itself at 11:00 P.M., jolting me awake with another blast of carnival music. A message on the screen said a Ford Escort was blocking the hotel entrance. I switched it off but woke twenty minutes later to the same music and message. When I called downstairs, a manager explained this Big Brother moment was not some snafu. He had himself programmed the central computer to activate every television in the hotel at twenty-minute intervals.

I could not unplug the set because it was plumbed into the socket. A notice underneath warned that any tampering would activate an alarm summoning security personnel. So I stuffed wads of toilet paper into my ears, pulled on an eye-patch, and lay awake marveling that only sixty-seven miles separated an island with a hotel refusing to put telephones in its rooms and this horror, and wondering how long islands like Jura could survive in the shadow of establishments like this, and resist becoming places like anywhere else.

7

HOLY ISLAND — PATMOS

The story of the Swedish doctor Axel Munthe on the Italian island of Capri is more evidence that a single island can change your life—and haunt you forever. While holidaying in Capri in 1875, Munthe climbed to the ruined chapel of San Michele on the grounds of the former villa of Emperor Tiberius. He gazed down at the Bay of Naples, Mount Vesuvius, and the snow-covered Apennines and reflected, "To live in such a place as this, to die in such a place, if ever death could conquer the everlasting joy of such a life!"

He imagined building a Greek temple, open to the sun and wind, with marble columns, avenues of cypresses, and statues of gods and emperors. He fell into what he described as "a rapture" and met the two-thousand-year-old spirit of San Michele, a tall specter wrapped in an elegant mantle who warned him that to possess this beautiful place would mean sacrificing his ambitions and becoming "a might-have-been, a failure."

"You take away from me all that is worth living for," Munthe protested.

"You are mistaken," the spirit replied. "I give you all that is worth living for."

Munthe returned to his medical studies in Paris and tacked a faded photograph of Capri to the wall of his room. He finished school, became a society doctor, and moved to Capri as soon as he had saved enough money to buy San Michele. His 1929 autobiography, *The Story of San Michele,* was a publishing sensation, reprinted sixty-three times. Instead of the love affairs, public triumphs, and private disappointments that are the usual stuff of autobiographies, it revolved around his obsession with Capri, and argued that the right island can supply "all that is worth living for."

The closest I have come to a revelatory Munthe-like moment happened on Patmos, one of four islands in the Dodecanese where my wife and I stayed during our honeymoon, and the only one we brought home with us. When we spoke about changing our lives, as young people living in New York apartments do, I always saw us there, in a whitewashed house near the monastery, hearing church bells and goat bells, and drinking rough wine on a terrace high above the Aegean.

"PATMOS" became the password for my ATM card, and whenever I typed it into a bank keyboard I saw the Monastery of St. John the Theologian, the mountaintop fortress with sheer black walls that dominates the island. Then I saw myself, standing on one of its flat roofs and circled by the white houses of the town below it, then circled again by a carpet of blue water and staring down on a miracle of islands and more islands, stretching like stepping-stones to Asia Minor.

For the next twenty years, this moment and this view kept reappearing in my thoughts and daydreams, particularly when I was under stress, during the birth of our twins, and when my mother underwent brain surgery, and it always calmed me.

When I read in Thomas Merton's *The Seven Storey Mountain* how the church of St. Antonin dominated its French town and forced anyone seeing it "to be at least a virtual contemplative," and how it fit into the landscape, "in such a way as to become the keystone of its intelligibility," and gave a supernatural significance to everything else you saw, I remembered the Monastery of St. John. I thought of how it

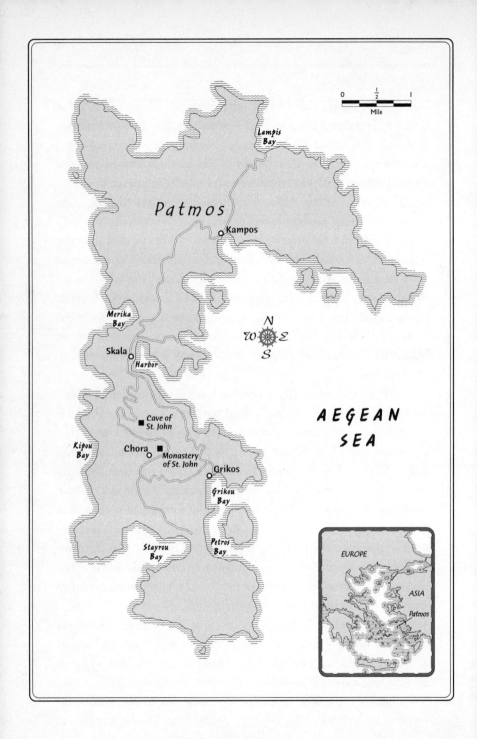

Lampis
Bay

Patmos

Kampos

Merika
Bay

Skala

Harbor

N
W E
S

AEGEAN
SEA

Cave of
St. John

Kipou
Bay

Chora

Monastery
of St. John

Grikos

Grikou
Bay

Stayrou
Bay

Petros
Bay

0   ½   1
Mile

EUROPE

ASIA

Patmos

never let you forget that Patmos was where, Christians believe, God spoke to St. John, providing the words and visions that are the Revelation of St. John the Divine in the New Testament.

It was also in *The Seven Storey Mountain* that I first read about the poet Robert Lax. He and Merton had been friends and classmates at Columbia University during the 1930s, working on the same campus humor magazine and belonging to a circle that included the publisher Robert Giroux and the poet John Berryman. Merton later wrote that Lax was "a potential prophet without rage," possessing a "natural, instinctive spirituality." Mark Van Doren, who taught them both, thought Lax gave the appearance of contemplating some incomprehensible woe. His real woe, Van Doren believed, was his inability to articulate his bliss, to explain "his love of the world and all things, all persons in it."

Merton became a Catholic in 1938. Lax, who was Jewish, converted to Catholicism six years later. Their lives diverged in 1941 when Merton entered a Trappist monastery in Kentucky. Before the end of the decade, Merton's autobiography had made him one of the most praised writers and solitaries of the century. Lax, meanwhile, was becoming one of the most obscure. He wrote for *Time* magazine and worked as an editor at *The New Yorker*, coached boxing, volunteered at a Harlem settlement house, traveled with a circus, and in 1962 moved to the Greek islands where, one literary critic said, he "fell off the map."

The novelist William Maxwell has called Lax a saint. A *New York Times* reviewer has described him as "the last unacknowledged major poet of his post-60s generation." Before returning to Patmos, I read some of his abstract, minimalist poems and immediately understood why he is better known in art than in poetry circles. They were poems as art, words and syllables arranged in narrow columns and floating on a page like archipelagoes of islands.

I was also struck by how his observations about Patmos echoed mine. In his journals he had written about "The view of the monastery up on the hill (a citadel) as seen from the far end of the bay" and "a feeling, a real feeling, of peace in the air."

I was encouraged to discover he was a solitary, but not a hermit. He believed a writer should be immersed in life, yet able to withdraw from it. When I read that he liked living alone, but surrounded by a busy community, I wrote asking if we could meet while I was visiting Patmos.

I returned to Patmos in June, as good a time for the Greek islands as May is for the Hebrides because wildflowers are blooming, buildings are newly whitewashed, taverna waiters are cheerful, and the sky is the blue of a Maldivian lagoon instead of a milky midsummer white. There was a welcoming letter from Lax at my hotel and the next day his assistant, who had been engaged by St. Bonaventure University, where Lax's papers are being collected, led me to his rooms.

I had known Lax lived in Skala, the island's busy port, but I had expected a solitary house on the outskirts, not an apartment in a whitewashed house facing a busy street above the harbor. The six freshly painted signs that stood drying in the sun across the street said TOPLESS NUDE BATHING IS FORBIDDEN ON THIS BEACH.

Lax resembled his poetry, a narrow and austere column of a man dressed in a black sweater and watch cap. His face was an Abraham Lincoln affair of starved cheeks, picked clean of fat as his poems are of adjectives. But instead of the sad eyes that usually accompany such a face, his were mischievous and joyful, and his voice was soft and young, perhaps because he used it so sparingly.

He was feeling poorly and had to struggle from his narrow bed to greet me. He took a straight-backed chair and put me behind his desk, among cardboard boxes labeled "Literary Interest," "New Poems," and "Ready for Archives." The room was a monk's cell: dark, and with thick walls and shuttered windows insulating it from the harbor. The most cheerful thing in it, aside from Lax, was a mosaic of postcards, epigrams, and photographs papering a wall. Among them was a white file card that read, "There are as many kinds of salvation as there are people to be saved." It was pasted next to an advertisement for a Marx Brothers film.

I said, "I don't think my daughters know who the Marx Brothers are."

Lax chuckled. "That's the worst news I've heard in years."

"Why did you choose Patmos?" I asked.

He described a Munthe-like moment. It had occurred in the early 1950s. He was living in a Marseilles hotel room and noticed how the rays of the setting sun illuminated a framed illustration showing St. John receiving the Revelation in a cave on Patmos. This small phenomenon was enough to fix Patmos, and Greece, in his mind. Afterwards, he returned to New York and worked at *The New Yorker*, winnowing poetry submissions, editing "The Talk of the Town," and "running out to the reception and posing as the editor in case anyone wanted to shoot him." He found himself gravitating to Greek restaurants without knowing why, except they somehow felt like home. He liked the way their waiters asked, "How are you feeling?" before demanding, "What'll you have?" In the end, he decided to move to Greece because he wanted good working conditions, and he thought he could find them on an island where you could be immersed in life, yet alone.

He settled at first on Kalymnos, a busier, warmer, and more populated island south of Patmos, staying there throughout the winter and moving to Patmos in the summer. The bustling Kalymnos port reminded him of Marseilles and encouraged his journals. Patmos was more quiet and austere, and inspired his poetry. He considered the Patmians ideal companions, friendly and chatty, yet respecting his need for solitude. Finally he settled here permanently, living first up in Chóra next to the walls of the monastery, then moving down to Skala when the walk up the mountain became too arduous.

I complained that Skala was no longer the sleepy three-taxi port I remembered from 1978, although it was admittedly a long way from becoming another Thíra or Rhodes. There were more cafés and pensions hugging the curve of its pebbly shoreline, and more motorbikes zipping through its narrow streets. Air-conditioned jewelry stores catered to cruise passengers, and the villas of absentee foreigners lay sprinkled across formerly empty hillsides. At Campos Beach a house with a FOR SALE sign carried the address of a Jackson, Mississippi, real estate agent and said WE KNOW JACKSON.

Lax sighed when he heard this and said, "I go out of my way not to notice some things." His Patmos was two islands: the crowded summer one of July and August, when every room was filled and every restaurant had a line, and a peaceful winter one offering a real island experience. "In summer," he said, "I see the tourists as smoke."

Even during the summer, he believed, the Orthodox Church saved Patmos from the carnival atmosphere of other Greek islands. Because the monastery owned so much of the land, the monks had been able to put a brake on new construction, and their insistence that everyone wear long trousers or a skirt to visit the monastery reminded visitors that Patmos was a holy island. Lax thought their religious life permeated the islanders' life, making Patmians "a very welcoming and respectful people."

After several days on the island I came to agree with him. Patmos was still a holy island, where escaping the church was impossible. I ate at an ouzeri in an alley off the busy waterfront and was surrounded by jolly parties of monks in black gowns and round hats. I took a caïque to Livadi Beach and swam to a barren islet where the only building was the domed white chapel where generations of monks had contemplated the divine. On other islands, you looked up and saw hotels and communication towers; on Patmos you saw a monastery that never let you forget this was where Christ had appeared to St. John, eyes aflame and feet the color of burnished bronze.

The cave where this miracle happened had been walled in and turned into a chapel festooned with the usual Orthodox trappings and icons. But through a small window I could see what St. John had

seen in A.D. 95: brilliant sunlight, a stony hillside, and an uninhabited
islet that reflected his exile here. The great relics of Patmos were
the hollow in the rock where St. John rested his head and the triple
cleft in the ceiling through which God spoke to him. If God had appeared to John, it was more proof that islands are inherently holy
places. If John imagined the encounter, it was more proof that the silence, timelessness, and isolation of an island encouraged authors like
St. John—and Orwell—to loosen the bonds of time, and imagine the
future.

I climbed to Chóra on a nine-hundred-year-old mule path. The
monastery towered overhead, a ship frozen in a sea of white houses.
There were more houses now, and more padlocked vacation ones.
But every alley and stone street still led to a church, a chapel, the
walls of the monastery, or the convent where nuns handed out Turk-
ish delight flavored with incense. Just outside Chóra, the barren hills,
twisted olive trees, wild thyme, and broken terracing said Palestine.

A monk at the entrance to the Holy Monastery of St. John the
Theologian gave me a flyer that called Patmos a "school and cure for
souls" and urged visitors to "Respect the Holy Places, our traditions
and our morals by your dignified attire, serious appearance and your
general behavior."

The buildings were the same warren of tiny rooms, narrow stairs,
and pocket courtyards I remembered. I climbed to the flat roof and
saw the view that had stayed with me for twenty years. From here,
Patmos resembled a piece of taffy pulled to the breaking point, with a
slender isthmus connecting two jumbles of coves, headlands, capes,
and mountains. There were more distant islands than I recalled, a
whole fleet, and more tiny islets floating in the bays and coves, some
of them just big enough to hold a solitary white chapel.

In the distance, Skala and several other compact communities appeared to be white islands. They were surrounded by rough, stony
ground, and surrounded again by the Aegean.

Lax's poem "One Island" perfectly described the view from the monastery. It repeated elemental words like "circle," "sea," "earth," "light," "dark," "land," "wave," "rock," "shadow," "wind," "hill," "cloud," and "one," and presented the result as columns of words or syllables framed by oceans of empty space. It was poetry for a castaway, by a castaway, the kind Selkirk might have written, had he been more literate. It captured the monotheism of a stark island and echoed the first verse of St. John's Gospel, "In the beginning was the Word, and the Word was with God, and the Word was God."

I decided that islands were natural monasteries. (After all, monasteries are often compared to islands, and are called islands of peace, or serenity, or civilization, so why should the reverse not be true?) This explained why Selkirk was "a better Christian in his solitude," why Marietta believed she could listen to herself on Isla Crusoe, and why Lax found he could write poetry on Patmos. And, like monasteries, islands were refuges offering the community life, silence, and solitude that encouraged contemplation and creativity. This explained why when islanders went to mainlands they suffered the dislocation of monks outside the cloister. Patmos was a double monastery: a natural monastery whose landscape and life was dominated by an actual one, and therefore doubly hospitable to miracles and visions, and to listening to yourself, and hearing God.

Lax had written that he never came to Patmos without feeling it was holy. When we met three days later, I asked if he believed islands were holier than continents, and God more knowable on them.

He bowed his head and said, "Let's start this like a Quaker meeting, with a few minutes of silent prayer."

I shut my eyes and saw my islands, first on a map, then flashing like colored slides on a screen. I was in Barnhill's kitchen as the setting sun turned the Sound of Jura the color of polished silver, then standing outside a church in Abemama while the choir practiced, then seeing Ambae from the veranda of the Octagon House, then sitting in this hushed room.

Lax broke the silence, saying he believed Patmos was holy because people had religious awakenings on it, life-changing ones. And it had a landscape of answered prayers. Patmians had built its 365 chapels, one for every day of the year, to thank particular saints for performing miracles. A sailor he knew who had been swept off a boat by one wave and swept back by the next built a chapel to thank God for his rescue. Another friend built a chapel to honor an aunt who had returned from the dead to lay her hands on his abdomen and cure a cancerous tumor. Reminders of the power of prayer and faith crowned every Patmian headland and hill.

A psychiatrist had told Lax that visitors and natives alike reported clear, significant, and memorable dreams on the island, and Lax believed everyone remembered their dreams because Patmos was peaceful. My room overlooked the harbor, so my sleep was often interrupted by the arrival and departure of late ferries. But on other islands my dreams had been just that—clear, memorable, and significant. At Barnhill and the Maulana Hotel, I had dreamed for the first time in years about an event that happened in 1975 when I lived in the West African nation of Niger. I had hitched a two-day ride from some English missionaries and as I was dozing and waking through the night I imagined stars in the shape of a cross burning bright over a distant village. When we reached it I learned that a recent truck accident had killed some refugees fleeing drought and famine. The destitute and malnourished villagers had adopted three suddenly orphaned children.

As for God being more knowable on Patmos, Lax would only speak for himself. "Whenever my eye goes to high points, to the mountains and the monastery," he said, "I am reminded of Him."

I should not have expected more from a man so famously stingy with words, but I was slightly disappointed, until I turned over an icon of St. John that hung among the photographs and postcards. On its back Lax had written, "Acquire the spirit of peace and thousands of souls will be saved around you."

I repeated it out loud.

He could not remember where he had found it, only that it sounded right and true, so he copied it. "And trust you'll be saved, too," he added with a sly smile.

I thought it was a good explanation for his poetry and life, and for moving to a remote island and becoming a solitary. It also sounded like something Thomas Merton might have said. I later found this passage in *The Seven Storey Mountain*: "I want to find a really quiet, isolated place . . . where I can get down to the thing I really want to do and need to do—from which, if necessary, I can come out to help others."

"If one man acquiring the spirit of peace can save the souls of thousands, can an island preserving that same spirit save a continent?" I asked.

Lax smiled. "Well, trying to get people to understand the spirit of peace has always seemed like a good thing to try."

■

There are so many Aegean islands, so close together and so different from one another that the temptation to visit the next one, and the next, is irresistible. From Patmos I went to Lipsos, an island visible from the roof of the monastery. I found a Pleasure Spot in the making and continued to Kos, a package-tour hell. Finally I landed on Tílos, which is such a perfect island that three hundred of the island-lovers who have stumbled onto it have founded the Friends of Tílos Association (FOTA), whose newsletter has called it "one of the last great jewels of the Dodecanese" and one of Europe's "last peaceful places."

The island inspiring this devotion is as remote as a Greek one can be, bypassed by larger ships and too far from Rhodes or Kos to attract day-trippers. From the deck of my ferry it looked so bleak and forbidding I imagined travelers changing their minds when they saw it and continuing to the next island.

Like all the best islands, Tílos was a complete and self-contained world. Its port town, Livadia, had a long and pebbly beach framed by headlands, small hotels and tavernas, and a pleasant little square. Inland, Megalo Horio was the usual anti-pirate huddle of sugar-cube houses and narrow lanes. There was a fifteenth-century monastery tucked into a valley of cypress trees and rushing streams, a long sandy beach that is among the finest and emptiest in Greece, a fertile plain filled with greenhouses and olive and fruit trees, and mountains criss-crossed by goat tracks and crowned by crumbling crusader castles.

Tílos had a wild beauty that reminded me of Espíritu Santo and Isla Robinson Crusoe. The mayor of Megalo Horio, Dr. Tasos Ali-feris, was a version of Des Alwi who had banned bird hunting and dreamed of making the island an "ecological park," a designation giving its local authorities more influence over water conservation, building permits, and garbage disposal. The Tíliots welcomed travelers and were almost as friendly as Abemamans. Snapshots of visitors covered the walls of a Livadia taverna, and Vasilis Economou, the son of its owner, told me: "We like looking at the photographs of our friends during the winter and thinking about them. But if they don't visit the next summer we worry, 'Are they still alive?' When they do come, even if it's three years later, we are very relieved."

Outside Livadia and Megalo Horio, Tílos was as silent as Jura. I walked for an hour east from Livadia on paths and goat tracks strung across the headlands and met only one person, an Englishwoman who was reading a book in the shady courtyard of a chapel. Two years before, FOTA had asked its members what attracted them to Tílos. The favorite answers were "Being close to nature," "Walking opportunities," and "Tílos people." Number one, cited by 100 percent of respondents, was "Peace and tranquility."

In addition to its ruined castles, Tílos had two marvelous sets of relics. At the beach at Adonis, low tide revealed slabs of sandstone rock containing the ancient skeletal remains of children and teenagers who had perished in a shipwreck or died of natural causes and been buried in a cemetery later flooded by the sea. In Megalo Horio, a small museum displayed some of the fourteen thousand dwarf elephant bones an Athens paleontologist had found in a nearby cave in 1971. These donkey-sized elephants had lived on this island between 50000 and 3500 B.C. Among the theories advanced for their extinction was that the gradual warming of the earth and resulting rise in sea levels had reduced the size of Tílos, submerging the elephants' pastures.

The largest Tílos relic was the abandoned hilltop village of Mikro Horio. Its 220 desolate stone houses looked bombed, in part because its departing residents had carried away their roofs, leaving fig trees to grow from parlors and kitchens. When I visited, goats were bounding through the rubble and poking their heads through gaping windows, and the graveyard silence was broken by a buzz saw wielded by a shirtless man building an extension to the Mikro Horio music bar. On summer nights, young people came here to dance. Most were Greeks from Livadia or Athens, and some were descended from Tíliots whose bones were visible in the Mikro Horio ossuary. They turned their baseball caps backwards to dance to rock numbers, then respectfully forward for the music of their ancestors, who probably would have approved of the festivities since they were famous for throwing impromptu parties ending when everyone collapsed from exhaustion.

I was told Mikro Horio had died because its residents grew tired of climbing home from their fields and hauling up water in olive oil tins yoked over their shoulders, because the Italians who seized the Dodecanese islands from the Ottoman Turks in 1912 built up Livadia, and because many families left the island in the late 1940s, as there was no high school. But other small Greek islands lacked high schools at the time and their communities survived, and other island villages built on high ground continued to be inhabited.

I asked Vasilis Economou, who is also the island's amateur historian, what had precipitated the abandonment of Mikro Horio.

"Land mines," he said. Sure, the town's location and a desire for higher education had been important, but land mines planted by German soldiers during the war had started the exodus. The Germans had mined the islanders' farms to discourage them from harvesting food needed by the German army, and three men had been killed while attempting to pick tomatoes. The Greek civil war and chaos in Athens delayed the clearing of the mines and many Tíliots, afraid to till their own land, had emigrated to Rhodes, Crete, Athens, and Australia. Had the Germans not mined Mikro Horio's fields, or had the Greek army swept them sooner, the exodus would have been more gradual, and the town might have survived.

And had Des Alwi not revisited Banda Neira in 1968, I thought, its perkenier mansions might still be ruined shells, and its nutmeg groves slashed and burned for cassava. Had rabbits and blackberries not been introduced to Más a Tierra, the path to Selkirk's lookout might have wound through thickets of endemic trees. And were islands less fragile and vulnerable, they might not engage our sympathies and allegiances so easily.

■

I had visited only about half my islands, but I already felt I was traveling through an insular version of "The Twelve Days of Christmas," in which each new island added a new verse while repeating earlier ones. And the more every island echoed the ones preceding it, and the more connections I saw between their charms, the more I began imagining myself traveling through a single homogeneous country.

I had been struck by the perfection of an island silence on Isla Robinson Crusoe and reminded of it again on Narrows, Jura, and Patmos; impressed by the ability of an island to preserve history and relics on Banda Neira, and then again on Narrows Island, Campobello, Jura, Espíritu Santo, and Tílos.

My suspicion that islands play tricks with time started on Banda Neira and was confirmed by Santo's Octagon House.

Richard Henry Dana had spoken of Isla Crusoe being his "true home," and Erik Kvick of Santo being his father's true home, while Tamalia and former Dutch residents of the Bandas kept jars of its soil on their mantelpieces. And whenever I climbed to a high point on Isla Crusoe, Jura, or Patmos, I was reminded that an island wilderness is more frightening, and complete, than any continental one.

8

FRIENDLY ISLANDS —
ABEMAMA AND KOSRAE

The fragility of remote islands means that returning to one you have loved can be risky. I had been lucky with Patmos and Jura, but I worried about Abemama, an atoll in the Central Pacific nation of Kiribati where I had spent an idyllic week in 1985. Its beaches had been a more brilliant white than any I had yet seen and its palms bent by the wind into more graceful curves. Nowhere except the Sahara had stars burned so close and clear. There had been no asphalt, litter, television, or air-conditioning; no power lines to distract from the cloud shadows sweeping its lagoon; and, as far as I could tell, no unhappiness. Its people lived in pandanus-thatch houses, traveled by foot or bicycle, and gathered in four-story-high traditional meeting houses, or maneabas, built from coconut logs, sisal, and coral. Its relics were a well dating from the early nineteenth century that had been taboo to everyone except the royal family, who drew water from it with a human skull lowered on a rope of hair, and the charred poles of a maneaba burned down by a British district commissioner in 1900. Its only accommodation was the Robert Louis Stevenson Hotel, six bungalows made of palm fronds, pandanus mats, and the bark of the sweet-smelling uri. It was named after Stevenson because he spent four months on Abemama and found it so pleasant he built himself a house whose ruins were still visible.

My days in Abemama were an agreeable succession of long beach walks, lengthy conversations with George Tokataake, the hereditary king of Abemama, and excursions to the sites of historic interest and natural beauty with his two grandsons, Willy and Donald. Every night I ate turtle stew, grilled fish, pawpaws, curried prawns, and other local dishes in an open dining room lit by candles and kerosene lamps. Only the one-room stores selling canned goods and necessities like matches and thread and a twice-weekly flight to Tarawa on a small propeller plane told you there was a world outside the reef.

One of Abemama's greatest pleasures was its gentle and friendly people. Stevenson had described them as having "a curious politeness, a soft and gracious manner, something effeminate and courtly." They still had this reputation and other islanders called them "the ladies of Abemama" because they abhorred violence and confrontation. King George believed they were the most polite people in Kiribati, perhaps in the Pacific, and easy to pick out in a crowd of other islanders because they were so quiet and patient. "We are famous for being quite harmless," George Tokataake boasted.

He was a perfect king for Abemama. With his wide grin, gap teeth, long bony face, and bald head he resembled a skull, but one of those jolly Halloween ones. He had tattoos on his arms, liked dirty jokes, and often reverted to the salty language of a merchant seaman, which is what he had been until coming home to Abemama. He reminded me of those Scandinavian monarchs who ride bicycles everywhere and are unmistakably royal, but have a common touch.

His subjects continued gathering in maneabas as their ancestors had, preferred grass houses to concrete ones, and followed a code of etiquette so strict children had to dismount from their bicycles and walk whenever they passed an elder or a maneaba. The taboos involving heads were taken so seriously that men cutting toddy from palm trees were forbidden to sing because they might appear to be lording it over those beneath them, and it was so unthinkable to use the same word to describe a human head and a fish head that the latter was called "the part of the fish where the lips are."

But even in 1985 I noticed that some customs were being discarded or weakened. When Willy Tokataake, one of the king's grandsons, gave me a tour of the island's largest and oldest maneaba, he kept apologizing for its shocking condition, pointing out its collapsing fence and shredded mats. He blamed the newest generation of elders, saying that although they continued attending meetings they were uninterested in making any repairs. On other islands people saved themselves the trouble of repairing a maneaba by replacing its traditional roof with tin and installing concrete pillars and cement floors. He worried this might happen here.

Willy and his brother Donald were also concerned that young Abemaman youth were becoming, in Donald's words, "too individualistic and ignoring the good of the community." To remedy this they held monthly meetings in maneabas around the island and lectured the children on their history and customs. Yet in the evenings, in these same villages, they showed the kind of video movies that are the enemy of traditional cultures, using a portable generator to power the television and charging admission. One night I attended a screening of the James Bond film *Live and Let Die*. In its opening minutes, a United Nations delegate died in agony as a high-frequency sound was piped through his headphones, another man was knifed, and a third tortured during a voodoo ceremony. Then the opening credits unrolled over a nude woman lying on a flaming skull. The lines of beetle-backed boys watched in reverent silence, little exemplars of Abemaman etiquette as they discovered the world beyond their reef.

I have no idea if by now every maneaba in Abemama has a tin roof, concrete floor, television, and VCR. But in the early 1990s I read that a foreign waste-disposal firm was offering to install a complete television network in Kiribati in exchange for being allowed to dump nuclear waste in its territorial waters. Even if impoverished Kiribati

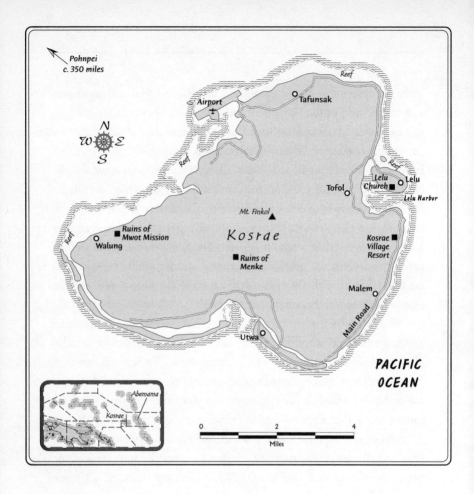

had the willpower to decline this poisoned apple (I later learned that it did), it was one of the atoll nations threatened with global warming submersion, and large numbers of shallow-water fish have already died near Abemama's reefs because of higher-than-normal salinity and water temperature.

I was reluctant to return to Abemama because I wanted to remember it as it had been. Instead of going back and risking disappointment, I looked for another Micronesian island famous for its friendly people and found Kosrae, an island with a population of eight thousand that is the easternmost of the Carolines and seven hundred miles northwest of Abemama.

Every island trolling for tourists claims its people are welcoming and friendly, but in the case of Kosrae there was dramatic proof that its inhabitants really were the friendliest on earth.

When the U.S. Navy was island-hopping across the Central Pacific during World War II, it bypassed strategically unimportant Micronesian islands like Kosrae and imposed a blockade, leaving their Japanese garrisons isolated and hungry. In the final weeks of the war, the Tokyo high command ordered troops on these islands to execute the native populations. The Japanese commander on Kosrae proclaimed a holiday and ordered everyone to gather the following morning for games and canoe races. That night, while some Japanese soldiers were setting up camouflaged machine-gun nests overlooking the meeting places, others went from village to village warning their Kosraean friends to hide in the mountains. When locals assembled the following morning for these "games," sympathetic Japanese soldiers mingled among them, placing themselves in the line of fire and saving a people who had enchanted them as much as they had earlier foreign occupiers and explorers.

Kosrae is so isolated that Europeans did not even know it existed until 1824, when a French scientific vessel appeared in Lelu's harbor. Louis Duperry and Edmond d'Urville went ashore and surprised a hundred natives holding a feast in a large meeting house. Until this moment—a transforming one similar to the appearance of the Dutch fleet in the Bandas in 1615—Kosraeans had believed they were the only people on earth.

Most people might reach for a weapon upon having their supper interrupted by the equivalent of men from Mars. But D'Urville said the Kosraeans shouted in "joy and admiration," stroked their visitors' white skin, and offered them platters of breadfruit. Then they led them through the canals, paved roads, great walls, and stone houses of Lelu, a wonder equal to Easter Island's stone heads, and one placing Kosrae among the most advanced civilizations of the Pacific.

The Kosraeans these first Europeans encountered were like Isla

Crusoe's endemic species, fragile and delicate plants protected by their isolation. D'Urville called them "a simple, peaceful, and generous people." Duperry raved about "generous and peaceful" vegetarians who lacked barbaric customs and warlike weapons and were strangers to hard work because their island was so fertile.

Three years later, the commander of a Russian scientific expedition, Fyodor Lutke, praised their hospitality and "astonishing decorum" and suggested their lack of oceangoing vessels indicated they had lived in isolation for centuries, explaining their peaceful demeanor.

In 1839, the second mate of an American brig stopping on Kosrae wrote: "The natives . . . had the name of being the most friendly of any of the South Seas to Europeans and whilst we remained, they certainly showed themselves deserving of it. They are one of the few peoples on the earth who know not of war and neither possess clubs, spears nor any of those weapons generally found among savages."

The journey to Kosrae is long and costly but I justified it by telling myself that even if its people were less delightful than those who had charmed the Japanese, it would be worth the trip to meet Thurston Siba, the recently retired governor. Whenever I saw Thurston Avenue or Thurston Circle in Honolulu, or noticed that the chairman of the *Honolulu Advertiser* was named Thurston Twigg-Smith, I was reminded that I am a distant relation of Reverend Asa Thurston, one of the first missionaries to arrive in Hawaii, who, as the shopworn expression goes, "came to do good, and did well." The Hawaii Thurstons invented the written Hawaiian language, introduced modern medicine, and opened the first schools, but they also outlawed the hula, wrapped generations of beautiful Hawaiians in ankle-length Mother Hubbards, orchestrated the coup overthrowing the Hawaiian monarchy, and perpetrated the Great Mahele, a slick land grab transferring land from Hawaiians to missionary families. This is why, in the custom of our times, I feel more guilty than proud of them, and when I learned that Asa Thurston had belonged to the same missionary church that sent the Reverend Benjamin and Lydia Snow of Portland, Maine, to Kosrae, I wondered if a visiting Thurston had lifted one of those Mother Hubbards and bedded a convert.

■

When the South Seas author and trader Robert Dean Frisbie traveled in 1924 from Rarotonga to Puka-Puka, the last and easternmost atoll in the Cook Islands, he spoke of the sensation of journeying to the end of something—to the insular equivalent of a mountain peak or the headwaters of a great river. As his schooner sailed northwest through ever more remote—and friendlier—atolls, he imagined himself crossing a barrier between corrupted and pure islands that was "as impenetrable as the jungle curtain which fell behind Mungo Park when he sought the outlet to the Niger." Finally, he arrived on Puka-Puka, where he became the only white man on another island of exceptionally friendly people, "beyond reach of even the faintest echo from the noisy clamor of the civilized world."

Now that airplanes have replaced schooners and tramp steamers, the experience of traveling slowly along a chain of Pacific islands has largely disappeared. A passenger-carrying ship still connects Papeete with the Marquesas, and field-trip vessels sail within island groups, but passenger ships no longer cross thousands of miles of empty water. The only trans-Pacific airplane route mimicking Frisbie's journey is Continental Micronesia's "island hopper," a three-times-weekly flight between Honolulu and Guam, calling at Johnston Island, Majuro, Kwajalein, Kosrae, Pohnpei, and Chuuk. Its real end of the line is not busy Guam but Kosrae, whose position 2,800 miles west of Honolulu and 1,500 miles east of Guam makes it the most isolated island-hopper stop.

My flight became emptier with each island and I was the only non-Micronesian to disembark at Kosrae, and for a week its only foreign visitor, just as on Abemama. From the moment I landed, my encounters with Kosraeans were characterized by such a natural intimacy I felt I was back on Abemama, among people who already knew me.

My first Kosraean was "Miriam," a talkative malcontent with the weary detachment of a Joan Didion heroine. She drove me to the Kosrae Village Resort, a grand name for nine thatched bungalows underneath some mangroves at the edge of the water. I had chosen it because it offered free accommodations on Sundays as a concession to the fact that there was nothing for a visitor to do then but go to church.

Miriam wished she were boarding my plane and returning to Virginia Beach, where she had waitressed for five years before being summoned home to care for her ailing father, the penalty for being the only unmarried child of five. "And the minute he dies, I'm gone," she said. Life in the United States had ruined her for Kosrae. She could never marry a local man because they drank and gossiped while their wives cleaned and cooked. Everything I had heard about the puritanical Kosraean Sunday was true. Fishing or drinking alcohol, even in private, got you a month in jail. Hiking, swimming, shell-gathering, biking, diving, waterskiing, or appearing in public without a shirt—they were all illegal. Her friends called Sunday "baby-making day" because what else could you do? But she liked it because the worst men headed into the hills to drink toddy, leaving the women in peace.

"Why have you come here?" she asked, her expression implying I must be crazy.

I mumbled something about escaping the first snows of an Adirondack winter.

"I would like to be in your Adirondacks right now. A few months of winter and my skin would be white again, like yours." She gave my arm a gentle stroke, like the one I imagined her ancestors giving D'Urville.

I quickly discovered I could not walk anywhere on Kosrae without being offered a ride. Two fishermen in a rust-eaten truck who picked me up giggled after every sentence. They wanted me to know they believed fishing with long lines or dynamite was cruel to the fish, so they would never do it. They had heard about me hours after my arrival and said Mr. Thurston Siba was already eager to meet me. "Thank you for riding with us," they chorused when we parted.

A retired teacher named Kingston tracked me down after hearing I was inquiring about the attempted World War II massacre. He remembered village elders begging his family to hide in the mountains and said Kosraeans were friendly to Americans because if they had not landed on September 8, 1945—still an official holiday on the island—the Japanese might have tried again to kill them.

The Kosraeans I met were as friendly as Abemamans, but a half century of American charity had swept away their palm-and-thatch dwellings, replacing them with concrete bungalows. It had also financed a diet of foreign canned and processed foods, and the importation of used cars from Japan. But whenever I left the road, I was on an island Duperry, Lutke, and the Snows would have recognized, one of the prettiest Pacific high islands, with cloud-shrouded mountains, forests so thick trees grew from trees, and a soil so fertile fence posts took root and sprouted.

The friendliness of the Kosraeans and their high spirits were all the more remarkable given a history that would have justified them stoning strange white men on sight. The crews of New England whaling ships had raped their great-great-grandmothers and brought the epidemics of influenza, smallpox, and venereal disease that reduced the population from five thousand to three hundred, leaving only a single infant alive at one late-nineteenth-century low point. European "blackbirders," or slavers, had sold Kosraeans to Australian plantations and South American mines, and had inflicted murder, rape, and vandalism on the island. In 1896, Spain seized Kosrae and sold it to Germany. After World War I, the League of Nations gave it as a mandate—a "Sacred Trust of Civilization"—to the Japanese, who paid slave wages and tortured plantation workers. After World War II, the United Nations handed it to the United States as a Strategic Trust Territory, beginning decades of corrosive charity.

Given this dismal history, why were Kosraeans so friendly?

They told me: "We have so few visitors that every one is entertaining for us." "Our culture celebrates sharing instead of competition." "Kosrae is so fertile we have never faced starvation."

I had my own theories. The months that Pacific Islanders once spent voyaging to new islands in open canoes had supposedly bred into them the distinctive rolling gait necessary for balancing yourself in a pitching boat, and the body fat necessary for surviving the chilling sea spray. Perhaps being jammed together in those pitching boats had also made them genetically more sociable. Or maybe they had such sunny dispositions because as children they were seldom spanked or criticized and spent most of their waking hours cradled in the arms of a relative. More likely, they embraced visitors and were so gentle and tolerant because the nearest inhabited island was over two hundred miles away and their watery horizons, empty in every direction, never let them forget they were on their own, dependent on one another for joy, love, and survival. Whenever a Kosraean showed me a kindness, I remembered his or her ancestors' "joy and admiration" at seeing D'Urville. It was the reaction of a goat ignorant of the lion. They were friendly because they had nothing to fear.

The local partner of the Californian couple who owned the Kosrae Village Resort was a stocky cherub named Madison Nena who had previously headed the Kosraean bureau of tourism and been responsible for starting the Utwa-Walung Conservation Area, a large protected area of mangrove swamp, rivers, and reefs. He believed Kosraeans were friendly for the same reason there had never been a murder on the island (at least one that was not "an accident"): everyone attended church on Sunday. "We are the friendliest people in the Pacific because we are the most religious," he said. "It's that simple."

Every Sunday, Kosraeans attended morning services, lunched on a Sunday soup prepared the day before (to avoid cooking on the Sabbath), and returned for "Christian Endeavors," an opportunity to discuss the sermon. "After all that, we come home feeling very holy," Nena said, adding that he could not think of anyone who *never* went to church. The heretics who had abandoned the Congregational Church of Asa Thurston and the Snows had become Seventh-Day Adventists or Jehovah's Witnesses. The Mormons were the real rebels.

Kosrae was the most observant Christian island I had seen—a Saudi Arabia of Christianity, but lots more fun. One of its great relics was the Congregational Church. A visiting church historian from Boston had been flabbergasted to attend services identical to those of nineteenth-century New England, and Nena introduced me to a parchment-skinned minister who boasted, "Church officials come from Hawaii to train us and find we are more religious than they are!"

The church had been accepted so quickly, and remained so powerful, because when the Snows arrived in 1856, Kosrae's popular ruler, Good King George, had grown tired of the drunken orgies of the white traders and whalers. He embraced the missionaries and after a single Sunday service ordered his subjects to begin observing the Sabbath. He gave the Snows land for a house and supported their demands that congregants wear long dresses and trousers, forswear alcohol and tobacco, and stop sending their women to the whaling ships. In their reports the Snows praised him as "a model of quiet unostentatious simplicity" who set "a high moral tone for his people."

Say what you will about missionaries smashing idols, shilling for colonial powers, and coming to do good and doing well, had the Snows not forbidden this trade in women, venereal disease might have completely depopulated Kosrae.

Nena drove me to the dedication of a new wing of the Lelu church at a steady twenty-five miles an hour, the island speed limit and one widely observed because no one was ever in a hurry, or wanted to risk hitting a child. When he noticed me eyeing the speedometer, he asked if he was driving too fast.

The church courtyard held the largest amount of food I have yet
seen in one place. I estimated there were already six thousand coconuts in palm frond cradles, three thousand bundles of sugar cane
and taro, and three hundred dead pigs, skinned and oozing blood,
stacked in piles of six, one for every twenty-seven Kosraeans, including babes in arms. Every minute, pickup trucks delivered more pigs,
which were tossed into heaps and sorted by village. Spectators circled
them like judges at a county fair, hands behind backs, whispering and
pointing. This massacre of pigs, like the islanders' abandonment of
vegetarianism and fondness for pork, started with the single pig that
Duperry presented to the king in 1824. Nena said the food was a
symbolic thanks offering for the new wing, proof of Kosraeans' faith.
Afterwards, it would be returned to the villages and devoured.

One glance at Thurston Siba, who stood among the dead pigs
wearing a careful Middle American wardrobe of polished shoes,
creased trousers, and tie pin, and I knew we did not share any missionary genes. I am balding and thin. He was papaya-shaped, with
sienna skin and a long Levantine nose. He explained he was a
Thurston for the same reason Nena was a Madison. They were both
named after famous Americans, and other popular island first names
included Kennedy, Lincoln, and Johnson. An American missionary
had suggested his name as a tribute to Asa Thurston. "But of course
you and I have a symbolic relationship," he added, not wanting me to
be disappointed, "so you must share my pew at services tomorrow."

On Sunday, the hotel locked up the liquor and boys appeared in
the street wearing long trousers. The interior of Lelu church was as
stark as any in New England, with white walls, a bare altar, and an
unadorned wood cross. Siba ran his finger along the Kosraean Bible
readings so I could follow them, and the minister delivered a sermon
describing a heaven resembling the landscape outside the window.
I have been to churches on other South Pacific islands, so I was
prepared for the marathon of hymns, readings, and prayers, for the
sumo-sized men, their hair still slick from the shower, the ladies in

ankle-length dresses moving like ocean liners, and the banknotes un-
folding like flowers in the collection plate after being clutched in
sweaty palms. But Lelu was distinguished by the quality of the singing. After the opening prayer, Siba and everyone surrounding us broke
into a lovely four-part harmony. Their voices were as transparent as
the lagoon, so clear and sharp they cut the humid air like a knife. The
service was a nineteenth-century Congregationalist one, but the singing was as exotic and hypnotic as watching any troop of whirling
dervishes.

I hiked to the ruined eleventh-century city of Menka with Tatao Morris Waguck, a middle-aged man with beef-jerky skin who had rediscovered it. As a boy he had heard stories about a jungle city haunted
by ghosts, and since stumbling on Menka's ruined foundations while
tracking a wild pig, he had made it his life's mission to educate Kosraeans about it and make them proud of their history.

He skipped over roots and rocks in his bare feet, using a machete
to slash at branches and vines as we climbed up the valley of Mt. Fin-
kol. When he turned around to tell me that these elephant-ear ferns
were the world's largest, and that he had returned to Kosrae from
Hawaii because he preferred picking fruit from trees to buying it in
stores, I saw the Nike swoosh on the front of his baseball cap, and
when he turned back, *Just Do It!*

Like many Kosraeans, he was so chatty I decided the steady and
pleasant hum of "happy talk"—to use Bloody Mary's phrase—helped
explain his people's reputation for friendliness. Most families lived
close together, often within the same compound, so there were few
moments in a day when a Kosraean was not talking, laughing, or
singing. Silence was a vacuum to be filled, and whenever our conversation flagged, Waguck said something, anything.

He declared, apropos of nothing, that missionaries had done good
things for Kosrae, "but their greatest contribution was teaching us to

sing four-part harmony because our singing before was terrible—just one tune!"

He said this land belonged to his family and they prohibited hunting. Did I notice the difference? The forest near the town of Utwe was silent but here birds fluttered and sang.

He asked if I had come to Kosrae because I shared a name with Thurston Siba. And was I aware that Kosraean people had names from Australia, Spain, Germany, Japan, and the United States, and that Mr. Ted Sigrah, grandson of Kosrae's last chief, was related to former president George Bush?

My first view of Menka was a disappointing one of shallow pits and low stone walls buried in underbrush. But then we climbed to a plateau and I saw a maze of higher walls stretching into the jungle. The most extensive ruins crowned a temple mound that had been the site of wrestling matches and sacrifices. On any mainland, and on most islands, Menka would have been a much excavated and celebrated attraction, but on Kosrae no archaeologist had bothered to stake a claim.

We sat on a pounding stone once used for grinding the seka root into a mild narcotic, lunching on cookies and coconut milk. Waguk said he had sponsored an open house here last year and eight hundred Kosraeans had spent the day dancing and eating traditional foods. Now he had even more time to promote Menka because a sharp reduction in American subsidies had forced him to take early retirement from his government job. He would not miss his paycheck because he could collect free food in the forest. And why did Kosraeans need money anyway? To buy more cars? Hundreds of wrecked and broken ones already littered the island. When the American subsidies ended in 2001, there would be no money for bringing these second- and third-hand cars from Japan, then everyone would have to walk or paddle a canoe. "And my response to that is 'Good!' " he announced, "because then we will all lose weight, live longer, and be much happier."

Kosrae had become dependent on American charity after U.S. Navy destroyers entered Lelu Harbor in 1945 and it became an American-administered United Nations Trust Territory. In 1978, its inhabitants and those of four other Trust Territory Districts had voted for a constitution that is the legal basis for the Federated States of Micronesia (FSM). Eight years later, the FSM and the United States implemented a Compact of Free Association allowing the United States a free military hand in the region in return for $1.34 billion in grants over the next fifteen years. This money was supposed to encourage ventures that would leave the FSM islands economically self-sufficient. Instead, much of it went for imported goods, prestige projects, and salaries for government employees like Tatao Waguck. By 1996, the last year for which I could find any statistics, three-quarters of Kosrae's wage earners were receiving government paychecks, and the island was exporting $500,000 in goods while importing $7.5 million. Half these imports, on an island of remarkable fertility, consisted of food, tobacco, and canned beverages, mostly soda pop.

The FSM islands lost their strategic value to the United States after the end of the Cold War and no one believed the U.S. Congress would vote to extend the grants beyond 2001, at least at anything approaching their current level. There would probably be money for health care and education, and the small fisheries and tourist industry would provide a trickle of foreign exchange, but by 2001 Kosrae would have only enough hard currency to buy 10 percent of its current imports. This would mean less petrol to run the rattletrap cars and fewer parts to repair them, less money for building new roads with coral mined from the reef, or importing tins of corned beef, tubes of Pringles, bags of Cheez Doodles, and the other sugar- and fat-packed convenience foods responsible for giving Kosraeans the highest rate of diabetes on earth. There would be fewer imported materials for building or repairing the stifling concrete houses that were so ill suited to the climate that many people lived in their yards, and fewer dollars for importing parts for broken video players, so fewer boys copying the tough guy stares of Kung Fu heroes, breaking their arms jumping from trees because they imagined themselves flying like Superman.

The consensus of foreign observers was that the Compact monies had disrupted the subsistence economies of the FSM islands without providing any sustainable alternative, and that the fault lay in poorly conceived plans, corruption, and administrative mistakes, in how the money was spent, rather than the money itself. It was believed Kosrae could of course participate in the global economy, and that the right mix of handicrafts, fishing, and ecotourism would provide a tiny island of eight thousand people in the middle of the Pacific, lacking any natural resources the rest of the world desired, enough foreign exchange to support a lifestyle based on imported goods, foods, and energy. "Micronesians are doing their best to become self-sufficient," a former American ambassador to the FSM had told the *Los Angeles Times*, but this would be "very difficult" because they lacked any resources. It had apparently not occurred to the ambassador or others that until quite recently Kosraeans had been magnificently self-sufficient, eating the fish they caught and the food they grew, traveling by canoe and living in houses they built from island trees.

A story about the FSM in the *Christian Science Monitor*, headlined "Trouble in Paradise," assumed that the end of American charity would be a catastrophe, and that Kosraeans dreaded losing the foods that were making them unhealthy, the houses making them uncomfortable, and the films leaving them dissatisfied with their lot. But many of the Kosraeans I was meeting shared Waguk's opinion that their island might be a happier place once the Compact money ran out.

No one stood to lose more than Thurston Siba, whose rental car agency, general stores, and cinder-block manufacturing works depended on imported goods. But when we met in his cavernous Lelu store and I asked what would happen when there was no hard currency to import the Cheez-It crackers, Betty Crocker cake mixes, and

Cap'n Crunch cereal lining his shelves, he shrugged and said, "I suppose we'll have to return to the old ways."

He made this future sound great. There would be less garbage and fewer junked cars. People would eat more local food and their diet would improve. They would still have coconuts and taro, fish on the reef, pandanus for thatch, and their religion, and if I returned in ten years for the dedication of another wing on Lelu's church, I would find just as much food assembled in its courtyard.

"How will you get around when you can't buy gas?" I asked a fisherman who drove me back to the Kosrae Village.

He laughed. "We'll walk more and lose weight."

Kingston, the retired teacher, told me he was looking forward to the day the American appliances disappeared because they made people lazy and fat. And when there were no more videos his former students would read more.

Madison Nena overheard us. "I won't miss the videos either," he added, saying they had encouraged secret binge-drinking and left people unhappier. And the fewer cars, the better. Most were junkers tricked up with a new paint job when they arrived. The salt and humidity quickly fouled their works and their new owners left them where they fell.

If anyone should have been worried about the reduction of the Compact grants it was George Singkitchy, Kosrae's director of commerce and industry, and the man responsible for overseeing its Departments of Consumer Service, Housing, Tourism, Marketing and Research, and Industrial Development. I met him in his office on the second floor of a two-story tin-and-concrete government building whose cracked windows, unraveling rugs, and groaning air conditioners already reflected the reduction in American charity.

The owlish Singkitchy seemed perplexed by his surroundings and responsibilities. He made some half-hearted excuses for Kosrae's fisheries industry, saying the Taiwanese ships had made the big money while Kosrae's dockworkers and cold storage facility earned scraps. He floated ecotourism as a solution, but conceded that given Kosrae's isolation it was unlikely to generate enough foreign exchange to support the government payroll or finance imports at current levels. He listened patiently as I argued that private automobiles on Kosrae made as much sense as the air-conditioned health clubs on Maldivian atolls and suggested Kosrae launch the kind of jitney service found on many small islands, with a fleet of vans cruising the coastal road.

"But how will we afford to buy these vans?" he asked.

I had no idea.

He leaned across his wobbly coffee table and whispered: "Listen, the honest truth is that what we have in Kosrae today is not making anyone very happy. In the old days, we worked a little on our farms, and had plenty to eat. We respected the napa tree, and used it for making our roofs. Now people cut them down and use them as fill. We lived in traditional houses—comfortable houses that were cool, cheap, and easy to maintain—and we liked them. I know *I* grew up in a thatched house, and *I* was happier then. But when American officials arrived after the war they insisted on concrete-and-tin houses, and soon everyone was copying them, and living in expensive buildings that are too hot."

Did this mean that if I returned in ten years I would find more traditional houses, fewer junked cars, less plastic garbage, and a healthier diet?

The director of commerce and industry raised his eyebrows. "Sounds great, doesn't it?"

It was easier for Singkitchy, Waguck, and Siba to imagine themselves enjoying a happy life without modern luxuries because their nineteenth-century Protestantism dismissed such things as unimportant, and perhaps returning to a precontact economy held fewer terrors for them because they lived in the shadow of Lelu, one of the most splendid ancient cities in the Pacific, and a constant reminder of what they could accomplish on their own. Even in the nineteenth century, it had been a thriving metropolis of walled houses, ceremonial compounds, artificial canals, and bamboo palaces whose size, beauty, and soaring peaked roofs stunned European visitors. D'Urville described well-paved streets and beautiful houses surrounded by high walls. The German artist, Friedrich von Kittlitz, who saw Lelu in the mid–nineteenth century, marveled at its scalloped roofs and graceful gables, "painted red like canoes with pleasing white decorations," the cleanliness of the houses, and furnishings "of the highest simplicity." Kosraeans abandoned Lelu in the 1870s, when their population fell into the hundreds, and some of its compounds have since been demolished and their rocks used for the foundations of concrete houses.

Lelu's vegetation is so luxuriant that when I walked around the islet for the first time I missed the ruins. I returned later with Madison Nena. We cut through a backyard and were suddenly standing in a labyrinth of twenty-foot basalt walls, paved roads, canals, and tombs, all built with boulders hauled from the other side of the island by a people lacking steel tools or the wheel. The walls and foliage blocked any views of the water and we could have been deep up a jungle valley. Lelu is often called "haunting" and "spooky," and its mossy walls and banyans did give it a graveyard feel, but the spookiest thing was the contrast between these magnificent ruins and the crude modern houses surrounding them.

Kittlitz described King George's compound as having acres of gardens and orchards, and reed-mat and thatched-roof mansions with pairs of "delicately worked, large canoes" that rested in scaffolds built into their gables. The king's thatch-and-bamboo palace had disappeared, but his descendants and their principal enterprise, an Ace Hardware franchise, occupied the same waterfront land.

I found Ted Sigrah, grandson of the last king of Kosrae, stocking shelves in a fluorescent-lit aisle, surrounded by the imported gadgets, parts, and tools that might become unavailable after 2001. He was so tiny and shriveled that his Ace baseball cap, tightened to its smallest size, rested on his ears. As the sound track from *Saturday Night Fever* rocked the store, he praised his grandfather as a strong Christian man who suffered torture under the Japanese rather than order his subjects to work on the Sabbath, and boasted that his grandmother had been a descendant of the nineteenth-century Maine trader Harry Skillings, making him a cousin of former president George Bush.

He lived next door, in an unfinished cinder-block house on the grounds of the former royal compound. Broken appliances and automobile parts obscured the backyard graves of Kosraean kings. Sepia-toned photographs of Sigrah's grandparents lined the walls of a parlor furnished with an electric keyboard, a video recorder, and a twenty-one-inch television. Two huge women and some children lay sprawled on the linoleum floor while credits for a movie rolled down the screen. The women chugged soda pop from plastic liter bottles while their kids rolled empty potato chip canisters back and forth. I realized that not a single thing in this room would be easily available on Kosrae in a few years, and it was not impossible that if I returned in a decade or two I might find it replaced by the kind of traditional house Kittlitz had praised.

It was suggested if I wanted to see the Kosrae of the past, and maybe of the future, too, I should visit Walung, a seaside village isolated by mountains and mangroves that was accessible only by flat-bottomed canoe. Everyone agreed it was a Shangri-la of palms and thatched houses whose three hundred people lived off the surrounding land and sea, and had so far resisted electrification and the extension of the coastal road.

Louis Becke, an Australian author of South Seas adventure stories, had launched Walung's reputation. He had started wandering across the Pacific as a fourteen-year-old stowaway, living on Samoa and trading firearms before becoming the supercargo (business manager) of the *Leonora*, a brigantine captained by Bully Hayes, a colorful American psychopath with a hair-trigger temper who had been stealing ships, blackbirding, and outwitting the law from China to New Zealand for decades. In 1874, after a hurricane sank the *Leonora* in Kosrae's Utwa Harbor, Hayes and his ruffians unleashed a reign of terror on nearby villages. Repelled by what he called "mutiny, treachery, murder, and sudden death," Becke walked around the coastline to Walung (then known as Leassé), and for the next seven months was its first and only white resident.

His descriptions of Walung's dense mountain forests, shrill parakeets, pale green sea, and clamoring reef make it sound like another Bali-ha'i. It faced "a curving beach of creamy sand," backed by mountains "wrapped in fleecy mist." Its friendly inhabitants hugged and embraced him, and his days were an idyll of fishing and kava-drinking. He fell asleep listening to the singing of women and hearing the "song of the surf" on the barrier reef. Years later he would insist that island villages like Walung were the "true home" of his generation of traders and adventurers, and write that he often wished he could relive those seven months and let his latter-day respectability "go hang."

To take me to Walung I hired a man named Nixon who had been born during Eisenhower's presidency to parents who found that name too much of a mouthful and so had settled on his vice president instead. The Kosraean Nixon was a solidly built man with a goatee, a shaved head, and a gentle nature, so he had nothing in common with the other Nixon. While we waited at a dock near the airport for his uncle, who would take us to Walung in his motorized canoe, he told me he had recently returned after twenty homesick years in Hawaii, and liked Walung because it reminded him of the Kosrae he had left behind, an island where people still traveled by boat, grew their own food, and spent evenings listening to the legend-tellers. His finances had become shaky after he had started a Little League team and bought uniforms and trophies for the boys with his own money, and he hoped to recoup his losses and support himself by becoming a guide. He had waited a month for someone to take his Walung tour and I was his first customer. The sheet of paper on his clipboard was a questionnaire, designed to measure my happiness at every turn. As we crossed the lagoon, as his uncle poled us through channels in the mangrove swamp, and as we finally slid ashore on Walung's beach, he kept asking, "Are you enjoying yourself *right now*, Mr. Thurston? Are you? Are you sure? Oh, I *do* hope so."

But once we landed in Walung Nixon had no idea what to do with me. Its charm was in what it lacked—shops, restaurants, electricity, cars, and roads—rather than anything you could see. "When the American money runs out, everyone will enjoy this simple life," he insisted, pointing out Walung's papaya, breadfruit, and tangerine trees as if they were rare specimens, and its wood-and-thatch houses as if they were palaces.

He loved its mile-long, powdery beach so much that he had brought a plastic bag along and we started by collecting garbage that had washed ashore. It was Kosrae's finest beach, he said, the only one suitable for a resort, although its waterfront owners had sworn never to sell.

I told him I was having a splendid time poking my nose into cooking sheds that proved Walung's people lived on fish, taro, and fruit. I said I loved how its forested hills rose so steeply, how its palms grew so thickly along the beach. I agreed Kosrae was one of the prettiest islands anywhere, and Walung its prettiest village. But where were its three hundred residents? I had seen a few children splashing in the water, an old man mending his nets, and two fully dressed women bathing in a stream. But where was everyone else?

He said the men were fishing and the older children in school, but many of these shuttered houses belonged to government employees who escaped here on weekends. When the money for their salaries ran out, perhaps they would move in permanently. Meanwhile, it was their refuge.

Shortly after Becke left Walung, some Congregationalist missionaries built the Mwot school on a plateau above the beach. The Baldwin sisters, who were its most famous missionaries, had combined the dedication and fanaticism that are often the hallmarks of such people, cutting photographs of women in revealing dresses out of the magazines donated by American parishes, and playing donated phonograph records on their wind-up Victrola before dumping them beyond the reef. Yet they had trained generations of Kosraean preachers and teachers, and always slept fully clothed in this hot climate so they could instantly respond to any emergency. Elizabeth Baldwin had gone blind while translating the Bible into Kosraean.

Mwot had been abandoned in the early 1960s when the government began providing universal public education. I told Nixon it sounded like the kind of attraction he should be including on his tour and asked to see it. He immediately raised objections, protesting that the plateau was overgrown, the climb was long and tiring (it was not), and his uncle had not bothered to return since graduating from Mwot in 1962.

I assumed they believed it was haunted, or nursed grudges against the missionaries. But it gradually came out that Nixon's uncle had loved Mwot so much he could not bear gazing on its ruins. He finally relented, leading us up the coral steps he had helped build as a boy, past an overgrown graveyard where an 1888 obelisk commemorated Mwot's founder, and a towering pine tree the missionaries decorated for Christmas.

Mwot was a Menka in the making. Every building was roofless, and a rusted refrigerator stood alone on a chipped tile floor, like a sculpture. Mwot's situation made it the first place on Kosrae to catch winds that had swept over thousands of miles of empty ocean. Later, as they crossed the island, these breezes would pick up the odor of decaying plants and animals, and the thick perfume of tropical blossoms. Here they smelled as fresh and clean as sheets dried by the sun and wind.

Nixon translated his uncle's comments.

"He says this is the best place on Kosrae because of its cool breeze and views of the lagoon."

"He remembers laying these tiles and has only the *happiest* memories of being here."

"The buildings were so beautiful that seeing them this way makes him cry."

His uncle turned away and began slashing at the vines with a machete.

That Mwot could fall to ruin so quickly made it easier to imagine a similar fate for Kosrae's modern infrastructure, although I doubted if thirty-five years from now anyone would shed tears for Mr. Singkitchy's offices, the Ace Hardware store, or the graveyards of junked cars. Singkitchy, Nena, and Siba had told me Kosraeans were already shifting gears—that more men were constructing their homes from mats, logs, and bamboo, and more women preparing traditional foods. Traditional canoe-building practices were being revived, too, and men were fishing from boats resembling those of their great-grandfathers. It is not inconceivable that by 2024, the two-hundredth anniversary of Duperry's visit, Kosrae will resemble the island he saw in 1824, or the Walung that seduced Louis Becke in 1874, or the Suwarrow that captivated Robert Dean Frisbie in 1934, or the Abemama that bewitched me in 1985—islands whose great charm is that they are, like Crusoe's, "removed from all the wickedness of the world."

3 SYMBOLIC ISLANDS

9

PRIVATE ISLAND — NIIHAU

We imagine that islands belonging to the same archipelagoes, chains, and lines, we imagine that islands that are close together will be alike, and often they are. But it can also happen that one island is an outsider: an ugly duckling lacking fresh water, a mysterious private island, a terrifying prison island, or one tainted by a history of cannibalism or murder; or that one island is believed to be more holy, or more sensual, than those surrounding it. Islands like these are scattered around the world and have more in common with one another than their neighbors. At least that was my theory, and my justification for choosing a single prison, utopian, frightening, undiscovered, and private island to represent the rest.

Private islands are as addictive as mixed nuts, and once I started searching through the twisted Utopias and sexual playgrounds for a good one to visit I found it hard to stop. My favorites were Beaver Island and Golondrina, and had either remained in the same hands I might never have considered Niihau.

Beaver Island, the largest in an archipelago of heavily wooded islands at the northern end of Lake Michigan, is where a hot-tempered and oversexed Mormon heretic named James Strang established a settlement in 1847 that he and his 250 followers called—what else?—

St. James. More Strangites followed, and a year later Strang was inaugurated king in a ceremony replete with throne, crown, and shouts of "Long Live James, King of Zion!" The Strangites built a road across the island, calling it the King's Highway, elected their king to the state legislature, and prospered by selling wood to Lake Michigan steamboats. But this utopian period was brief. A group of Irish Catholic fishermen who had preceded Strang ignored his royal edicts, acts of vandalism between them and the Strangites escalated to murder, and rumors reached the mainland of sexual debauchery. (Strang claimed God had commanded him to marry often and well.) Strang instigated his final downfall by issuing an edict requiring women to wear smocks and pantaloons. Conservative members of his community protested that this was a scandalously revealing costume. Strang horsewhipped the leader of the anti-smock faction, who in return lay in ambush and mortally wounded him.

Equally bizarre was Golondrina, a tiny Mexican island near southern California where Princess Der Ling, of the Manchu Dynasty, re-created the imperial court of Peking. She had escaped China during a turn-of-the-century revolutionary outbreak with the assistance of an American Marine lieutenant, under what were characterized as highly romantic circumstances. She leased Golondrina in 1927 and, hoping it might encourage the writing of her memoirs, populated it with an all-female court of 150 retainers and dancers overseen by a palace guard of twenty ex-Marines, commanded by the same lieutenant who had rescued her from Peking. She presided over this court from a gilded throne, settling the intrigues and quarrels that were the inevitable fruit of throwing 150 women and 20 men together on a small island, and providing an audience of one as her ex-Marines drilled and her court performed classical Chinese dances. At the end of the day, she stepped out of her Manchu princess regalia to reveal an elegant Western evening dress, her orchestra shifted to jazz, and her ladies-in-waiting and Marines danced a mad Charleston.

Golondrina was one of twenty-five islands profiled in "Island Kingdoms," an article in the 1930 inaugural issue of *Fortune* that began by declaring, "Our wealthier . . . citizens are coming to realize that in this industrious age there is only one means of living to one's self, to retreat to a body of land completely surrounded by cold, deep water. . . . As a symbol of great possession the privately owned island may yet supplant even the steam yacht."

Some of *Fortune*'s tycoons wanted a simple life, like the Boston Brahmin who outlawed electricity on his Maine island, or the owners of an island off Boothbay Harbor who boasted of working and sleeping in the same flannel shirts. More often they wanted to create a more perfect world or impress their contemporaries. Waldorf-Astoria hotel owner George Boldt ordered his Heart Island, one of the Thousand Islands in the St. Lawrence River, carved and bulldozed into the shape of a heart and built a granite castle surrounded by fishponds and an Italian garden. Henri Menier, the "Chocolate King of France," awarded himself a second title, "King of Anacosti" after buying the large island with that name in the Gulf of St. Lawrence. He imported a thousand French farmers, outlawed alcohol, stocked the interior with elk, reindeer, buffalo, and moose, named the main landing Port Menier (a name it still carries), and built a Norman mansion with a window shaped like a fleur-de-lys.

Some private islands suggested eccentricity bordering megalomania, or even insanity. After building the largest ballroom in the United States on Catalina, William Wrigley Jr. leveled a large hill that interfered with his view of the water. The proprietress of Bogue, a barrier island off North Carolina, instructed her guards to shoot picnickers on sight. The laird of St. Catherine's Island, off Georgia, gave visitors a tour of the old slave quarters where they found, according to *Fortune*, "old-style Southern darkies who think in terms of 'the Boss' and 'the chillun' living in the barracks that once sheltered their slave ancestors."

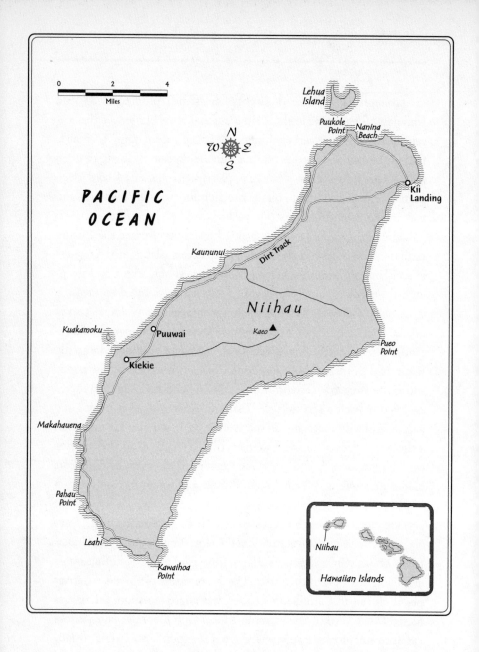

Since the *Fortune* article, private islands have become even more popular and prized. Diana Ross, Ted Turner, Peggy Rockefeller, various Mellons and Du Ponts, and numerous high-tech moguls have at one time or another owned private islands on which they could hide from stalkers, kidnappers, nosy parkers, and people like me. These modern lairds' obsession with privacy and security made it difficult to find an island whose population was more diverse than its servants, and where I would be welcome, even for a few hours. I finally chose Niihau, one of the Hawaiian Islands, because it was the largest private island on earth and I liked the sound of its owners, the Robinson family. Instead of building mansions and naming things after themselves, they had used their island to preserve an endangered language and culture.

■

Niihau had caught my attention while I was researching the attack on Pearl Harbor and read that after crash-landing on it a Japanese pilot had imposed a brief reign of terror. When I attempted to interview eyewitnesses to this event, I discovered that Niihau could be reached only on the Robinsons' decommissioned World War II landing craft, and visitors were prohibited. At the time, I liked the idea of an island where everyone lived a simple life, spoke Hawaiian, and performed hulas for their own pleasure, but I was also suspicious that it was so taboo to outsiders.

The Niihau familiar to everyone but its inhabitants is the sinister and unbroken wall of cliffs visible across the Kaulakahi Channel from Kauai's Kekaha Beach Park. It is the type of island a child might draw to represent words like "forbidden" and "mysterious," the same ones commonly used to describe Niihau. Seen through binoculars it appears even more inhospitable. There is nothing green and no sign of life. It is fascinating only if you remind yourself that behind those cliffs are two hundred people whose language and customs have made them as rare as pandas, and whose privacy is so jealously guarded by the Robinson family that you stand a better chance of winning the lottery than of spending a day in their company.

The Robinsons' Scottish ancestors bought the island in 1864 from

King Kamehameha V for $10,000 in gold coins after a stretch of un-
typically wet weather turned it briefly green, convincing them it would
make an excellent ranch. They built a house and church, offered jobs
to every male resident, and acquired more land on neighboring Kauai
after discovering that Niihau's aridity made it unsuitable for large
numbers of cattle. In 1915, a severe water shortage combined with a
desire to protect its inhabitants' traditional Hawaiian lifestyle persuaded Aylmer Robinson to place it off limits to visitors, even to
family friends who had been coming over on weekends. This policy
has continued to the present, and has served to magnify the resentment, envy, and suspicion that often attach themselves to private islands: resentment because placing an entire island off bounds seems
more greedy than surrounding a mainland property with fences and
NO TRESPASSING signs; envy because private islands promise a more
perfect freedom and independence than public ones; and suspicion
because such islands remind us of James Bond villains, Dr. Moreau's
Beast Folk, and the smutty Capri of sex-mad Roman emperors.

Suspicions of the Robinson family have been widespread in
Hawaii ever since a committee of the Hawaii Territorial Legislature
visited Niihau shortly after World War II. The Robinsons sensed the
politicians' hostility. They hurried them through Puuwai, Niihau's
only town, and prevented them from entering the church or school.
When a photographer snapped an island family, Aylmer Robinson refused to reveal their names, explaining that Niihauans objected to being used "for exhibition purposes." The tour concluded with a mean
lunch of sandwiches and coconuts served on the back steps of the
Robinsons' ranch house. Afterwards, the *Honolulu Advertiser* compared the island to Alcatraz, treating it as a scandal that its cowboys earned a dollar fifty a day and its children left school at fourteen
(although such things were common throughout the islands), praising
the legislators for seeking "to transplant the benefits of modern science and transportation," and speaking darkly of an "iron curtain" of
private ownership.

The legislators' report charged Niihau with being "out of step" with American concepts of freedom, and expressed outrage that the Robinsons denied its inhabitants the right to drive a car, although the only island roads were horse tracks. It recommended that the territorial government seize Niihau through eminent domain and drag it into the twentieth century by building a public pier, an airstrip, a police station, and a prison for juvenile delinquents. Sixty-two Niihauans, half the adult population, signed a petition protesting that this would "bring bad influences to the island." The territorial legislature backed off, and for the next twenty years the biggest changes came when the coast guard closed its station, forcing Niihauans to communicate with the mainland by carrier pigeon, and when a Federal poverty grant provided a movie projector and portable generator, allowing them to see their first motion picture, *The Last of the Mohicans*.

Aylmer Robinson and his brother Lester died in the late 1960s, and Lester's sons, Bruce and Keith, assumed management of Niihau and the Kauai properties. The developers assumed the boys would be pushovers and lobbied the state to condemn Niihau so they could build casinos and high-rise hotels along beaches superior to Waikiki's. They argued that the rest of Hawaii could reap the rewards of casino gambling while remaining uncontaminated by it.

Governor John A. Burns countered with a plan for the state to buy Niihau and restore its landscape to that of a precontact Hawaiian island, then open it as a cultural park in which the Niihauans—speaking Hawaiian, riding horses, and dancing hulas—would be the exhibits. If they rejected this role they could become park rangers, Burns said, and move "into the mainstream of contemporary island life."

The young Robinson brothers surprised everyone by hanging tough and refusing to sell. Burns died of cancer and his successor tabled his scheme for turning Niihau into a Hawaiian Williamsburg, in order to save it from becoming a Hawaiian Las Vegas.

Ruth Tabrah, who visited the island in 1967 and 1977 as a member

of the Hawaii Board of Education and has written the best book
about it, claims even Franklin Roosevelt had a plan for Niihau. Roosevelt saw it only once, while cruising down the Kaulakahi Channel
during a presidential visit to Hawaii in 1934. But its dramatic cliffs
and "forbidden island" mystique made such an impression that ten
years later, around the time he was spinning stories about his boyhood on Campobello, he wrote a note suggesting the United Nations
consider building its headquarters on Niihau.

Niihau is forbidden, but not that mysterious. Outsiders who have
visited it have reported their experiences with a dedication once common among travelers to Tibet. A one-day visit by Governor Lawrence
Judd and his entourage in 1929 resulted in numerous reports, articles, and memoirs. A plantation manager from Kauai kept a diary of a
week he spent there during 1942 while discussing land management
with Aylmer Robinson. In 1957, a *Honolulu Star-Bulletin* photographer crash-landed on purpose and his story, "Free Though Feudal.
They're Happy on Niihau," carried the subtitle "Iron Curtain Lifted
for the First Time." Two years later, the *Honolulu Advertiser*'s night-
club reporter made a midnight landing on a remote beach and was
apprehended by Niihau cowboys convinced he was a Russian spy.

Because Niihau has changed so gradually, these travelers' tales
are remarkably similar. The Niihau of the 1920s, 1940s, and 1990s is a
"paradise of smiling faces" where you find "compassion, respect, and
love rather than fortune-seeking, greed, and envy." It is "so precious
and naïve it sounds like a fairy tale," so "timeless" a visitor feels he
has "opened an album whose pages walked him into the life of a century ago," and so uncorrupted that one visitor left echoing Selkirk
and Crusoe, wondering "if we have to indulge in so many of the
so-called necessities of civilized life." In 1998, a Niihauan living in
Honolulu remembered "very giving, mellow, shy, and humble" people living on an island that was "what Hawaii was like a hundred
years ago."

Ilei Beniamina, a native Niihauan living on Kauai, planned to retire on Niihau because, she told a reporter, "the rocks are in about the same place they were when I was a child." She explained that her mother had already returned, "because she feels it's closer to God."

I thought the biggest mystery surrounding Niihau was not why its inhabitants liked it so much, but why the Robinsons had held on to this money-losing relic so fiercely and for so long, particularly after decades of vilification as "colonial masters" who were "running an Alcatraz."

A *Honolulu Advertiser* reporter had petitioned the Robinsons for fourteen years before being allowed one short visit in 1985, a mistake they were unlikely to repeat, since his mention of plastic garbage washing ashore had led to environmentalists invading Niihau to clean its beaches. I did not expect the Robinsons to let me roam around asking Niihauans if they felt like freemen or serfs, but I went through the motions anyway and wrote Keith Robinson a crawling letter. When he did not reply I tried booking a seat on one of the Niihau Ranch helicopter tours that permitted a visitor to fly over Niihau in the Robinsons' helicopter, then land for a brief visit on a remote beach, but not mingle with the inhabitants. The Hawaiian woman (Bruce Robinson's wife, I learned later) answering the telephone at Niihau Helicopters was discouraging, saying the tours had a four-person minimum and no one had signed up for weeks. I flew to Hawaii anyway, attracted by the consolation of at least spending some time on neighboring Kauai, an island that has appeared in more Hollywood movies than any other, and whose landscape has become synonymous with paradise for millions of filmgoers.

Perhaps it was because George Orwell had written "Pleasure Spots" in response to a magazine article praising Honolulu that I imagined him sitting beside me as I flew there en route to Kauai. But there he was, scrunched into a plastic seat at Hartsfield-Atlanta International Airport, unable to escape the overhead televisions tuned to CNN, then on the receiving end of a flight attendant's order to lower his shade so not a shaft of sunlight could fall on *Son of Flubber*, unreeling as we crossed the Grand Canyon, unseen below us.

Flying to Honolulu is one of the few travel experiences the jet has not robbed of its drama. Because Hawaii is the earth's most isolated archipelago there is nothing for 2,400 miles to the east or 5,000 miles to the west. For hours you see the shadows of trade wind clouds on the Pacific, then Mauna Kea, land clouds mimicking the shape of Molokai, and finally Honolulu's skyscrapers.

I dozed fitfully on an evening flight from Los Angeles, waking often to stare down at the moonlit ocean through a lace of clouds. I pictured the crew, staring into their dials, being guided to this lonely string of islands by radar and computer, and thought about the earliest travelers to these islands—the Polynesians, making for these same islands in fleets of voyaging canoes, or vakas, without compass, maps, or sextant, using the same stars to guide them across three thousand miles of empty water from the Marquesas to Hawaii. The vakas were the jumbo jets of canoes, a hundred feet long, double-hulled, steered with giant paddles, and powered by huge sails woven from pandanus leaves. Their open decks carried families, livestock, plants, and household possessions, everything for beginning a new life on an unknown island. Their captains navigated by the stars and moon by night, the ocean swells and currents by day. They looked to the sea for drifting twigs and phosphorescence, to the sky for birds and land clouds. They circled an island checking for treacherous currents and breaks in its fringing reef before sailing into a lagoon and unloading passengers, who immediately erected shelters, planted taro, and rolled coral rocks into circles for their temples. The Polynesians' myths say they traveled to escape overpopulation, land disputes, and warfare—the usual island plagues. But anyone mesmerized by an empty horizon knows they must also have been restless and curious, sailing beyond their reef for the same reason boys who grow up hearing train whistles in prairie towns head for Chicago.

After months of empty horizons, Hawaii's Polynesian discoverers saw snow-capped Mauna Kea and the towering green cliffs of Molokai. They could easily have missed Hawaii, and no doubt some did, sailing toward the Aleutians and vanishing forever. Compare them to the early Greeks, who had the courage to put to sea only because they could always see another island on the horizon, or to Columbus, who discovered an already inhabited continent. Unlike him, the first Polynesians on Hawaii were like astronauts on the moon, the first humans to walk there, the most daring island discoverers of all.

As we descended toward Honolulu, the pilot suggested we raise our shades so we could see the planets, "lined up like a string of pearls." Then he banked, showing us the red taillights of jammed traffic on the H-1 freeway, and added: "Thought you might like knowing that to get here we've used as much fuel as you'd need to drive a car fifteen thousand miles a year, for twenty-three years. Aloha."

The next morning, I saw Waikiki through Orwell's eyes, imagining his grim satisfaction at finding such a perfectly realized Pleasure Spot.

He had predicted, "One never does anything for oneself." Well, here was Kalakaua Avenue, thick with touts for "adventures" requiring helicopters, Jeeps, dirt bikes, and motorized rubber rafts.

He had written, "One is never alone." Here were eighty thousand people packed into a reclaimed swamp the size of Central Park where lifeguards placed orange traffic cones in the sand to open a path to the ocean.

The Royal Hawaiian Shopping Center showed Waikiki was working hard on fulfilling the Pleasure Spot sine qua non of no wild vegetation and natural objects. It had the charm of a multistory car park and dwarfed the whimsical turrets of the Royal Hawaiian Hotel, whose gardens it had largely replaced. Similar concrete bunkers lined Kalakaua Avenue, giving Waikiki a Las Vegas atmosphere of every inch dedicated to profit.

What vegetation Waikiki did offer was neither wild nor natural, thanks to the Great Hawaiian Tourist Myth, which promises an impossible combination of perpetual sunshine *and* a Garden of Eden landscape. The Hawaiian islands do have both, although not in the same place. Their leeward coasts are sunny and dry, but with a climate and natural vegetation closer to Death Valley than to Fantasy Island. Their windward coasts have the flowers and foliage, but also the rain that keeps them alive. The earliest attempts of Hawaii's visitor industry to turn its sunny leeward coasts into versions of its greener windward ones were goofy but endearing. In the 1920s, Norman D. Hill, Hawaii's "Doctor of Photography," used etching knives, razor blades, and brushes to add waterfalls, orchids, and palms; to enhance rainbows; to erase utility lines; and to create a paradise that was, in the language of a 1925 brochure, "An Eden of peace and pleasure . . . love and laziness . . . and plumbing that is American." In later decades, the compulsion to realize the tourist myth led to leeward-coast resorts tricked out with windward-coast flora. A wild, distinctively Hawaiian landscape became a manicured Eden of golf courses, recessed sprinklers, and transplanted palms, and an anti-Eden of tidepools polluted by the fertilizers needed to keep the bogus landscaping green and fresh.

Two hotels built during the 1980s tourist boom elevated the foolishness to an almost sinister level, and make Kuda Huraa's excesses seem trivial. On a field of lava rock on the Big Island's leeward coast, a developer constructed an oasis of windward coast foliage tricked out with an art museum and an air-conditioned monorail. There were artificial lagoons where guests could swim with bottlenose dolphins (imported from the Atlantic Ocean), and artificial canals where Venetian vaporetti glided on underwater rails. On Kauai, a similar hotel had carriages pulled by Clydesdale horses, zebras and kangaroos incarcerated on artificial wildlife islands in the middle of a golf course, more vaporetti, and enough fiberglass urns and columns to give it the feel of a Greek temple, one devoted to the worship of money.

Both resorts floated like space stations, orbiting outside Hawaii's culture, environment, and geography, much as the Maldivian tourist islands orbit outside theirs. Their message was that not only did the real Hawaii lack enough natural beauty and exotica to delight a visitor, but even the bogus one of mai tais and ukuleles fell short. These resorts have since changed ownership and eliminated the more egregious excesses, but no one is tearing them down, or restoring their coastlines.

■

I do not need to describe Kauai to you because, whether you know it or not, you have already seen it, again and again.

The exterior of Emile de Becque's house in the film version of *South Pacific* and the terrace overlooking Hanalei Bay where he and Nellie Forbush courted were both on Kauai's former Birkmyre estate. A few miles up the coast is Lumahai Beach, where Forbush washed that man right out of her hair. Still further north is Ha'ena Beach Park, the site of Bali-ha'i, complete with a dramatic mountain now known as Bali-ha'i Peak. Kauai's parched leeward coast has been Australia in *The Thorn Birds*, its rain forest *Jurassic Park*'s Costa Rican jungle, its soaring green mountains the Andes in *Raiders of the Lost Ark*, its taro fields the Vietnamese rice paddies of *Uncommon Valor*. Peter Pan's Never-Never Land in *Hook* and the waterfall in *Fantasy Island* are both on Kauai. If you have seen *Lord of the Flies, Lt. Robin Crusoe, U.S.N., The Wackiest Ship in the Army, Islands in the Stream, She Gods of Shark Reef*, and the 1976 remake of *King Kong*, you have seen Kauai. In fact, whenever you see in the movies a tropical island with jagged mountains, crashing waterfalls, and lovely beaches, you are probably seeing Kauai. When you land on a tropical island, you probably expect Kauai. When you dream of a tropical island, it is probably Kauai.

I could have driven myself to Kauai's *South Pacific* locations, but I decided to join Hawaii Movie Tours's "Kauai Through Hollywood's

Eyes" tour because it promised a chance to watch movies filmed on the island on an in-van monitor and compare them to their actual locations. It came with the usual drawbacks to sharing a van with fifteen strangers—fogged windows, post-breakfast farts, and seniors taking forever to disembark—and several unique to Hawaii Movie Tours—being shamed into singing "Puff the Magic Dragon" as we approached Hanalei, watching the *Blue Hawaii* wedding scene three times (because Elvis is in it), and enduring endless jokey references to my namesake, Thurston Howell III of *Gilligan's Island*, a television series I loathe.

The genius behind this tour was Bob, a leonine man with a mane of salt-and-pepper hair who boasted of playing Julius Caesar at Caesar's Palace, in Las Vegas. His tour taught two unintended lessons. The first was that no matter how spectacular the rainbows, waterfalls, and mountains outside the van, the passengers considered whatever was appearing on the screen inside to be more beautiful and interesting. I just glanced at the film clips, but the eyes of the other passengers almost never left them. Given the choice of the real Hanamaulu Bay or the one in *Donovan's Reef* (John Wayne and Lee Marvin, 1963) or *Pagan Love Song* (Esther Williams and Rita Moreno, 1950), they preferred the Hollywood version. And why not? The movie showed a Hanamaulu Bay with outrigger canoes, beautiful natives, towering palm trees, and grass shacks. The real beach was more brown than white, and lined with ironwood trees instead of the palms the *Donovan's Reef* film company brought from Los Angeles. Instead of hula dancers and grass houses, there were squatters living under blue plastic tarps who had run extension lines into the public toilets to tap electricity for their television sets and Mister Coffees.

Bob's second unintended lesson was that mainland Americans were buying Kauai. We drove through three miles of the former sugar plantation acquired by a California couple for $19 million, then parked at an overlook above a beach purchased by a Hollywood producer who had used it as a location and was leaving in place the palms and tropical plants his company had transplanted to make it resemble Tahiti, or perhaps Bali-ha'i. As we walked down the beach appearing in the *Gilligan's Island* pilot, Bob described the island homes of Charo, Barbra Streisand, and Clint Eastwood, and said Sylvester Stallone had used a laser to level his polo field.

The climax of his tour was Black Pot Beach in Hanalei, a spectacular curve of sand where *South Pacific*'s sailors sang "Bloody Mary" and "There Is Nothing Like a Dame." The view across the water to an escarpment of green mountains laced with waterfalls is a scenic wonder comparable to the Grand Canyon or the Great Rift Valley, and was the backdrop to Emil de Becque's terrace. Bob apologized for not taking us to this terrace. It had sat on a ridge just above Black Pot Beach, but the former Birkmyre estate buildings had been demolished after a time-share scheme fizzled. Some ruined foundations remained but the road to them was impassable, and the terrace had vanished.

Bob's tour ended in Hanalei. Two days later I was preparing to drive farther north to Lumahai, one of the *South Pacific* beaches, when I read a front-page headline on the island newspaper, the *Garden Island*, saying, "Partying Kids Challenge Cops—Massive Beach Bashes Feature Drugs, Booze, Fights." Four hundred teenagers had gathered at Lumahai two nights before for binge drinking, narcotics, and music blasting from speakers powered by a portable generator. The outnumbered police could only transport the wounded to the hospital and stop the intoxicated from driving. According to the article, parties like these were a relatively new phenomenon on Kauai, and during an earlier one, revelers had fed an entire wooden playground set into their bonfire.

The message of a second article, "These Kauai Teens Say There's Nothing Else to Do," was that although Kauai had its youth centers, programs, and dances, they were unpopular because they banned drugs and alcohol. A boy identified as Jim whined, "What for to do on this island? Nothing." Melissa bitched, "They should do something for us kids," and suggested someone build them a place to hang out. An ice-skating rink would be nice.

The riot was blamed on Kauai's economic woes. Only one sugar plantation remained, and the previous year its visitor count had declined from 1.2 million to 900,000, a catastrophe for an island betting everything on tourism. A radio station kept a weekly tally of people leaving for the mainland and it was implied that Kauai's travails, like those of other Hawaiian islands, were unusual and unexpected. Attempts to lure high-tech industries had been hurt by Kauai's high costs (it has the highest electricity prices in the United States) and low educational standards. There was desperate talk of legalizing cockfighting, and of making an end run around the animal activists by putting boxing gloves on the birds' claws. Unemployment, welfare rolls, and crime had risen, and a new organization, the Kauai Visitors Aloha Society, announced that its mission would be to ensure that "visitors who are victims of crime leave with a little aloha despite their misfortune." Its members gave clothes to tourists who had their luggage stolen, and went to hospitals to present leis to the victims of violent crimes.

In Hanalei, everyone was talking about the riot. The Chinese-Hawaiian owner of the café where I stopped for lunch rattled the newspaper in her daughter's face and shouted, "The police should do more, they should clean up this problem!"

The girl rolled her eyes. "Maybe if they gave us kids something to do—"

"Do? Do! What you mean, 'do'? No one give us anything to do. We work. We fish. We swim. We make fun. Why you need something to do?"

"Whatever."

Stacked on the counter were copies of a free magazine titled *101 Things to Do on Kauai.* Most of the Things to Do involved climbing into a helicopter, zodiac boat, jeep, or some other form of motorized transport and spending money, lots of it. So perhaps it was not strange that Kauai's teenagers, who lived with helicopters overhead, shiny rental cars cruising their roads, and resorts hogging their best beaches, complained of nothing to do. If hiking, swimming, and fishing were not good enough for the tourists, well, why should they be good enough for them? If tourists wanted Pleasure Spot hotels, why not Kauai's teenagers? And what was more ridiculous, really, vaporetti and kangaroos, or an ice rink?

Among the great pleasures of islands are the stark differences between neighboring ones in the same group, and the way you can take a short plane or ferry ride and suddenly arrive on one with a landscape, customs, and an economy that are entirely different. This is particularly true in the Aegean and Caribbean, where neighboring islands can be friendly and welcoming or closed and suspicious, depending on their histories, and short distances can separate Pleasure Spots from beachless backwaters. The same holds true in Hawaii, where rural Molokai is less than forty miles from Waikiki, and only seventeen miles separate Kauai, whose teenagers burn down playgrounds and dream of ice rinks, from Niihau, where the children consider competitive hymn-singing a treat, where everyone travels by foot or horse, lives by the sun instead of the clock, gathers to dance the hula by oil lamps, and runs simple appliances on solar power or generators tricked up from lawn mower engines, and where there is no need for a Visitors Aloha Society because there is no crime.

The more I heard and read about Niihau, the more determined I became to see it, if only from the air for a few minutes. I began calling Niihau Helicopters twice a day to check if they had scheduled a last-minute flight, but it seemed that out of the tens of thousands of tourists vacationing in Hawaii on any given day, the only one willing to pay to see a real Hawaiian island was me.

Keith Robinson and his brother Bruce, who manages the Niihau Ranch, both live at Makaweli, the family sugar plantation on Kauai's west coast. I had assumed people owning an island without telephones would themselves have unlisted numbers (if they had telephones), so I was surprised to find a K. Robinson listed in the Kauai phone book, and even more surprised when he answered himself.

"You're lucky to get me," he snapped, explaining he was at home only because his mother was sick. Usually he worked from early morning until after sunset in his Kauai Wildlife Reserve. He had not received my letter because he collected his mail only once a month, but if I met him at the Makaweli post office in thirty minutes we could drive into the reserve together. He doubted I would see Niihau. His brother was too busy trying to prevent the Niihau Ranch from going broke to entertain me, and the helicopter tours were a bust because, he complained, "All we get are travel writers demanding freebies!"

I knew that Robinson was in his late fifties, and that he had created a nature reserve for endangered Hawaiian flora. His family was one of Hawaii's top five private landowners, and his father and grandfather had attended Harvard. I expected a smoothie environmentalist in a luxury sport utility vehicle, not a sinewy man in a sweat-stained work shirt, threadbare blue jeans, and green hard hat driving a dented Nissan truck carpeted with old newspapers and leaking oil so badly we started by adding several quarts.

He was as tense as a sprinter before the gun. As we turned onto a rutted cane road, he demanded, teeth clenched, "So, what's the deal? What's the deal?"

"I want to know why people love islands, and why your family loves Niihau."

He relaxed. "That's the deal? Okay. That's okay."

The cane fields surrounding us were the electric green of a tropical fish, the earth the color of dried blood. A double rainbow arched over the valley. It was a landscape from a children's book—the mountains too big, the colors too bright.

The road was filled with ruts and boulders and we continually scraped the undercarriage. Robinson made kissing noises to attract doves and scattered birdseed from a bag held between his legs. He said he had repaired this road himself, hauling in 4,800 pounds of concrete, strapping a flashlight onto his hard hat, and working into the night to fill ruts and remove boulders. It had taken months, a labor of love.

He apologized for the eroded pastures and scrawny cattle grazing on dirt. But if the family rested this land, they risked defaulting on their taxes. It was Kauai's last sugar plantation and probably doomed. Its yields were good but taxes and regulations were killing it. They were already furloughing employees.

We parked and crossed a stream over a plank bridge to reach the reserve. He had built it alone, he said, clearing land, planting seedlings in oil cans, and installing a solar-powered electric fence to deter wild pigs. He had worked here almost every day for twelve years, once missing a week because of heavy rains, and two days after he sprained an ankle while carrying buckets of water on a moonless night. If I had come last week, before the rains broke a drought, I could have helped him unload fifty-gallon water drums.

I tagged along for several hours while he blasted leafhoppers with Raid, scattered rat poison, and pulled up cotton plants, all the while muttering, "Miss a day, and the pests and pigs take over. I'm turning fifty-seven. How long can I continue? What will happen to these plants then?"

It was a good question. Hawaii has more than 70 percent of all recorded endangered plant and animal species in the United States and is known among botanists as the "endangered species capital of the world." The Oahu Nature Conservancy could not preserve the *Solanum sandwichensis*, but Robinson had spirited a cutting into his reserve ("real cloak-and-dagger stuff"). Botanists believed there were only two Niihau fan palms in existence, but he had hundreds. Officially, only twenty-five native Hawaiian gardenias survived, but twenty grew here, as well as two dozen specimens of a hibiscus presumed to be extinct.

Sightseeing helicopters frequently passed overhead while I was in the reserve. Bob had told me Kauai's flightseeing business began after Elvis Presley played the owner of an aircraft-sightseeing business in *Paradise Hawaiian Style*. Since then, helicopters had become the largest segment of Kauai's "Activities Industry," a group of enterprises that made it impossible to find a valley or beach where you could escape the whoop of a helicopter or buzz of an outboard motor. The helicopters were air-conditioned and outfitted with compact disc players, so passengers were never without the sound of music as they swooped over canyons, waterfalls, and the Kauai Wildlife Preserve. The contrast between tourists listening to Bolero as they zoomed above us and this ornery man hand-spraying the leafhoppers that menaced the last earthly specimen of some orchid was dizzying.

As a helicopter's shadow flitted across the ground, Robinson looked up and said, "You know, I've mislabeled many of these plants, so I might be telling you the truth about which is which. Then again, I might not."

He boasted that his mislabelings were plausible enough to fool an experienced botanist. One visiting scientist had been so appalled he begged him to undo them or destroy the reserve. He worried that after Robinson died the Kauai Wildlife Reserve might contaminate scientific literature for years.

Robinson said he told the scientist it was only temporary and would die when he did.

"Then why do it?" I asked.

"I don't know!" He looked confused. "These plants were all around when I was a kid, so I guess I don't want them to disappear."

The threat to destroy everything was no bluff. He had been declared in violation of the Endangered Species Act for breeding endangered species on private property, and been threatened with fines and imprisonment. Because he was growing the last species of a *Caes alpina* on Kauai, government agents had claimed the right to "secure and manage" the reserve. "Three days later, the *Caes alpina* was mysteriously destroyed," he said, flashing a brittle smile.

He had threatened to resist any intrusion by government agents, and reminded his enemies he had been a sharpshooter in the Hawaii National Guard. "They would have got me in the end," he conceded. "But they would have lost some men too. And how would it have looked, killing a conservationist protecting rare species on his own land?"

His reserve was an island within an island, a Niihau-like enclave for plants. He tickled the blossom of a rare hibiscus and suggested it was like the Hawaiian people, delicate because it had evolved in isolation, and doomed once nonnative plants more efficient at getting water and nutrients were introduced from outside the chain.

I suggested that perhaps the same biological principles were at work in the human realm, explaining why some island peoples and cultures faced extinction. He agreed. Native Hawaiians were noncompetitive, like the endemic plants on their islands. They were not lazy, just uninterested in squeezing the last dime out of every transaction. This made them easy on the environment, but left them vulnerable to more energetic immigrants who had overwhelmed a language and culture that could only survive in its purest form on a human reserve, like Niihau.

We discussed Niihau more over dinner at the Wrangler, a timeworn steakhouse where a film of dust and grease covered the saddles and wagon wheels that were a tribute to Kauai's vanishing cowboy culture. We were the only diners, but Robinson waited until the waitress was out of earshot before whispering, "I shouldn't be saying this, but Bruce and I are making preliminary plans, exploring our options. . . ." He looked around again. "We are thinking of giving up."

Niihau Ranch was close to financial collapse, he said. It could be operated with twenty employees, but the Robinsons had to find work for as many as fifty. They guaranteed a job to any working-age, Niihau-born male, and provided every resident with free housing, medical care, and meat. Their expenses far exceeded the ranch's modest income, and they had reduced the landing craft from two runs to one a month, but soon they might be unable to afford even that. "And if you can't afford to run a boat, how can you afford to own an island?" he asked.

Meanwhile, they were "flat broke!" He lived with his mother in a bungalow near the helicopter hangar and survived on $10,000 a year. Many plantation employees owned larger houses and drove better cars than he did. After seeing his truck and witnessing his delight at being treated to a restaurant meal, I believed him. The Robinson in line to inherit Niihau was his nephew, Bruce Robinson's son. But he had just graduated from college in California and was starting a high-paying job as a computer programmer. "I don't blame him," Robinson said. "Hell, I'd take that job!"

The Robinsons were not like one of those land-rich ranching families in the American West who bitch about taxes but live in grand style by selling off a few hundred acres for ranchettes. Owning a private island like Niihau that was also a human preserve was an all-or-nothing proposition. It was either an island where everyone spoke Hawaiian and lived a simple life, or it was not. The Robinsons knew if they sold even a few hundred acres they would expose the Niihauans to the modern world, threatening their culture and language.

Niihau had always been an expensive hobby and the family had lost more than $8 million supporting it since 1945. The Makaweli plantation had helped subsidize the island before, but with the sugar industry prostrate, it was having trouble supporting itself. The family had once hoped its other Kauai property, Koolau Ranch, would support Niihau. It contained some of the most beautiful island landscape on earth, including the mountains and valleys appearing in *South Pacific*. Keith Robinson had managed it for seven tumultuous years during the 1970s, battling marijuana cultivators and hippie squatters who out of spite castrated his bulls and destroyed his rare native plants. Finally the state declared it a conservation area, ending any chance it might sell for its real value.

Koolau had left Robinson so bitter he ended every sentence about it with an exclamation point. The squatters should have been "thrown in the gas chamber!" His battles with the dopers had been "a virtual war!" He took a deep breath. "I wasted seven years there—a time when I should have been getting married and having children!"

The last, best hope for saving Niihau was a Navy proposal to use it to test missiles. The Navy already maintained an unmanned radar station on the island and sometimes trained commandos there. But the missiles promised a more reliable source of income. The proposed facility would only launch target rockets that would be intercepted miles above the earth by others fired from offshore naval vessels. No missiles would hit Niihau, and its residents would have no contact with Navy personnel. Yet the proposal had outraged environmentalists and anti-nuclear and native Hawaiian activists. The latter condemned the missiles as an assault on Niihauans and a desecration of their lands, and accused the Robinsons of "exploitation and domination," and holding the island in a "colonial chokehold."

The Robinsons and their defenders responded that the only way to preserve Niihau's traditional way of life was to keep the island in sympathetic private hands. Had the state owned Niihau, they argued, the taxpayers of Hawaii would have to be allowed free access. Had Niihau been owned by a more avaricious family, it would have been sold long before, and there would be no traditional Hawaiian-speaking community left in the world, and no direct and unbroken link between the Polynesians who discovered these islands and those living on them. But this very fact, that the Hawaiian people owed what one Kauai politician called "a debt of gratitude" to the Robinsons, only made their ownership of Niihau appear a greater humiliation to some.

I doubted there would have been many complaints had a Nevada rancher allowed the military to test nonnuclear rockets on his range-land. But because Niihau was an island, its land seemed more precious and unique. The phrase "military testing" is also one that elicits particularly strong reactions in Hawaii, where Navy ordnance has blasted uninhabited Kahoolawe into a moonscape, and throughout the Pacific region, with its tragic history of nuclear testing.

I understood that no missiles would hit Niihau, but when I heard "Pacific island" and "military tests" I remembered General Groves, newsreel footage of mushroom clouds rising over atolls, and Billy, a drunk with a face marked by suspicious blemishes whom I met in a bar in the Marshall Islands. He had been a teacher on Rongelap atoll when it received a dose of radiation from the 1954 "Bravo" hydrogen bomb test on Bikini. He spoke of the sky turning blood red and a ferocious wind knocking his son over. Other children ran into the schoolyard, competing to gather the white flakes falling from the sky. Soon they were scratching, rolling on the ground, and screaming in agony as Americans in orange overalls disembarked from a seaplane and held Geiger counters to their writhing bodies.

The nuclear powers chose Pacific islands for their tests so that mistakes like Rongelap could be confined to small populations of distant, dark-skinned people, and because it was easier to place a radioactive remote island off limits than to sacrifice a piece of a continent. The United States and Britain halted their Pacific tests after a 1963 treaty, but the French continue testing on their Polynesian atolls, every year adding to the more than 250 nuclear detonations that have occurred above or below Pacific islands since World War II, and leaving more islands wounded or uninhabitable than have yet been lost to global warming.

▪

After our dinner, Robinson's truck would not start. He tried to jump it by pushing it down an incline in the Wrangler's parking lot while holding the wheel with one hand. He shook off my offer to help, shouting that he did this all the time. The engine kicked in, and he drove away without waving, and I was reminded of journalist Noel Barber's account of visiting Tom Neale, the famous hermit of Suwarrow, the same atoll in the Cook Islands where Robert Dean Frisbie had lived in the 1920s. "As he [Neale] talked," Barber wrote, "I realized with something of a shock that although he was obviously pleased to see me, and was delighted with the stories I had brought him, he would not miss me when I left."

I had dismissed Robinson's talk of shooting it out with government agents as middle-aged bravado. But after reading the two letters he handed me before we parted, I was not so sure. He had written them in response to questions from a European journalist. In them, he accused the Hawaiian political machine of treating his family as "public enemies." The authorities had only backed off from threats to seize the reserve, he wrote, because they feared "an ex-sniper fighting in dense jungle on his own home territory." Honest people had no future in Hawaii and the government would use condemnation to seize Niihau and the reserve. When this happened, he would "die fighting for freedom, either alone or as a member of some militia unit."

I had misjudged Robinson. He was not merely a Tom Neale puttering around a remote island. He had sacrificed everything to save Niihau and Hawaii's rare plants. For the last twelve years he had spent almost every waking hour of every day alone, a Crusoe on the island-within-an-island world of the Kauai Wildlife Reserve, nurturing a paradise that would vanish with his death. His islomania was the passionate and obsessive kind of *The Man Who Loved Islands*, and his life an illustration of what D. H. Lawrence called "the danger of becoming an islander."

I was also wrong about him not caring if he saw me again. Two days later I found myself staring at the back of a familiar green hard hat as the Niihau Ranch helicopter swooped over Niihau's eroded gullies while he said, "My father wore out a pair of shoes every week chasing sheep here."

My rented room on Kauai had no telephone, so I had continued to call Niihau Helicopters twice a day, hoping for some last-minute companions. The trip suddenly materialized when a party of four tourists from the hotel with the bogus urns and fake lagoons, decided they wanted to see Niihau. Before we took off, the pilot told us we were lucky because Robinson rarely accompanied a tour.

Robinson's narrative scrambled attacks on the government with an elegy to his childhood that was so detailed and passionate it made me wonder if he had come along because he thought it might be his last chance to see Niihau from the air before his brother sold the helicopter. As we crossed the channel he told us, almost in the same breath, that we were approaching the last intact and undeveloped shoreline in Hawaii, that he had never bought a new car in his life, and that his family received a call a day accusing them of enslaving the Niihauans.

As we flew low over a forlorn stretch of coast where the wind had bent the kiawe trees backwards and scoured craters in hillsides, he said, "I spent many happy hours here as a boy, camping and beachcombing."

We skirted an African Sahel–like interior of desiccated water holes and stunted trees and he said, "When I was a boy, the cowboys went all day without drinking and anyone who took any liquids from sunrise to sunset was a sissy." Below, wild pigs darted across the cracked earth, frantically searching for food and water.

We passed over the abandoned Robinson homestead and he said, "The women of our line last into their mid-eighties, although they usually turn into vegetables, but the men all die early from cancer."

He drew our attention to the beach where he had fished as a boy, and to derelict hunting camps, fish ponds abandoned after gypsum poisoned all the fish, dry lake beds plowed up for agricultural projects, abandoned sheep corrals, and sheds where cowboys had bagged charcoal, all failed Robinson family schemes to make Niihau Ranch self-sufficient.

We saw the beach at Keawanuhi Bay, a potential Waikiki, according to the developers. "Oh yes, they'd just love getting their hands on this," Robinson said. "They've already raped the shoreline everywhere else, so why not here? One company even offered to buy our sand, but we refused because it's our protection against tidal waves."

We headed inland to avoid overflying Puuwai and disturbing its residents. In the distance, I saw roofs scattered among thorn trees. We were too far away to make out the horses tethered in backyards, stone walls covered in bougainvillea, or the shrub whose white flowers bloom in the moonlight. We veered back to the coast and startled four cowboys on horseback. They looked up, shielding their eyes and waving, and I felt I was staring into the past.

Like many islanders, Robinson believed his island was uniquely beautiful. I suppose you could praise its "stark beauty," but it was really the runt of the Hawaiian litter. The most unusual thing about its eroded hills, crumbling cliffs, and shadeless beaches was that every single one had a name. Every spring, cave, barren valley, formation of rocks, and patch of sand also carried the name of a god, event, ancestor, or physical property. If you knew their meanings, as the Niihauans and Keith Robinson did, you knew Niihau's history. You knew that Kaunuakane, or "Altar of Kane," were ledges in the side of a cliff where fish spotters had sat, acting as guides for fishermen in canoes, and that the rock "Tahiti Moe" was part of a lost continent Niihauans believed had once been their home. "Kapena Kuke" was where Captain Cook landed, and where the Niihauans who met him scratched lines in a rock to measure the height of his jawline and the top of his head. And once you knew this, you understood why it is so important for Niihauans that the great relics of their island—their rocks—remain in the same place. On other Hawaiian islands, the smallest and most insignificant features had also been named and venerated. Many are remembered, but many others are forgotten because the rocks, ridges, and tide pools have been leveled and paved. None of Niihau's beaches was as beautiful as Lumahai, but for a

Hawaiian, beauty lies less in a landscape's appearance than in the fact that it remains undefiled.

We landed at Nanina Beach, on the northern tip of the island. The bushes were knee high and the wind was unceasing. Scientists had identified it as the driest place on earth after Death Valley. "I spent the happiest moments of my life here, fishing off those black rocks," Robinson said. His father's favorite fishing ground had been Lehua, a rocky islet across a strait from Nanina. He often swam there through whitecaps like these, kicking at sharks attracted by the fish in his burlap sack.

As we trudged to a picnic table shaded by a tin roof, the pilot said, "Some people on the tour want to stay forever, but some are like, 'Okay, we've set foot on Niihau, let's go!' "

After the others had left to swim and beachcomb, Robinson leaned across the table and whispered that his family had received signals that the Navy might abandon its plan to use Niihau for testing missiles. Selling the helicopter had become a possibility. If they did, and if the Navy left Kauai, Niihauans would have no way of being evacuated in a medical emergency.

"I shouldn't be telling you this," he said, still whispering, even in this lonely place, "but we are already making contingency plans for moving to the mainland." One exit strategy involved letting the islanders stay on and live off the land, like a tribe of Crusoes.

After lunch he led us to a shelf of rocks and tide pools to bait eels, a family tradition. He had planned this entertainment in advance, buying squid that he placed in a wire cage and dangled into the pools. When no eels had appeared after fifteen minutes he became increasingly frantic, bounding between rocks, murmuring endearments to the unseen eels, and complaining that this was "Mickey Mouse," a major disappointment. When a large eel at last darted from a cave he whooped like a boy landing his first fish. A 1908 photograph in a book about Niihau showed some Robinson ancestors fishing from these same rocks. In it, a woman in black stockings held up a giant eel, with an identical look of triumph on her face.

"The monk seals, where are the monk seals?" Robinson shouted while scanning the beach with my binoculars. This was the first time he had visited Nanina without seeing one of these shy and wary beasts. They were an endangered species and Niihau was the only place in Hawaii where they felt secure enough to come ashore and breed. He feared intruders had scared them away.

Traditional Hawaiian fishing rights, or koa, extend the limit of free diving from the shore to a depth of fifty feet. Although state law allows public access to any beach in Hawaii, the Robinsons had argued that koa should be enforced in Niihau because they had purchased the island from King Kamehameha before annexation. But the courts rejected their petitions and upheld state law, and incursions into Niihau's waters and landings on its beaches became so frequent and threatening to the Robinsons that they invited Philip Meyer, an expert in traditional fishing cultures, to spend ten years investigating the island's cultural and material life.

Meyer was the only outsider since 1915 to enjoy such lengthy and unrestricted access to Niihauans. His report concluded that Niihauans did not feel coerced or "governed" by the Robinsons. Instead, his predominant impression had been of "satisfaction, rich social relationships, and happiness." He provided no great revelations about life on Niihau. The men hunted pigs, rode horseback, and surfed. Women drove the landing barge and collected shells for the necklaces that could sell for as much as $10,000. The island was a traditional Hawaiian community. It was not static, simply evolving at a much slower pace than Hawaiian communities on other islands. Its people took what they wanted from the outside—computers for their school, transistor radios, and solar panels—and rejected the rest. They did not mind the small Navy presence because a Niihauan accompanied Naval personnel whenever they left the radar station. But the strangers who caught their fish and picnicked on their beaches terrified them.

These incursions had increased threefold between 1970 and the mid-1980s, and by 1997 an average of one boat a day was entering their waters. During one Labor Day weekend, Meyer had conducted an "Intrusion Survey," counting twelve boats with a total of forty-one passengers dropping anchor, and eighteen people coming ashore. The trespassers scared Niihauans off beaches where they gathered shells and collected opihi, spooked the monk seals and turtles, and reduced the catch in nearshore waters. Like the people of Jura who feared the Overland Route, Niihauans considered incursions by outsiders a threat to their security.

After leaving Nanina, we flew over the dry northeastern coast, past scores of named rocks, landings, coves, and beaches. Robinson's eyes never left the shoreline. As he recounted the time he had fished off that rock, come ashore at that landing, or ridden with his father along that beach, I finally understood the hold Niihau had on him. It was a Hawaiian island, and he was both an islomane and a nineteenth-century Hawaiian who preferred preserving native Hawaiian plants and culture to living the sweet life in Honolulu, and who wanted to nurture and protect this Hawaiian Utopia.

UTOPIAN ISLANDS — EIGG AND SVALBARD

One of the most encouraging island stories of recent years unfolded in 1997 when donations from island-lovers everywhere enabled the Isle of Eigg Trust to buy this tiny Hebridean island for $2.5 million from the last of its nine lairds, an eccentric German artist who called himself "Maruma" because the word had appeared to him in a puddle outside a Stuttgart nightclub. The press delighted in the triumph of the canny Scottish islanders, whom a previous laird had dismissed as "drunken hippies and dropouts." The buyout by the Trust, a partnership among Eigg's sixty-eight residents, the Highland Council, and the Scottish Wildlife Trust, was front-page news in Britain, and bulletins announcing it interrupted Australian television. The next morning, the Trust's secretary, Maggie Fyffe, found her answering machine jammed with messages from the lonely looking for community, the rootless searching for home, and island-lovers ready to move to Eigg tomorrow.

The ferry crossing to Eigg is one of Britain's most spectacular, with whales and seals sporting around a group of small and mountainous islands. I saw nothing of this at first because a mid-April snowstorm drove me into the lounge, where I met Iain Campbell, one of those fireplug-shaped Scotsmen who shrink and widen with age.

After decades as a Glasgow bus driver, he was retiring to Eigg because he had been born there, and, he said, "It's an island you cannot confuse with any other."

The sky cleared and I saw what he meant. A black rock called the An Sgurr loomed over a spine of hills, giving tiny Eigg great character. The formation resembled the funnel of an ocean liner, the rippled back of a dinosaur, a lion's head, or the fin of a shark, black and menacing. Without it, Eigg probably would have attracted fewer Viking raiders, Celtic saints, clan chiefs, and eccentric lairds, and had a less busy and colorful history. The An Sgurr may also have been the inspiration for *Treasure Island*'s Spyglass formation. In that novel, Robert Louis Stevenson, who had traveled widely in the Hebrides, described the Spyglass as "strangely-shaped" and "running up sheer from almost every side, and then suddenly cut off at the top like a pedestal to put a statue on." This is a perfect description of the An Sgurr.

I stayed at Kildonnan, a whitewashed farmhouse facing the water and a wild tangle of mainland mountains. When Keith Schellenberg, the laird preceding Maruma, had put Eigg on the market, a brochure written by his estate agent called it "one of the most famous and romantic islands in Scotland." Kildonnan, with its dramatic views of An Sgurr and pleasant walled garden, was called "one of its jewels."

Colin and Marie Carr now leased Kildonnan from the Trust instead of occupying it at the pleasure of a laird. He ran the farm and she took in guests. He was from the mainland. She was a Kirk, a member of a local family accounting for almost a third of Eigg's residents. The Carrs themselves were almost 10 percent of the population. Their oldest son lived on the mainland, their next son, George, worked with his father on the farm. Amy was home on vacation from the mainland secondary school at Mallaig, and Frances and Donny attended the Eigg primary school. They were cheerful children who were either performing chores, kicking a soccer ball, or playing board games. The Carrs were the kind of multitalented people who anchor

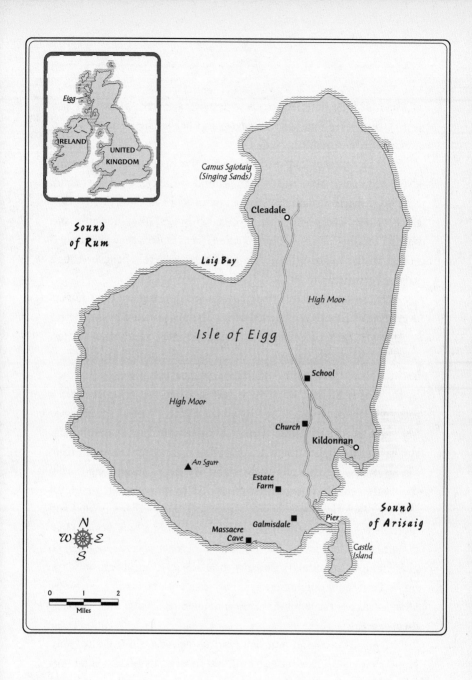

Eigg

IRELAND

UNITED
KINGDOM

Sound
of Rum

Camus Sgiotaig
(Singing Sands)

Cleadale

Laig Bay

High Moor

Isle of Eigg

High Moor

School

Church

Kildonnan

An Sgurr

Estate
Farm

Sound
of Arisaig

Massacre
Cave

Galmisdale

Pier

Castle
Island

N
W E
S

0   1   2
Miles

an island. Marie doubled, or tripled, or whatevered, as Eigg's registrar of births, deaths, and marriages, and her kitchen was the island party room and wedding chapel.

Her sister-in-law Sue Kirk managed the Eigg store, a tin-roofed shack occupying some windy high ground at the center of the island. Kirk told me the islanders were grateful to have even this modest store with its sparse stock of tins, cereal boxes, long-life milk, and bags of cookies. During a stretch when it was closed, they telephoned orders to the mainland and lived off their larders whenever rough weather canceled the ferry.

Her customers all dawdled and absentmindedly ran their fingers over the merchandise while chatting. Their faces were as distinctive as An Sgurr, with prominent chins, piercing eyes, and unusual noses.

Two schoolgirls pawing the candy wore identical British Airways backpacks and had been tanned by a tropical sun instead of burned by the North Atlantic wind. Kirk said they had just returned from a fortnight on Mustique, the Caribbean island favored by Princess Margaret and Mick Jagger. Three children from Eigg had gone and she had accompanied them as a chaperone. The trip was a gift from Felix Dennis, a publishing tycoon who had heard about Eigg during the Trust's Eigg Appeal and was tickled by the idea of a gang of "barmy revolutionaries" buying the island, and perhaps tickled still more by the idea of sending schoolchildren from a bare-bones Hebridean island to a jet-set Caribbean one. Tycoons were less likely to give children attending mainland rural schools Caribbean holidays, but at least, unlike rich men who have made islands their playthings, Dennis was not demanding that its inhabitants give him their labor, or love, in return.

Eigg's jetty, community hall, and its gentlest climate and landscape were all on its southern end, but most of its people lived four miles to the north in the scattered croft houses and caravans of Cleadale. I walked there from the store, head bowed against the snow squalls. At the edge of an escarpment, I looked up and saw a road twisting down into a landscape as spectacular as Kauai's. From this distance and height, Cleadale's cottages appeared to be white seeds, scattered across a carpet of moorland rolling down to a stretch of deserted beach. Behind them rose an amphitheater of eroded cliffs. Five miles across a strait, the mountains of Rum rocketed from a boiling sea. Eigg was another double wilderness, a savage island circled by a savage sea.

One of the newest houses belonged to Camille Dressler, a quick-witted Frenchwoman with Arab blood and flamenco-fierce eyes who reminded me of Valeria. Like most Eigg incomers, she and her husband had arrived in the 1970s to work for the laird, who was then Keith Schellenberg. He had attempted to attract tourists to the island with bike rentals, a tea shop, and a crafts center, never suspecting that the free spirits he was hiring to staff these enterprises would one day become his bitter enemies and buy his island.

After a year on Eigg, the Dresslers had decided to stay. They towed a trailer to Cleadale and lived in it for twelve years without piped water, garbage collection, or electricity. Twice they moved back to the mainland, twice they returned. Finally they bought this land from a neighbor and built a house. Dressler thought there was something irresistible about seeing water from every window. That was why she loved this island, and this house. She and her husband were educated people who could have earned a living elsewhere, but their minds were buried as deeply in Eigg as José Maria's and Valeria's were in Isla Crusoe.

Dressler worried that as the 1970s incomers like herself and her husband aged, no one was replacing them. At present, there were only one infant, two toddlers, and a preschooler living on the island, and soon the school might shrink to these four. One of the biggest challenges facing the Trust was attracting new people and preventing Eigg from becoming another depopulated nature reserve like Rum, or suffering the fate of St. Kilda, a Hebridean island evacuated in 1931 that is the bogeyman of every lightly populated island in Britain.

The Trust had received dozens of letters from people applying for crofts. But how could you know if someone was right for Eigg? she wondered. Or if they had the internal resources to be comfortable with a silence broken only by the rattle of a cattle grid? Many had questionable skills and motives. Perhaps Eigg needed an islander-in-training program, so a family could rent for a year and experience the isolation.

I believe it was Dressler who said, "It's when you're on your own that you get to know yourself," but it could have been almost anyone on Eigg, or on Isla Crusoe. Whenever I met any Eigg resident outdoors, I noticed the long pauses and shifting of eyes to the horizon also common to inhabitants of Isla Crusoe. Eigg's children had a spooky self-sufficiency. A single basketball hoop stood near a rise in the road beyond Dressler's house, framed by whitecaps and mountains, and on several occasions I noticed a single child shooting baskets into it, playing with great intensity, oblivious to the weather and wearing only a T-shirt against the bitter wind.

Sending children to the mainland for secondary school was almost as wrenching on Eigg as on Isla Crusoe. The ferry schedule made weekend visits impractical, so for weeks on end Eigg's teenagers lived on the mainland as boarders with families who had no responsibility to entertain or supervise them. When I paid a call on Iain Campbell, the retired bus driver I had met on the ferry, he told me he still remembered the trauma of being sent to a mainland school. He had left Eigg again to find a wife, because sixteen years separated him from the next-youngest island girl, and again when his oldest child turned twelve, because he did not want to inflict the same pain on him. And he might leave a fourth time if his health deteriorated and he needed more care than the island doctor could provide.

Who, then, *were* the right people for an island like Eigg? Younger pensioners, but not elderly ones? Families with young children, but not teenagers? It was not enough, as Fishers Island was discovering, to provide a secondary school on the island, because many parents insisted on the stimulation of a larger school. It was not even enough

to have a resident doctor, because as medicine became more sophisti-
cated islanders faced the choice of a longer life among mainland
strangers, or taking their chances on Eigg.

■

The laird's former farm at Galmisdale, with its rusting and broken
equipment, collapsed sheds, and gutted Land Rovers, reminded me
of Santo's Million Dollar Point, and disposing of garbage had become
as big a nuisance as it was on Kosrae. There were recycling bins outside the store, but no matter how much tin and plastic the islanders
collected, more washed ashore. Dressler fought it by taking children
on beach picnics that ended with bonfires of plastic flotsam. A priest
on South Uist, an island west of Rum, considered this litter a blessing,
and beachcombing a great Christian activity. "You're not interfering
in anybody else's life, and if you're a thinker it's a marvelous opportunity for thinking," he told a Scottish magazine. Combing beaches left
him amazed at the wonder of God's creation, but it only left me
amazed at the variety and quantity of the plastic bottles once holding
sunscreens, shampoos, dish-washing liquids, and soda pop.

Eigg was almost as rich in relics as Jura, and like Niihau, its
rocks had remained in the same place, particularly at the famous
Massacre Cave, where there had been a massacre almost as horrific as
Banda Neira's. In 1577, a party of men of the MacDonald clan had
been carrying a pitchstone rock from the An Shurr to the Kildonnan
graveyard when they saw the ships of a MacLeod clan raiding party
nearing Eigg. Believing themselves outnumbered, they gathered their
clansmen and hid in this cave on the south coast. A light snowfall
enabled the MacLeods to track them down. The MacLeods lit a
brushfire in the cave's mouth and suffocated 398 MacDonalds. Two
hundred years later, a clergyman visiting the cave reported, "the bones
are still pretty fresh, and some of the skulls entire, and the teeth in
their sockets." Sir Walter Scott retrieved a young woman's skull from
it in 1814. Another nineteenth-century visitor found "a few teeth . . .

sticking fast in a jaw"; another spoke of a "charnel house" of bones. In the 1970s, someone unearthed the skull of a child.

After Banda Neira and Espíritu Santo, I had become so blasé about island relics I was not surprised that the pitchstone rock the MacDonalds had been carrying in 1577 remained where it fell. More surprising was the sorry condition of the Lodge, an Italianate villa of ocher-colored stucco walls, columns, and arches that had been home to Eigg's lairds since the 1920s. It sat at the end of a long driveway bordered by palms and flowering trees. It looked more suited to Capri, but felt more haunted than Massacre Cave.

Its former gardener, Neil Robertson, still came to weed and prune. He said no other garden in the Western Isles had as many exotic specimens, and he was relieved that they continued blooming in this warm, sheltered vale despite years of neglect. But he wondered why Eigg's lairds had planted their ornamental trees and shrubs so close they blocked any view of the coastline. "Don't you think it's a funny thing, owning an island and not wanting to see the water?" he asked.

The Lodge *was* at odds with its location, a house for people wishing to forget they were on an island. From inside, you heard songbirds and a stream instead of waves beating on the rocks. The luxuriant gardens and lawns visible from the downstairs windows (and only servants lived in the small upper story) belonged on an estate in southern England or the South of France.

Walter Runciman, a politician and shipping magnate whose ownership of the island had been a golden age of prosperity and enlightened management, had built the Lodge in the 1920s, and his son Steven inherited it on his death and used it for many years as a writing retreat. It became briefly the property of one English farmer and then another before being acquired by Keith Schellenberg, the Yorkshire businessman who finally sold it to Maruma. All these owners professed great affection for Eigg, yet none had bothered to thin the trees surrounding the lodge so he could enjoy what Camille Dressler

and most island-lovers would consider to be one of the great pleasures of any island, a view of the water.

Steven Runciman had believed his father haunted the Lodge and
claimed to have heard footsteps. But I thought Keith Schellenberg
haunted it more. (Maruma had never slept here.) A young Edinburgh
solicitor named Sue Hopkins, who had worked on Schellenberg's domestic staff one summer and happened to be visiting Eigg at the same
time I was, told me she was stunned by its deterioration. The exterior
remained solid and imposing, but inside, wallpaper had peeled, rot
had buckled floors, fixtures had been yanked out, and sofas ripped
open. The ruined rooms made it difficult to picture the parlor games,
house parties, and handsome young men in blue blazers she remembered. Only the gardens had preserved what she called the "other-
worldly atmosphere." What stuck in her memory most was the briefing
Schellenberg gave the staff when they arrived. He told them liquor
and pop music were prohibited from the Lodge, and because he was
a vegetarian, meat was never to be cooked where he could smell it.

After selling Eigg to Maruma, Schellenberg had returned to collect what he considered to be his belongings. Among them was a map
of the island dating from the early nineteenth century that previous
lairds had treated as part of Eigg's patrimony, or so the islanders
claimed. To prevent him removing it, they used an old bus to block
the door of the storeroom where it was kept. Journalists alerted to the
confrontation arrived by helicopter. A policeman already on Eigg to
check its polling station told Schellenberg he could not move the bus
for thirty days. Camille Dressler re-created the scene in a book she
wrote about Eigg. The islanders cheered Schellenberg's final and con-
tentious departure, she wrote, and as his boat pulled away from the
dock he shouted at them, "You never understood me. I always
wanted to be one of you."

Like most men who own islands Schellenberg had no doubt
wanted other things, too. Like Des Alwi, he had probably wanted to
save an island. Like the title character in *The Man Who Loved Islands*,

he undoubtedly wanted to make Eigg a world of happiness and contentment. Like the upper-class mothers of Fishers Island, he perhaps wanted roots. And like any newcomer to an island he wanted its inhabitants to love him, and at first, maybe, they did.

During his early years, he had banned hunting and declared the island a wildlife preserve, reopened the community hall, converted abandoned crofts to holiday homes, and hired the artisans and laborers who would hoot his departure twenty years later. The population almost doubled, there were three marriages between locals and his incomers, and even Dressler would concede he gave the island "an attractive vitality." But he also had a fondness for the country-house high life of the 1920s, and unsettled some islanders when he told the *Highland Free Press* in 1991 that he had "Kept its [Eigg's] style slightly run down—the Hebrides feel."

By the early 1990s Eigg was more than slightly run-down, and Schellenberg's divorce from his second wife had left it in a legal and financial limbo. Tenants could not negotiate leases, and the estate farm suffered. When Schellenberg recovered the island in 1992, its people were hostile and suspicious. When a mysterious fire destroyed his beloved vintage Rolls, he and they became the kind of desperate enemies small islands are so good at making. He called them "rotten, dangerous, and totally barmy revolutionaries." They responded with "mean-spirited playboy" and "landlord in the worst tradition of nineteenth-century feudalism."

The more I learned about the feud between them, the more it appeared to have been inevitable from the moment he began recruiting these mainland artists and free spirits. Monarchs of All often want to ban things from their island kingdoms—cars, meat, rock music, hunting, or whatever. They want to dress girls like Ming dynasty princesses or put them in revealing pantaloons, preserve nineteenth-century Hawaii or the louche country-house party life of the 1920s. Just as it is in their nature to stage-manage their islands, it is in the nature of islanders to resist being managed. Men who own islands want to be kings, but islanders are natural republicans. After investing a fortune in a fish-processing plant and dairy industry on the Isle of Lewis, its laird, Lord Leverhulme, was astonished to learn that his islanders resented these grand schemes. In 1910, he summoned them to a famous meeting at Stornoway that came to a climax when a crofter shouted: "We are not concerned with your fancy dreams that may or may not come true. What we want is the land."

No laird had fancier dreams for Eigg then Maruma. He was fascinated with fire and wombs, and the press reported he had bought the island because the opening of its Massacre Cave resembled a vagina. He arrived by helicopter and promised to build a bakery, brewery, distillery, swimming pool, and pier-side complex with coffee houses, shops, and two hundred hotel beds. He spoke of more ferries, electricity from wind and solar power, and an Isle of Eigg Bank making low-interest loans. When he promised a new community hall, something the islanders wanted very badly, they hired an architect with their own money to design it. He told a Scottish newspaper Eigg would become "a pilot in self-sufficiency and efficient practice that will be an inspiration." It would be "the Ruhr Valley of the Hebrides."

On a second and even briefer visit he ordered everyone to gather the island's abandoned cars on the pier and promised to send a barge to remove them. It never arrived. When he next ordered the islanders to remove all the cow flop from Eigg's beaches on the grounds it was unsightly, they lost hope.

Instead of creating jobs, Maruma reduced them by selling off the estate cattle. His academic credentials turned out to be suspect, and it was revealed he had borrowed heavily to buy Eigg, then immediately pledged the island as security for a $500,000 loan from Hong Kong businessmen. Fifteen months after buying the island for $2.5 million, he put it on the market for $3.2 million. Within a year, Eigg's barmy revolutionaries had bought it from his creditors.

Keith Schellenberg brought Maggie and Wesley Fyffe to Eigg in 1976 to staff his craft studio, a mistake I imagine he is still chewing on. They are poster hippies. Wesley has the long face and bushy beard of an Orthodox monk. Maggie is large and dimpled, and is usually either rolling a cigarette, smoking it, or giggling about the marvelous triumph of the Eigg Appeal.

Their cluttered Cleadale house had been the cradle of Eigg's revolution, and I spent a rainy afternoon sitting in its parlor, drinking tea, and reading Maggie's news clippings. A grown daughter who had moved back from Edinburgh to help with the Eigg Appeal, and now lived in a trailer, sat toweling her hair after the luxury of a hot shower. Wesley came and went. People stopped to chat, borrow something, plan tomorrow's fair at the community hall, or add to Maggie Fyffe's account. She said the appeal started with a kick-off at the community hall attended by politicians and reporters. The islanders made T-shirts, printed leaflets, and launched a Web site. Contributions arrived with every post. She dumped the envelopes onto her dining table, parceling them out to people volunteering to tally money and write thank-you notes. Schoolchildren sent pennies, and large sums came from abroad. An anonymous donor contributed $1.5 million.

She believed they had succeeded because of the Internet and all the marvelous publicity. Had there been no burned Rolls or fire-worshiping German, the articles would have been less colorful and prominent, and fewer people would have heard about Eigg. It helped that Eigg had a funny name and every British schoolchild learned to recite, "Rum, Eigg, Muck, and Canna," and that some contributors wanted to strike a blow against Scotland's feudal system. "And being an island was important, too," she added, "because even someone who has never seen us likes knowing we're here."

I thought being an island was almost everything. There was something noble about buying an island for its inhabitants, and I doubted schoolchildren raised on *Robinson Crusoe* and *Treasure Island* would have contributed their candy money had Eigg been as the Appeal described it, "7,400 acres of heather moorland, woodland glens, fertile fields, and spectacular beaches" on the Scottish mainland. The ten thousand strangers answering the Eigg Appeal might have bought a mainland estate so that it could be turned into a park or conservation area, but not so sixty-eight crofters, artists, and dropouts could simply continue living on it and enjoying its wild beauty.

After the glorious buyout celebrations of June 12, 1997, after the Minister for the Highlands and Islands unveiled a bronze plaque and announced, "Game, set, and match to the islanders," the children sang a Gaelic song, the raucous party in the hall ended, and the pipers, musicians, politicians, journalists, and well-wishers left, the Isle of Eigg Trust inherited fields choked by bracken, a Lodge more expensive to repair than demolish, and an estate farm without animals or a tractor. Yet Maggie Fyffe and the people drifting through her parlor that afternoon were optimistic. They said the Trust would balance conservation and community interests and only agree to development that strengthened the community and protected the landscape. They would not let Eigg become the Pleasure Spot of Maruma's heady dream, or, like Rum, a nature laboratory without a permanent human community. The Trust had already leased the farm, and a grant from the Highlands and Islands Enterprise Fund was financing a new store, tearoom, and ecotourism center on the pier. The trustees had applied to the National Heritage Lottery Fund for another grant to protect Eigg's wild areas. Forestry, tourism, and farming would sustain Eigg, they said. But underneath all the optimism was the expectation that charity would continue to flow from the mainland, and young families would move here.

■

I left Maggie Fyffe for an appointment with Angus MacKinnon, a courtly and intelligent man with a full head of white hair and the authority that comes with being the oldest man on an island. His family had arrived in 1650 and he knew Eigg's history and legends better than anyone. He sat me in a straight-backed chair in his spot-less kitchen and critiqued the former lairds. Eigg had been a paradise under the benevolent Runcimans, he said, with every house occupied, every field plowed, and every man employed. The estate's roads were graveled, the hedges trimmed, and the fences all new. It had resembled a picture in a glossy magazine. His definition of a good laird was one with deep pockets who was "noninterfering." He had supported the Trust, but wondered where the islanders would get money to repair and maintain Eigg, now that they were their own lairds. There was work for the moment because of a government grant to build a tearoom and store at the pier. But what happened when they were finished? Before, they had been dependent on the laird. Now, he complained, "We're dependent on charity for every damn thing we do."

Maggie Fyffe knew the identity of the anonymous donor, but would tell me only that she was a woman in the North of England who was not a celebrity. There was no escaping the fact that Eigg's salvation had hinged on her generosity. Had she not heard about the appeal, or not been moved to make the donation, Maruma's creditors would have sold the island to another absentee landlord, its infrastructure would have probably decayed still more, its population declined, and it might have eventually become another St. Kilda.

St. Kilda is the outermost of the Outer Hebrides, 110 miles west of Eigg and so remote that even in the 1920s its most reliable communication with the mainland remained the famous St. Kilda "mail boats," homemade toy boats that floated on sheep bladders and carried cans holding letters the islanders launched when the wind blew from the northwest. For the last two centuries, St. Kilda's population had fluctuated between seventy and one hundred people who, like Niihauans, once ran for the hills at the first sight of a stranger. Crime, swearing, and drunkenness were unknown, and a visiting clergyman reported their morals were "purer than those of great and opulent societies, however much civilized," and that everyone shook hands at least once a day.

Organized religion and tourism began undermining St. Kilda's culture and economy in the mid–nineteenth century. Scottish Free Church missionaries persuaded St. Kildans to spend so much time attending services they had little left to trap seabirds and harvest eggs, and almost starved. Excursion boats brought tourists who showered them with gifts. A West Indian gentleman donated £600 and a laird gave every family a new cottage. The crews of trawlers and whaling ships left coal and fish. Sailors stationed at a World War I naval station handed out food. During the 1920s, when the laird, government, and charities were satisfying all of St. Kilda's material needs, its population plummeted to thirty-six.

Yet these survivors appeared determined to hang on. When two Australians of St. Kildan descent visited the island during the summer of 1929, they were unable to persuade even one person to accompany them back to Australia. Six months later everything changed when an island woman named Mary Gillies suffered an attack of appendicitis. A passing trawler alerted the mainland, but she could not be removed for several weeks and died soon afterwards in a Glasgow hospital. That spring no one planted crops and the entire adult population signed a petition to the secretary of state for Scotland asking to be evacuated. On August 27, 1930, they herded their sheep and cattle onto a chartered steamer and left open Bibles in their homes. Then they locked their doors and drowned their dogs. It is those drowned dogs, more than the tears shed on the deck of the warship as St. Kilda grew faint on the horizon, or St. Kildans' habit of returning in the summer to camp out in their former houses, that speak to the brutal finality of abandoning an island.

In his book *Island on the Edge of the World*, Charles Maclean turned St. Kilda into a cautionary tale for islands, blaming its end on "the malign and cumulative influence of tourism, religion, and disease," and on an indiscriminate charity that undermined St. Kildans' faith in their way of life. "The first tourists were charmed by the innocence of the people and [were] consequently liberal with money and gifts," he wrote, "leaving those who came after to deal with the dollar-hunger they had created." But I thought the St. Kildans had also been unlucky. Their reluctance to move to Australia only months before suggested that if Gillies had survived her appendicitis, some might have stayed through World War II and into the 1950s, when the government built a missile tracking station on the island and lengthened its pier, lessening the isolation that spooked people into leaving in 1930.

Eigg narrowly escaped St. Kilda's fate. After a visit to the island in 1949, the American author Russell Kirk described abandoned crofters' cottages and fields overrun by bracken. "Almost all communal spirit is lost," he lamented, reporting that Eigg's people seldom saw one another. They gathered only twice a year at the community hall, and the most remarkable event of 1949 had occurred when an elderly man traveled four miles to the other end of the island to visit a sister he had not seen in two decades.

Kirk blamed Eigg's perilous condition on the preference of big governments for big mainland institutions. He argued that small and cantankerous islands represented a symbolic criticism of the centralized and industrialized mainland, and he predicted their eventual depopulation and abandonment. He never imagined the phenomenon of Nantucket, Key West, and other Pleasure Spot islands, of mainland culture annexing and taming islands, or that a half century later, Eigg itself would symbolize a rare triumph for the small and eccentric.

■

The Eigg community hall was a rectangular shed near the Lodge with a history of being opened and closed at the whim of the laird. The forty-six people gathered inside for the annual spring fair represented almost the entire population of the island, considering that about a dozen were away on the mainland. To my surprise, I knew or recognized almost everyone, and I liked them all.

The fair offered the usual British amusements—a lottery, lucky dip, bake sale, and rummage tables. You could win a cake by guessing its weight, or a can of beer by driving a nail into a board with three blows. More unusual was the pleasure everyone squeezed from these simple games, and their reluctance to leave. Iain Campbell and his wife sat with Angus MacKinnon in a circle of tea-drinking pensioners. Camille Dressler managed the rummage, Maggie Fyffe took chances on the cake, and Marie Carr supervised the lucky dip while her sister-in-law, Sue Kirk, sold slices of her famous cheesecake, and her husband played darts with Neil Robertson and Colin Carr's son, George. No one sat alone, and even the children who had visited the island of Mustique delighted in the flimsiest used toys.

Midway through the afternoon twenty middle-aged-to-elderly strangers strode into the hall. They wore new hiking boots and parkas, and were passengers off the *Hebridean Princess*, a small cruise ship calling here once a year. They peered at the bakes and rummage, hands clasped behind backs like royals inspecting a primitive village at the far reaches of the Commonwealth. When the islanders invited them to drink tea and throw darts they shook their heads and forced thin smiles. According to Charles Maclean, the nineteenth-century St. Kildans had learned "to lay it on thick" for the passengers of the excursion boats. But on Eigg no one wheedled these visitors for anything, and afterwards it was agreed they had not spent a penny.

Maggie Fyffe had told me that Eigg's beauty and "the way we're a big family" were what kept her on the island. Its busy social life often surprised newcomers, she said. When she lived in a rural part of mainland Scotland, she sometimes went days without seeing a neighbor. Here, she kept bumping into the same people on the jetty, at the store, at a community event or a neighbor's house. One reason this happened was that on a small island the postman driving the school bus might also be the only electrician, the wife of the farmer who was the constable might be the town clerk and operate the tearoom, while the doctor played in the ceilidh band and fixed computers. A diagram showing how, when, and where everyone interacted during an average week on an island like Eigg would be a confusing blur of crisscrossing lines. But it would be a good representation of the kind of freedom people find on such an island—the freedom to pursue a number of interests, fill a number of jobs, use a number of talents, and become, like Crusoe, accomplished in many fields.

I looked around the room at the mixture of incomers and natives who made up Eigg's "big family" and realized how unusual it was. Anyone who needed more entertainment than books, music, and conversation could provide, or who wanted an island hermitage instead of an island community, had probably left. In the Maldives, it was illegal for an incomer to join the community. On Niihau, it was forbidden. On some islands, incomers gained acceptance by summering on the same island for years, like the Roosevelts, or marrying a native, as Dahl had done on Tuvalu. But even on those islands, incomers remained separated from natives by the fundamental fact that natives bore the isolation and material privations of an island in order to live where they had been born and raised, while incomers were free spirits who, by coming to an island, had cut precisely the kind of geographic, community, and family ties that island natives prized. But on Eigg this chasm had been so successfully bridged that the only person unable to join the community was the laird.

I left Eigg with an Anglican priest with furry ears and a cracked smile who came four times a year to hold services. As we shivered together in the boat taking us to the ferry, he exclaimed, "Wonderful island! Wonderful people, too! But my goodness I could never bear to live here."

"I think I could," I said.

His smile said, "You Americans . . ."

I was serious. Eigg really *was* a Utopia where no one was very rich or poor, and where everyone ate a similar diet, lived in similar dwellings, and acted like members of an extended family. Castaways face the horror of solitude without community (which is why so many used the pistols those humanitarian captains left behind), but community without solitude could be a Sartrean *No Exit* of people trapped for eternity in a brightly lit room. Eigg's inhabitants enjoyed the balance of community and solitude Robert Lax had found on Patmos, living in a landscape as wild as Jura's and as beautiful as the Bandas, yet shaking hands every day.

■

I traveled to the island of Spitsbergen in Svalbard, a Norwegian-administered archipelago six hundred miles south of the North Pole, expecting to find the opposite of Eigg, an island of rugged individualists. I could understand why you might maroon yourself on Abemama or Banda Neira, or how a splendid run of spring weather could make you forget Jura's damp winters, but I was flummoxed by Svalbard's appeal. Its polar night stretched from mid-November through January and was followed by weeks of twilight and months of midnight-sun daylight. In summer, mists and fogs obscured the sun for days, wildflowers bloomed for a few weeks on 10 percent of the terrain, and the presence of six thousand polar bears made it imperative to carry a loaded rifle outside the town of Longyearbyen. In winter, high temperatures ranged from −4° to −22° Fahrenheit, "mild," according to a government publication, considering that Svalbard is 10° latitude above Barrow, Alaska, almost 5° above Thule, Greenland, and home to the northernmost year-round community on earth.

I reasoned that Svalbard had to be offering some spectacular compensations for all these hardships, particularly after I read that Norwegians competed to live in its principal town, Longyearbyen, then schemed how to extend their contracts rather than return to

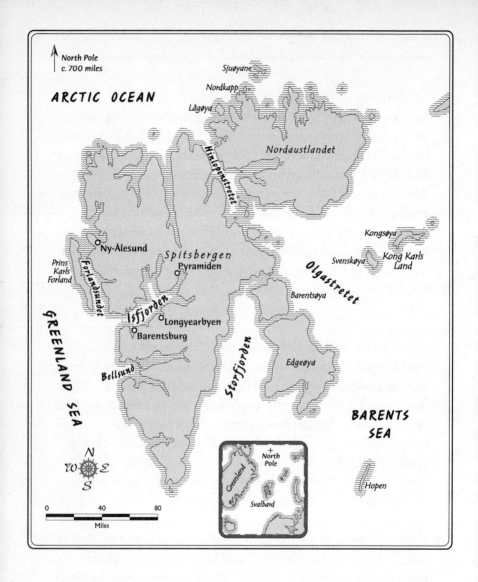

their wealthy and enlightened mainland. I imagined dropouts, solitaries, and people gripped by a particularly virulent strain of islomania, like Dr. Petrukov, a bear-sized man with a flowing white beard who had spent ten years studying the aurora borealis from an underfunded Russian research station while scrounging food and battling polar bears and earning the title Robinson Crusoe of the North.

I thought Spitsbergen, where both Longyearbyen and the Russian settlement of Barentsburg are located, would be an island beyond the scrutiny of polite society, where even the sober Norwegians dropped their inhibitions. It would be an island where you could get away with things, even faking the first flight over the North Pole, as Admiral Richard Byrd may have done. (After Byrd's death, one of his early associates claimed his 1926 flight was a hoax, and even the *Encyclopaedia Britannica* will say only that he "claimed this accomplishment.") There would be icebergs drifting down cobalt fjords and mountains shooting from the sea, glaciers white enough to blind, and snow-capped peaks piercing the clouds like bayonets—a Santa Claus landscape of untracked snow and sparkling ice—and this was more or less the Svalbard I saw as my plane crossed eastern Spitsbergen.

Even at 4:00 A.M., when I landed at Longyearbyen, the crisp air was just above freezing but the sun shone high in a cloudless sky and felt hot enough to burn. The settlement sat near the head of Adventfjord, a narrow finger of water in Svalbard's "banana belt" where a whisper of Gulf Stream water cleared pack ice and melted the snow during the brief arctic summer, enabling lichen to grow and poppies to bloom.

I hitched a ride into town with a gorgeous policewoman who said, "I've only been here two weeks, but I want to stay forever. I guess I have that polar bug bad." She left me at a wooden miners' barracks converted to a hostel. Outside, birds sang and the sun blazed. The curtains in my cubicle-sized room were thin, and I soon gave up trying to sleep and went out searching for what made Longyearbyen so wonderful.

It was certainly not the setting. Eroded mesas and slag-heap mountains flanked its valley, and the supports of a dismantled ore tramway marched up one hillside like a line of gallows. A forlorn cemetery with the permafrosted corpses of coal miners who had perished during the 1918 flu pandemic sat near some charred logs, the remains of a previous settlement flattened by the Nazis.

The new Longyearbyen had two neighborhoods. At the top of the valley, where I was staying, were lines of barracks stark enough to give any ex-POW the willies. Scattered higgledy-piggledy near the water stood dozens of prefabricated houses with the primary colors and absence of whimsy of a sensible Scandinavian toy, inhabited by a people with the rosy-cheeked, doll-like handsomeness of the policewoman.

I had arrived during the mud season, before the last filthy patches of snow had melted or the first flowers bloomed. Instead of kennels of barking sled dogs or racks of cross-country skis, there were hundreds of snowmobiles resting on wooden planks or sinking into the boggy earth. Back at the hostel the clerk boasted that Longyearbyen had twelve hundred snowmobiles, one for every man, woman, and child, the highest snowmobile-to-person ratio on earth. The environmentally sensitive Norwegian government banned them from the mainland, but on Svalbard anyone could own one and they were one of its major attractions. They zipped up and down this valley all winter, whining like buzz saws. "Sometimes I think I am living in an enormous, dark, and very noisy factory," the clerk said, deepening the mystery of why people loved this island.

An excellent little museum displayed the pre-snowmobile relics. The gangly Espen Nordhammer, a student intern already scheming to extend his time in Longyearbyen, showed me his two favorites: a wooden doll a trapper had fashioned from scrap and driftwood, and some permafrosted underpants and a woven belt clinging to the skeleton of a seventeenth-century whaler—clothes that forced you to imagine the person wearing them, and to picture those teeth chomping on seal steaks, and that pelvis making love to a woman.

He led me outside so I could admire a busted motorcycle a Spanish expedition had planned to ride to the North Pole. After a few hundred yards it had spluttered and died. Other "explorers" had arrived expecting to ski to the pole or take taxis. "They all had the polar bug," he said in a tremulous voice, "and maybe I have it, too."

Like everyone infected by this bug, he had trouble defining it. Maybe it was the dry air, or the contrast between total darkness and total light. But no one seeing these exhibits could deny it existed. It had certainly infected Hilmar Nois, another "Crusoe of the North," who had wintered on a remote Svalbard beach thirty-eight times, seven with his wife. He had built tools from driftwood and an alarm clock from the gears of a wrecked ship, and had designed the booby-trapped rifle still used to protect camps from polar bears.

The bug had also infected Georg Nilsen, who had disappeared in 1921 while traveling from his camp to a radio transmitting station for a Christmas celebration. The two men who set out from the station to rescue him starved to death in a snow cave. Their diary's final entry, on exhibit at the museum, read, "Don't put us in a white coffin, we have seen too much snow."

The polar bug was often lethal. The museum's list of fatal accidents showed 112 lives lost between 1950 and 1991 to bears, avalanches, air crashes, thin ice, snowmobile accidents, glacial crevasses, and mine and maritime disasters—a huge number for such a small settlement. And this did not include the 141 Russian and Ukrainian coal miners and their families killed when their chartered jet crashed into a mountain opposite Longyearbyen in 1995, or a young woman eaten by a polar bear the following year while hiking near Longyearbyen— a tragedy persuading even its most seasoned residents to carry loaded high-caliber rifles outside town.

If I wanted to see the polar bug at work, Nordhammer said, I should meet Harald Soleim, Svalbard's longest-serving trapper and the northernmost hermit on earth. He had lived for twenty years across Isfjorden at Kapp Wijk, in a cabin surrounded by antibear trip wires and flares. He generated power with a windmill, trapped seals, and collected eider feathers for sleeping bag manufacturers. He was eccentric but sociable, setting off a small cannon to celebrate the arrival of a visitor. He was also something of a rebel, protesting a fine levied against him for shooting the polar bear (a protected species in

Norway) that had killed one of his dogs, and petitioning the Norwegian king for permission to shoot two bears a year. But he also had a cell phone and computer and traded stocks over the Internet. He sounded a lot like Longyearbyen, a jarring mixture of harsh climate and luxury, pioneering spirit and government regulation.

The polar bug had bitten some Longyearbyen residents, but others came for more mundane reasons. Until 1990, the government discouraged visitors and there had been no hotels, shops, fresh vegetables, or anywhere to eat except the coal miners' mess hall. Outsiders came on scientific missions or business related to the mines, and anyone without an invitation was deported to the mainland. Since then, all but one mine had closed, and the production costs for this remaining one were so high it would have been cheaper to operate Longyearbyen's power plant on coal imported from third world countries. Coal was a touchy issue for a government that prohibited burning it on the mainland and criticized the coal-burning industries of other nations for contributing to global warming. It would have been more economical to close Svalbard's last mine and maintain a small community of scientific researchers. But national pride, the possibility of undiscovered natural resources, and rivalry with the Russians, who continued mining coal elsewhere in the archipelago, had persuaded the Norwegian government to lavish money on Longyearbyen.

During the 1990s, three hotels, an arctic research center, and a small university branch campus had opened, transforming Longyearbyen into a middle-class boomtown with more amenities than a mainland city ten times as large. A transient middle class of scientists, functionaries, and the twenty-somethings who pour drinks and make beds at ski resorts and Club Meds around the world arrived, and because of them, Longyearbyen offered such urban and mainland pleasures as bar-hopping, disco dancing, fine dining, and withdrawing cash from an automated teller machine and spending it in a department store with all the plastic-wrapped, designer-logoed comforts of home.

Wealthy Norwegians flew in to celebrate anniversaries and birthdays, and mainland companies held conferences at the Polar Hotel. Longyearbyen became fashionable and desirable. Wages were high, alcohol and tobacco untaxed, and income taxes a low 15 percent. Government subsidies made the school and medical services superior to mainland ones. And where else, I was repeatedly asked, could you live in a friendly small town, take university courses, drive a snowmobile, have access to a health club with an indoor swimming pool, and also catch the polar bug?

As in everywhere else I have been in Scandinavia, I preferred the women in Longyearbyen to the men. They were breezy, hardworking, handsome, and flirtatious, while the men were broody, suspicious, overly formal, and overly fond of drink. The women also ran the restaurants and bars where, given the oppressiveness of the midnight sun, the bleakness of this valley, and the threat of polar bears outside it, I spent more time than I care to admit.

Elisabeth Aaraesther at the governor's office won me over by showing none of the caution that usually grips a bureaucrat facing someone with an open notebook. Sure, she said, Norway subsidized Svalbard to keep its population even with the Russian mining settlements of Pyramiden and Barentsburg; sure, many people came for the low taxes and because it was trendy; and sure, everything here was better than on the mainland. "To be honest, sometimes I'm ashamed we live so well," she admitted.

She would also admit that the increase in tourists and scientific expeditions threatened the fragile environment. Helicopter tourism spooked the wildlife and brought noise and air pollution. Scientific expeditions left garbage that would require centuries to decompose. Cruise ship passengers had trampled the tundra, and all-terrain vehicles and motorized sleds had leaked gas onto it. Some people believed an island so close to the North Pole could not support even this mod-est level of exploitation, but every year more Norwegians wanted to visit Svalbard and live on it, and her office handled more inquiries from people wanting to winter in one of the remote government-owned cabins. Environmental officers tried to screen out applicants lacking basic survival skills. They entered into lengthy correspon-dence with the finalists and chose the winners depending on the sin-cerity and persuasiveness of their essays.

I also liked Kari Angemo, who had the hefty good looks of an Olympic athlete and was as candid as an old friend. She worked at the Info-Svalbard, a government agency charged with making a success of tourism. Yet she was willing to say, "I often wonder why Mr. Longyear put his town here because it is not that pretty. You see much better scenery flying over the mountains when you leave." She would even concede that some Svalbardians preferred the dark months because the midnight sun threw too much light on their television screens.

She showed me all the sights visible from Longyearbyen's three roads. We stopped at a memorial to an inebriated boy who had frozen when his snowmobile ran out of gas within sight of the lights of town. We stared through a chain-link fence at the remains of the Tupolev that had crashed with the Russian miners. Nearby, the carcasses of slaughtered seals, food for the dogs that took tourists into the interior, dangled from the wooden supports of another defunct cableway.

I became fond of Veronica, too. She spoke English with an Australian accent and either was a great actress or was genuinely happy to see this middle-aged baldy drag himself into the bar of the Funken Hotel every afternoon. She had worked on a Bali-based cruise ship but now preferred Longyearbyen's frenetic social life. Everyone followed the same schedule, she said. First a brief stop at the motel bar near the mini-mall, then more drinks in the smoky Po-lar Bar. After midnight everyone moved to the Huset ("House") for dancing and more drinking. There was usually an after-party, then time for a nap before going to work, with never a thought given to the fact that a monument to a student eaten by a polar bear was less than a mile from where everyone was enjoying the drink currently all the rage in Longyearbyen, Long Island Iced Tea.

It was pathetic to travel thousands of miles to become a barfly 650 miles from the North Pole, but what else was there to do on Svalbard in early June? Too much snow had melted in some places and not enough in others. I was too late for ski trekking or "snowmobile safaris," too early for boat trips to remote fjords and islands. I wanted to meet Harald Soleim, but he was not answering his cell phone or e-mail, which meant that his power pack was low or he was away, and I was reluctant to spend a fortune chartering a boat only to find no one home. So I followed Veronica's advice and joined Longyearbyen's sunlit bacchanal, emerging tired and boozy from one dark, smoky bar until the crisp air, sunlight, and twittering birds slapped me in the face and I recovered enough to push on to the next.

As I walked into the Huset at 1:00 A.M., a boy spread his arms and shouted, "Svalbard is wonderful!"

"Why?" I asked.

"Because I can drink and walk home without worrying about the police checking my breath!"

By 2:00 A.M. the dance floor had filled with kids flapping their arms to Norwegian versions of "Mockingbird" and "Hungry Heart." The grunge look is problematic for Scandinavians but these willowy boys had done their best, growing sparse blond mustaches and wispy goatees. Explorers on dogsleds, hollow-eyed trappers making camp in snowfields, and soot-faced miners stared from grainy black-and-white photographs covering the walls as the boys played air guitars and stuck their tongues into their girlfriends' ears.

The following evening, I dined at a restaurant food critics had voted one of Norway's ten best. The small, elegant room had peach walls and pinpoint lighting. A large party of businessmen in bankers' suits and shiny office shoes toasted their accomplishments with champagne and photographed their seal steaks. The waiter warmed my Côtes du Rhône over a candle and ladled overcooked vegetables from an aluminum foiled swan. Just when Longyearbyen was starting to remind me of Kuda Huraa—another island defying climate, geography, and common sense—the waitress told me that Harald Soleim himself had trapped the bird used for my breast of wild goose.

According to a booklet published by Svalbard Polar Travel, the Polar Hotel was "the world's northernmost full-service hotel." Its meeting hall, "a stylish location for groups of 160 people," made Longyearbyen "one of Europe's most exclusive locations for meetings and conferences," the copy said, adding that "motivation, personal relations and teamwork are the key words here," and group activities could be arranged that would encourage participants "to work as a team, helping them to improve their attitudes toward customers, colleagues or employees."

The next morning I watched the businessmen from the Huset restaurant build teamwork by hiking along a ridge above Longyearbyen. We each had our own armed guard and we passed within sight of a memorial cairn to the young woman devoured by the bear. My guard, the dour Joern Dybdal, believed this woman had been "very unlucky." Bears usually kept to the shoreline, but this one, a cub, had wandered from its mother and became hungry and disoriented. "It should not have been up here," he said.

But who or what *should* be up here? Businessmen wearing suits under their parkas and marching through the thin snow cover in wing-tip shoes?

Dybdal muttered about the damage shoes inflicted on the yellow poppies and purple sorrel, more than was caused by decades of snowmobile travel. Lichens and grasses in the most accessible regions were showing wear from groups like these. Every new party, ours included, made it worse, and the tundra would need centuries to recover.

Longyearbyen's tour companies also promised to build worker motivation and solidarity with fossil-picking trips to the glacier, wilderness barbecues, and excursions to Barentsburg, a Soviet-era relic the Norwegians considered at once mysterious and pitiable. The Svalbard Treaty of 1925 had granted its forty-two signatory states the right to exploit the archipelago's natural resources. Besides Norway, only the Soviet Union built mining settlements, and during the Cold War the two nations competed to have the largest population in the archipelago. The collapse of Communism and the air crash had brought Barentsburg to its knees. Its population fell to 850, its shops closed, its newspaper folded, and flights to Murmansk were suspended. Its generating plant and mines were so inefficient that one-fifth of its coal went for local consumption. A supply boat had not called in a year, and, a few months before, its officials had asked the Norwegians for winter clothing.

Barentsburg was three hours by boat and less by snowmobile, but for most Norwegians it could have been Timbuktu. No one knew who ran it. Was it the Russian consul? The mine manager? The men monopolizing the sale of handicrafts to tourists? Or the shadowy Stalinist apparatchik who had once rejected a gift of cross-country skis on grounds there were not enough for everyone?

Islands divided by religion, race, or nationality have been spectacular disasters. Judged against the standards set by Timor, Ireland, Cyprus, and Ceylon, the Russian-Norwegian rivalry on Svalbard was polite and restrained. Still, there was a triumphalist atmosphere, a sense of going slumming, permeating my excursion to Barentsburg on the M.S. *Langysund*. A large party of Germans, and another of silver-haired Norwegian doctors and their wives, filled most of the ship's forty-five places. The Norwegians' constructive group activity involved getting howling drunk on Jägermeister in the stuffy salon and giving the stink-eye to the Germans, who reciprocated.

I fled to the deck and met our guide, a Valley Girl Norwegian named Nadine who also had the job of making sure passengers bought drinks at the bar instead of coming up here to sneak nips from their flasks. She was relieved that everyone was getting drunk rather than asking her to identify the birds swooping overhead. "Black and white, gray and white, they're all boring. Does anyone really care what they're called?" she asked. This was her third year in Svalbard and she loved its low taxes and partying. She even made enough money to take a winter vacation on a Caribbean island. But this excursion was her least favorite. It made her sad that the Russians could not afford to shop in Longyearbyen.

The weather changed in a snap. We left in dazzling sunshine, then hit a fog bank that was blown away minutes later by a bitter wind. Everything was prettier than Longyearbyen. Glaciers licked at valleys. A wall of craggy mountains, snow-covered from top to bottom, could have been a line of Rocky Mountains sliced off just below their peaks and set afloat.

Barentsburg sat on a plateau above the dock where we landed, squeezed between the fjord and the mountains. Three Russian guides divided us up and led their parties up rickety stairs to the town. Several of our number were too inebriated to make the climb and stumbled back to the ship.

My guide, Ala, was a pinch-faced Ukrainian granny who had smartened herself up by yanking her gray hair into a bun and painting the cracks in her leather jacket with shoe polish. Her Intourist patter began, "Welcome to the Paradise of the North where everyone is enchanted by its beauty!"

I asked why she had remained in Barentsburg for ten years when most people went home after a two- or three-year contract.

She ignored me.

Could she direct me to Doctor Petrukov's research station, so I could interview this Crusoe of the North?

"Gone home," she snapped.

"This is the best place on earth!" she shouted, sweeping an arm toward the vista of forlorn apartment blocks. "We are clean, do you hear me, *very clean,* and in Barentsburg, unlike *other* towns, everyone helps each other."

A plume of black smoke rose from the generator. Coal dust covered sidewalks and tailings had piled in drifts. The Russian and Ukrainian miners wore gray and black clothes. Only their gold teeth sparkled. It was midday, but many were as drunk as passengers off the *Langysund*. Breathalyze Barentsburg and half the town, residents and visitors alike, would have been judged unfit to drive.

A faded mural of heroic workers crowned with a hammer and sickle and *CCCP* (the Cyrillic initials of the USSR) decorated the façade of the community center. The bust of Lenin in the forlorn square was of a type Muscovites had pounded to smithereens. "But why shouldn't he be here?" Ala asked with a thin smile. "He is our dear Lenin."

There were no children in the park, no mothers pushing strollers, or crying babies. Ala said the air disaster had discouraged parents from bringing children to Svalbard. But the truth, whispered the Norwegians, was that the Russians could no longer afford a school.

Ala led us into a canteen smelling of cabbage and dirty socks where she announced: "Our greenhouses produce cucumbers, tomatoes, and even flowers for holidays. We have our own cows and pigs in heated barns. We drink fresh milk. That's why we live better—we have fresh food, all we want!"

The contrast between Longyearbyen and Barentsburg was stark: a shabby Russian village versus all-the-comforts-of-home-and-then-some Longyearbyen; pasty-faced people in nylon windbreakers who could no more leave this island than Selkirk could escape Más a Tierra versus hip Norwegians in peacock parkas; a plugged-in town pampered by the richest country in Europe versus one ignored by one of the poorest. But at least in Barentsburg you could discern, in the mural of birch trees evoking a Russian forest, the wooden gingerbread tacked onto apartment blocks, the garbage cans painted to resemble open-mouthed penguins, and the jewel-box mansion of the Russian consul, the remains of a more ambitious dream.

"Our pride and joy!" Ala cried as we entered the Palace of Sports. "We built it with our own hands. We took nothing, nothing from outside!" The pleasant swimming pool had a glass ceiling, a garden of tropical plants, and blue tiles in the shape of reindeer.

She led us in and out of changing rooms and storage areas, searching for someone enjoying himself. Finally she ushered us into a stifling weight room the size of a motel bedroom. We leaned against its padded walls, watching two young miners with fabulous bodies and repulsive complexions lift barbells, adding the halitosis of our drunks to their stale perspiration.

Ala blocked the exit. She was determined we appreciate this tableau of socialist workers at play. One of the men scowled and made a show of spitting on his hands and rubbing them together before lifting the next weight.

I have permitted myself to be driven miles into the Gambian bush to see a holy crocodile that never appeared, and traveled to an Ambonese village for the pleasure of wading into a pool and touching a sacred eel. I have paid admission to visit a Zairean zoo whose keepers had eaten the exhibits and searched for crabs at Kuda Huraa, but crowding into a foul-smelling room in a bleak Russian mining town to watch two Ukrainians lift weights pushed the definition of a tourist-worthy attraction to some new frontier.

When the second weight lifter also shot us a dark look and blew a gob of spit onto his hands, Ala cried, "To the museum, my dear friends." This attraction, in the former school, charged an inflated admission to see sixteenth-century sled runners and pipe fragments proving the Russians had beaten everyone else to Svalbard.

I ditched Ala and befriended a guide named Tami whose group had abandoned her to hunt down some vodka. She stood alone, pretending to examine a trapper's chess set and wiping away tears.

She was a busty blonde with a pockmarked face who spoke flawless English and wore the tatters of a superior wardrobe—a pilled white sweater that was losing its embroidery and scuffed red high-heeled shoes. She had arrived ten days before and this was her first tour. It had gone poorly, but she was not crying for that. She was crying for her beautiful, long-legged boy. "He is only eleven but when I see him again he will be almost fourteen, a different person," she said. "No, don't try making me feel better. I know these are the years when a boy changes, and I am losing them forever."

We sat on a bench overlooking the gray fjord and crumbling mountains. She had no choice but to leave him in Moscow with her sister, she explained. Her husband was an engineer, an educated man, but the textile plant where they both worked had not paid their salaries in six months. After exhausting their savings to pay for their son's piano lessons, they each took the first available job. But Barentsburg had some consolations. It was a *real* community, the kind that had disappeared in Russia, the kind that made the Russians "better people," she said. Everyone helped each other and real friendships were possible. Women she had known for ten days had shown her more kindness than mainland friends she had known for decades.

"Even the drunks are sweet and generous," she said with a faint smile. "But have you noticed the dead eyes?" The chief engineer had lost his wife and three children in the crash. The woman selling tickets at the museum had lost her only daughter. Their eyes were dead, but at least they were kind.

To cheer her up I suggested she and her husband might save enough money to buy a house.

She gave me a pitying look. The state-owned company, Trest Arktikugol, had paid the last group of returning miners only after they threatened to picket company offices and call the media. By the time she and her husband left, it might be bankrupt. What did it matter, anyway? Their salary was fixed in increasingly devalued rubles and would be virtually worthless in a few years.

"No, we have not come to this island for the money." She lowered her voice. "We have come, my dear friend, to eat—for the food in the canteen, the meat, the vegetables."

So Barentsburg was Tami's Devil's Island, except the food was better and the inmates nicer. The view from this bench was more depressing, and tantalizing, than what Captain Alfred Dreyfus had on that island. He saw an empty ocean. She saw an arctic wasteland, and would spend her summers guiding tourists who could fly to Moscow tomorrow if they wanted.

Below us, the passengers in their colorful parkas reboarded the *Langysund*. Tami's eyes teared again. "Why does God torture the Russians?" she asked.

I said I hoped she would be paid. I hoped Barentsburg would be good for her husband. I hoped her long-legged boy would . . .

"Oh hope, hope, hope." She waved a hand. "Hope will be the last to die."

"Look at them," a Norwegian doctor crowed as we left the dock. He was pointing to Ala and Tami, who stood together waving handkerchiefs. "It's just as we were told. They're certainly hurting. Could anyone believe they're as happy as we are?"

"It's much poorer than our Norwegian town," his wife added. "And most of the men were drunk!"

■

Back in Longyearbyen, a twin-engine propeller plane soared across a cloudless sky. Flying over Svalbard's glaciers in a small plane struck me as the bravest thing I had seen here, so I tracked down its pilot, a septuagenarian retired mining engineer named Alfred Tiefenthal, who had lived on Svalbard since 1955. He was a thin, fragile-looking man, but he had built this twin-engine plane during seven polar winters. Yesterday he had taken it on its maiden flight.

The plane sat alone in an airport hangar. Its wooden propellers glistened and its streamlined fuselage was unblemished. It was the most beautiful aircraft I have ever seen.

I asked Tiefenthal why he stayed in Svalbard when most mine employees retired to the mainland. He shrugged. His son had been born here and his wife continued teaching in the school. He supposed anywhere you lived for four decades was home, and he had caught the polar bug.

"I have that polar bug, too," said Sven Nordhal, a middle-aged man with an early Beatles haircut who had helped Tiefenthal assemble the plane and was here to witness its second flight. Ever since reading about Spitsbergen as a boy, he had dreamed of living on it. When he developed a revolutionary technique for translating books into Braille, he was able to persuade officials at the coal company that then ran the island, Store Norsk, that he would be self-sufficient, and he was permitted to become Svalbard's first independent businessman. He liked the island so much he pitied anyone forced to leave when his or her contract expired. He even hated to leave on holiday. "The polar bug is like falling in love," he said. "There *is* no scientific explanation. You tell someone you're moving to Svalbard for three years and fifteen years later, if you're lucky, you're still here!"

I was beginning to understand Svalbard's polar bug, and it was sounding suspiciously like a Utopian strain of islomania. When Nordhal spoke of community spirit, new arrivals putting down roots, and Longyearbyen having more clubs than a mainland town ten times its size, I remembered Kari Angermo at Info-Svalbard. She had surprised me by saying that most residents, herself included, preferred the "dark time" of the polar night, when there was no hint of twilight, snowmobiles roared, and streetlights blazed around the clock, "because then everyone is social and there are lots of activities." And she reminded me of Joern Dybdal, who claimed that in twelve years here he had never been bored. He had arrived as a coal miner and stayed to launch a pony-trekking business. "I will remain here until my ponies die," he said, "and Icelandic ponies live a long time." He believed leaving Svalbard, rather than black lung, smoking, or drink, killed its miners. "They retire to the mainland and go downhill fast. They have big hearts, so they die of loneliness."

Dybdal reminded me of Kjell Mork, a schoolteacher who had been here twenty years and said most longtime residents preferred to vacation in the summer. They returned after the late August blizzards, eager for another dark season marked by a rich community life of drama and singing clubs, book groups, and dance troupes. He insisted that Svalbard did not attract "stubborn or angry people" and that 97 percent of its residents were overjoyed to be here, perhaps because everyone lived in roughly equal material circumstances. His comments, in turn, reminded me of Nadine, who had said, "This island just grabs and enchants you." The attraction for her was the dark season, "because that's when we joke there's a club for everyone in Longyearbyen, and you find a community spirit that has disappeared from our mainland."

11

FRIGHTENING ISLANDS —
MALEKULA AND PHU QUOC

A story my wife brought to our marriage about the shipwreck of her great-grandfather, the Right Reverend Henry Holme, off the coast of Central America in 1891 had a sunny *Swiss Family Robinson* beginning, but ended just short of a *Lord of the Flies* conclusion.

Bishop Holme, his wife Eliza, and their three children had been passengers on the steamship *Aguan* when it strayed off course and ran aground on Roncador Cay, a six-mile coral and sandbar island one hundred miles northeast of Greytown (now San Juan del Norte), Nicaragua. The lifeboats leaked, the captain was incompetent, and Roncador lay outside the regular shipping lanes, in the western Caribbean's "Empty Quarter." A party of men set out in the best lifeboat to row ninety miles to Old Providence Island to find help. The other boats shuttled back and forth to a sandbar island with the remaining passengers. Bishop Holme suspected some of the crew members of planning to abandon the black passengers and refused to leave the ship until everyone was brought ashore.

Once on the island, passengers and crew sorted themselves into two factions. Holme and his family, a party of distinguished Americans, the ship's officers, and the women and children gathered around some thatched huts used by itinerant fishermen. The second-class passengers and ordinary crewmen gathered at the other end, taking shelter in a coral blockhouse built centuries earlier by buccaneers.

The island was treeless and waterless, far less promising than the one Defoe gave Crusoe. Still, the better class of Victorian castaways scrupulously followed the Crusoean script, salvaging casks of water and provisions from the wrecked ship, erecting a tent, and turning the booby birds into soup. Their children collected shells and swam. Eliza Holme remembered her husband holding Easter Sunday services, delightfully cool evenings, and "the moon and stars shining on us in sympathy."

The riffraff at the buccaneers' fort returned to the *Aguan* to salvage liquor and loot the other passengers' luggage. Holme reported a worrying "outbreak of drunkenness" at their end of the island. Men at the first-class end stood guard every night with loaded pistols. Rescue came after six days. Had it been much later, the castaways might have finished each other off before thirst and hunger did the job.

I had a premonition of evil, perhaps like the one Bishop Holme experienced when he worried about the *Aguan*'s black passengers, while I was training for the Peace Corps on Djerba, a Tunisian island that like several Mediterranean ones claims to be the *Odyssey*'s Island of the Lotus Eaters. Its Lotus Eaters were a colony of Peace Corps volunteers who had spent three years there teaching English and avoiding the Vietnam-era draft. I cannot recall why I found them so sinister, only that they spent much of their time drinking beer and surfing the island's gentle waves. They gave me the creeps, and as I sat with them one evening in the deserted basement discotheque of a new package-tour beach hotel, chilled by the ferocious air conditioning, and even more by the sight of them becoming increasingly inebriated and belligerent, I decided to resign and go home.

The *Odyssey* contains some of the greatest island horror stories of all time, and bears some responsibility for the notions that an island's temptations are more fabulous than those of a continent and its dangers more terrifying, but that even a frightening island can be seductive.

Odysseus encounters numerous insular horrors, including the Cyclops who devours his sailors, and Scylla, the six-headed monster who eats at least one crewman from any ship passing near her cavern. But the Sirens, who lure sailors to the jagged rocks of their island with their enchanting voices, have beautiful female faces. The island of Ortygia, where Calypso imprisons Odysseus for seven years and makes him her lover is so beautiful "even a deathless god . . . would gaze in wonder, heart entranced with pleasure." The sorceress Circe detains Odysseus in her palace on Aeaea for a year of feasting and lovemaking, and the honey-sweet lotus that robs his crewmen of all desire to return home is the most delicious fruit in the world.

It is astonishing how many islands, particularly beautiful tropical ones, have a horror story in their past. Many of these stories involve shipwrecked sailors who attempt to subjugate the natives and are murdered by them, or romantics who come searching for paradise and become mortal enemies.

On Pitcairn Island, the *Bounty* mutineers fought over the Tahitian women who had arrived on the uninhabited island with them, murdering one another and the jealous Tahitian men. On beautiful Mili Atoll, Samuel Comstock and his companions, who had already murdered the officers of their whaling ship, began killing one another before being slaughtered by the outraged natives. Palmyra, an uninhabited atoll in the central Pacific, became the site of a notorious 1974 double murder when two yachting couples, who each hoped to live a Crusoean life on it arrived at almost the same time.

In the nineteenth century, Floreana in the Galápagos Islands was briefly known as Charles Island when it was ruled by a Creole named Charles who intimidated his eighty subjects with a pack of vicious dogs. In the 1930s, the same island attracted a colony of German nudists and romantics, including a Dr. Friedrich Ritter, who called

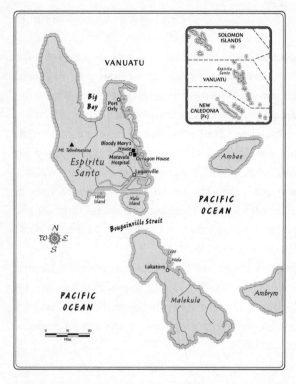

himself "der Robinson auf Galápagos," and his lover and disciple, Dore Strauch. Her articles about their idyllic life led the German press to name them "the Adam and Eve of Floreana." The publicity attracted a bourgeois German couple and their sickly son, as well as a sexually adventurous German baroness and her retinue of young men. The final fruit of their disputes, jealousies, and rivalries was the suspicious disappearance of the baroness and a companion, the mysterious appearance of the mummified corpses of two other members of the community, and the agonizing death of Friedrich Ritter from food poisoning (or just plain poisoning), during which he scribbled a note to Dore Strauch saying, "I curse you with my dying breath." She titled the book she wrote about these events *Satan Came to Eden*.

I could not count on stumbling on another Floreana, nor could I hang around a remote island waiting for its misfits and beachcombers to murder one another. The Monarchs of All had vanished with the European colonial empires, as had the days when a castaway could bamboozle the natives into worshiping him as a god. This left prison islands and cannibal islands as the only places I could hope to brush against some island horrors and meet, if not the cannibals, then at least their children, and if not the prisoners, at least their jailers.

I chose the island of Malekula in Vanuatu because it was near Espíritu Santo and two documentaries filmed on it at the beginning of the twentieth century by Osa and Martin Johnson had once made it the most notorious cannibal island in the world, turning its Big Nambas into legendary island horrors and reinvigorating the connection between islands and cannibals made by Defoe in *Robinson Crusoe*.

The Johnsons were legendary pith helmet and high boots motion picture explorers of the early twentieth century who decided to stop at Malekula during a 1917 swing through the South Seas because, as Osa Johnson later wrote, it promised savage peoples "completely untouched by civilization." They disembarked on Vao, one of several islets lying just off the east coast of Malekula that was home to four hundred Small Nambas who had fled to escape the even more ferocious Big Nambas. There the Johnsons stayed with Father Prin, a French missionary whose thirty years on untamed Malekula had produced only seventeen converts.

When the Johnsons finally went ashore on the main island, they immediately heard "the low pulsing beat" of jungle drums. A hundred "armed savages" surrounded them and, as Martin Johnson cranked his camera, Chief Nagapate stepped into a clearing. He was the cannibal king of every white man's nightmare. A bone pierced his nose, a mass of greasy black hair fell around his shoulders, and a large namba, or pandanus leaf sheath, protected his penis.

Martin Johnson captured their encounter on film. It showed Osa Johnson holding out a piece of bright calico cloth and murmuring how it would make "a very nice shirt" for this naked man; Nagapate grabbing her arm and trying to rub away her whiteness with his finger, then scowling as Martin Johnson shook his hand, then pinching and prodding Osa's body; the Johnsons leaving the clearing in haste as the Big Nambas retreated; the Johnsons and their porters dashing down the trail, pursued by the Nambas; Osa screaming as she was dragged into the bush; a British naval patrol boat steaming into the bay, causing the Nambas to release their catch; and finally, the Johnsons' mad dash for the beach, pursued so closely by the Nambas that Osa claimed to have heard the slap of heavy sodden leaves against their bare flesh.

Several months later, *Cannibals of the South Seas* opened at the Rivoli Theatre on Broadway and as Osa Johnson tells it, "Nagapate's scowling face was looking from the screen . . . and within a year had sent shudders around the civilized world."

The Johnsons returned to Malekula in 1919 to film a sequel. Father Prin had abandoned Vao, so they camped out in his house, passing the time by filming the slaughter of seven hundred pigs for a feast. They walked down to the beach on an evening Osa Johnson would remember as one of the most beautiful she had known. A full moon had thrown a golden path across the water, the air had a "bloom-like softness," and a luminous trail of phosphorescence marked the course of a shark. Suddenly, the Johnsons heard the soft swish of paddles and saw six silent men beaching a canoe and lifting out a long and heavy object wrapped in leaves. The drums began beating and Martin Johnson sat awake all night, holding a loaded rifle across his knees. The next morning they learned they had watched the unloading of the main course for a cannibal feast.

The Johnsons returned to the same bay where they had escaped the Big Nambas. This time Chief Nagapate met them on the beach and relations between them were more cordial. Osa now considered Nagapate a "screen personality" and no longer feared him. He invited himself aboard their schooner and Martin unrolled one of the colored movie posters that had advertised *Cannibals of the South Seas* on Broadway. For an hour, Nagapate and his warriors sat squatting on their heels, staring in silence at this miraculous object, sometimes gathering the courage to touch it.

The Johnsons set up a screen and projector on the beach. A beam of light shot though the black night and Nagapate and his warriors began watching *Cannibals of the South Seas*. First they saw the Johnsons at the Waldorf Astoria Hotel, racing cars and airplanes, and pictures of Armistice Day celebrations. When Nagapate's face filled the screen, Johnson signaled for his guards to explode radium flares. For several minutes the beach was bathed in white light as Johnson filmed the fear and amazement of the Big Nambas as they watched themselves flicker across the screen. The pièce de résistance was the appearance of a man who had died the year before, a phenomenon surely as terrifying for the Big Nambas as the tom-toms and cannibal feasting had been for the Johnsons. Afterwards, Osa Johnson sensed "a definite change in the attitude of the Big Nambas" and observed them becoming quiet and respectful toward whites.

After this revolutionary moment, white missionaries were successful in establishing several large mission stations on Malekula and most Nambas, Big and Small, became at least nominal Christians and largely abandoned traditional customs like cannibalism. The last officially recognized instance of one Malekulan eating another occurred in 1969, and led to the arrest of some Big Nambas on Vao.

Sharks have replaced cannibals as Malekula's great terror, and whenever I told anyone on Espíritu Santo I was planning to stay on Wala, an islet a few miles down the coast from Vao, I could count on hearing about the Swiss gentleman who had been eaten an hour after arriving on Malekula, and the infant son of an American yachting couple whom a shark snatched from their hands as they bathed him over the side of their boat.

The first advice I received from Peter Fidelio, the scholarly-looking ni-Vanuatu who owned the Wala Island Resort, was to stay in the shallows on the leeward side of the island. "Here is okay," he said, pointing to one stretch of beach. "But not there," he continued, gesturing to a spot a hundred yards away. His "resort" was a half dozen thatched houses with mosquito nets and kerosene lamps, set in a palm grove so close to the water a shark could have jumped through the window. During my four days there, the breeze never slackened, the sea never calmed, and I enjoyed nine hours of cool and untroubled sleep every night. During the day I crossed to the main island to make some dutiful excursion, only to be driven back early by the heat, the mosquitoes, and an oppressive landscape of wild mountains that turned coal black in the flat midday sun.

The inhabitants of Wala appreciated its advantages. Given the slightest chance, they would expound at length on how their paradise of thatched huts and crushed coral compounds was safer, cooler, and less mosquito-plagued than Malekula. Most of the men were descended from people who had originally canoed across the choppy strait to avoid being eaten. They saw no reason to leave now, and their children rarely set foot off the island until they were six and had to attend school on Malekula.

One night I heard drums beating and followed the sound to a plateau above the beach where two boys were pounding them to summon worshipers to a Catholic church made from woven mats. The congregants were almost exclusively women. Nearby, their husbands played *boule* on a patch of level ground between two lines of mango trees. I heard hymns, then the click of the balls. I shut my eyes and could have been in provincial France.

The word "custom" becomes *kastom* in Bislama and refers to traditional magic, rituals, and practices, many of them eradicated or driven underground by missionaries. The two great remaining pillars of *kastom* are the ritual slaughter of pigs and the superiority of men. Pigs on Malekula suffered an agonizing life during which their tusks were encouraged to grow through the roofs of their mouths. Then they were brought to a nasara, a sacred meeting and dancing ground, and clubbed to death. A Nambas woman did not fare much better. She spent her days bent double and working in the gardens, crouching low whenever she passed a man, and squatting low when sitting next to one. She was excluded from important ceremonies, could be traded for a pig or a basket of yams, and if she was lucky her husband showed his appreciation by arranging a ceremony during which she had her front teeth knocked out.

I persuaded Reuben, the grandson of the last traditional chief of Wala, to show me the island nasara. He led me to some flat ground in the center of the island surrounded by huge banyan trees and infused with the melancholy atmosphere of a ruined church. Dozens of tom-toms lay rotting in the underbrush. Many of the sacred pig stones, the flat slabs of rock a family earned by slaughtering pigs, had fallen on their faces or sides. Reuben became increasingly morose as he showed me the seventy rocks his grandfather had earned for his slaughtered pigs, the "grand place" where couples had been married, and the rows upon rows of pig stones bearing an unsettling resemblance to a field of tombstones for children.

He told me that Vao, the island where Osa and Martin Johnson had lived, remained a *kastom* holdout despite its large Catholic mission. It was only ten miles up the coast, but the next day it took us most of the morning to travel there, first by boat to the mainland, then by truck over washboard roads and across a strait in another boat. The reward was the opportunity to visit its *kastom* house, or nakamal, probably the spot where the man the Johnsons saw being spirited ashore in 1919 had been lashed to a tall hollow drum and covered with a batter of pounded yams before being cooked and eaten.

A local man whose name sounded like "Harvey" showed me around Vao's nasara. There were hollow tom-toms painted with red and green harlequin faces, carved wooden bowls used during feasts, heavy clubs for killing pigs, and more stones representing dead pigs. Harvey ushered me into the nakamal, a dark and gloomy hut where twelve-year-old boys underwent a circumcision rite. He said the iron bracelets hanging from its walls were for restraining the boys during the festivities.

Carved masks and model canoes bearing optimistic price tags lined the shelves of a meeting room. Harvey shut the door and announced I could either buy something or pay an inflated "fee" for photographing the circumcision hut. I paid twelve dollars for a wooden mask whose mouth was frozen wide open in a scream, presumably like one of the boys handcuffed to the wall in the nakamal.

"Where is everyone?" I kept asking Reuben as we walked down Vao's empty lanes.

He said they were at work, in the mission school, perhaps at home.

Finally, I asked the question I had wanted to all along, "Where are the cannibals?"

"Gone," he said, shaking his head sadly, making it clear I had diminished myself in his opinion. But if I was truly interested in *kastom*, he added, a group of Little Nambas had left a mission station on the mainland and returned to the old ways, everything *except* cannibalism. If I paid them a little, they would dance a lot.

The next afternoon we sat on logs under a huge mango tree while Stephen Lelactei and six prepubescent boys danced, and danced. Only he and a teenager wore a namba, the rest were stark naked except for anklets of corn husks that made them sound like rattlesnakes. They banged tom-toms, stamped their feet, and jabbed spears at the sky. Lelactei wore feathers and a double necklace of tusks and resembled King Nagapate in the Johnsons' poster. The boys changed costumes frequently, appearing several times in headdresses of carved pink and white fish. I saw "Chasing the Fish" and "Death of the Fish," then a quartet of dances about hunting and killing wild pigs. After each performance Reuben asked, "Another song?" and seemed relieved when I nodded. He sat motionless, his eyes never leaving the boys, applauding loudly and unable to hide his disappointment when I called a halt after an hour.

Chief Lelactei led me into the meeting house and, with Reuben translating from Bislama to what he imagined was French, said, "You must ask me questions."

I learned that his tribe had come down from the mountains to a nearby mission station twenty years before. The missionaries had ordered them to abandon their *kastom*, but his grandfather had secretly taught him the old dances and legends. Two years before, he had taken his family away from the mission and built this traditional village. Since then, his brother's wife had died, and his wife had become unwell and moved in with her father. The only inhabitants of this village now were himself, his brother, and their twelve sons and three daughters. He believed more people would be leaving the missions. They felt abandoned because the white missionaries had returned to Europe. There would soon be new *kastom* villages like this one all along this coast. What I had just witnessed was Malekula's past, and its future.

The cannibals may be gone, but most of us have prison islands in our backyards. The same isolation and freedom from mainland scrutiny that make islands so appealing also make them great places for a prison. In fact, so many islands have served as prisons that the words are almost as inseparable as "island" and "paradise."

Nelson Mandela spent eighteen years in a closet-sized cell on Robben Island, and Dr. Samuel Mudd, who set John Wilkes Booth's leg, spent four years on Fort Jefferson in the Dry Tortugas. Thailand shipped its political prisoners to Ko Tarutao, the Chinese banished out-of-favor officials to Hainan in the South China Sea, and nineteenth-century Chilean regimes incarcerated opponents on Isla Robinson Crusoe, where they languished in caves hacked from a cliff above San Juan. Australian Aborigines went to Rottnest Island, prisoners thought too incorrigible for Australia served out sentences in leg irons on Norfolk Island, and the Union held Confederate prisoners on Johnson Island near Sandusky, Ohio. The British turned the Andamans into a penal colony after the 1857–1858 Indian Uprising, and used St. Helena as a prison camp during the Boer War. There is even a Prisoners Island near my home, an islet in Lake George that the British and French both used during the French and Indian Wars.

The connection between islands and prisons has contributed to islophobia. When Napoléon Bonaparte saw St. Helena, the South Atlantic island where he died in exile, he remarked that it rose from the sea "like an enormous black wart." It is a pretty enough island, but for islophobes, no island can ever be pretty, sunny, or friendly enough to outweigh its baggage of exile and confinement. For them, an island's small population promises a hell of repetitive social encounters, its silence is worse than tinnitus, its insulation from the mainland a painful exile, and its limited space an Alcatraz cell writ large.

Even native islanders are not immune to these emotions. José Maria had told me that Isla Crusoeans who had never flown became nervous when storms suspended flights to their island, and I heard that when the ferry to Islay from Jura had suddenly been taken out of service for emergency repairs, people who had not left the island in months turned testy. There are practical reasons for this reaction. On a weathered-in island, routine medical emergencies become catastrophic, and there is always the danger, as on Niihau after Pearl Harbor, of intruders seizing control of an island until links with the mainland are restored.

Tami's Barentsburg exile reminded me of Devil's Island, and accusations that the Robinsons had turned Niihau into an Alcatraz brought the real one to mind. Two of the most frightening and heartbreaking island sites I have ever seen are the bench at Devil's Island, where for many years the unjustly imprisoned Captain Alfred Dreyfus sat staring out to sea toward France, and the solitary confinement cells on the D block in Alcatraz that allowed a prisoner to see, through bars, the Golden Gate Bridge, soaring seagulls, and a bay busy with ferries and sailboats. When the wind blew in the right direction, he could even be tortured by the sound of bands playing in waterfront music halls. The bench offered empty horizons and the despair of imprisonment thousands of miles from home; the cell, the torture of imprisonment surrounded by beauty and joy.

Many of the island jails I have seen have a similar appearance and

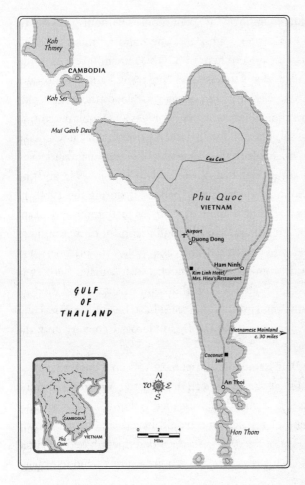

atmosphere. On both Devil's Island and Senegal's Île de Gorée, where slaves were held before being sent to the New World, fingers of hibiscus slithered through iron bars, lizards raced through the empty cellblocks, cicadas screeched like subway brakes, and walls, damp and green with fungus and clutched in vines, were still releasing a miasma of suffering and despair.

Several displays at the War Remnants Museum in Ho Chi Minh City (which I will call Saigon from now on because everyone else does) reminded me of the "bear pits" on Devil's Island, cells where inmates sentenced to solitary confinement spent months without speaking or seeing the sun. At Con Son, an island one hundred miles off Vietnam's south coast, the government of South Vietnam threw its worst enemies into similar "dog kennels" and "pig traps," and the museum re-creations of these were realistic enough to silence the largest parties of chattering schoolchildren. Next door was an exhibit memorializing the "Coconut Jail," a much larger prison on Phu Quoc, a teardrop-shaped island forty-five miles west of the mainland. The French colonial authorities had opened this prison in 1953 and the government of South Vietnam had expanded it during the 1960s to twelve sections capable of holding as many as forty thousand Communist prisoners. A card underneath photographs of former inmates strangled by steel wire declared, "The camp policy for prisoners was very cruel. Guards applied electric shocks, beat inmates with steel rods, and burned them alive." Four thousand prisoners had died on Phu Quoc, and the remains of a thousand have been disinterred and buried under a white obelisk at the Dead Heroes Cemetery near the Phu Quoc airport.

For me, the War Remnants Museum served up a confusing double helping of guilt: at what had been done by the Americans and the South Vietnamese, and that I had escaped doing it. It was a tricky place for someone of my age who would have seen Vietnam thirty years before had it not been for a medical deferment based on three large carbuncles on my rear that had required surgery and left major scars.

Many exhibits at the museum offered the through-the-looking-glass experience of seeing Americans play roles usually reserved for Germans and Japanese. A hollow-eyed American sergeant in a diorama resembled a debauched ape, and in one photograph some freckle-faced boys held up severed heads. Other pictures showed Americans dragging corpses behind tanks and pressing guns to the heads of Vietnamese. In the courtyard, kids ran their hands over a captured American helicopter, tank, and fighter plane, and souvenir stalls sold American shell fragments, dog tags, and Zippo lighters. I had been warned these were mostly fakes manufactured for the tourist trade, but I pawed through them anyway, searching for a familiar name.

The engraved Zippos were as repellent and fascinating as shrunken heads, and like them made you want to know more. What had happened to the soldier who had engraved on a lighter, "We are the unwilling, led by the unqualified, doing the unnecessary, for the ungrateful"? Or to the one choosing as his motto, "When the trooper dies he will rot in the mud like any other fucking animal"? And was the man whose Zippo declared "When I kill the only feeling I have is the recoil from my rifle" responsible for any of the crimes in the Hall of Atrocities?

Before coming to Vietnam I had corresponded with a Vietnam veteran I will call Roger Sayle who had served in a detachment of sixty Air Force personnel based at Phu Quoc's Duong Dong airport, located about twenty miles north of Coconut Jail. At first, he made Phu Quoc sound like Vietnam's Bali-ha'i, telling me how he and his buddies passed the time body-surfing, visiting local families, and observing a live-and-let-live policy with the Vietcong. When one of their jeeps hit a land mine they declared it a loss and painted it pink, turning it into a beach buggy. He had arrived in Vietnam a Goldwater Republican and left married to a Vietnamese woman and convinced America was on the wrong side.

But the more we spoke and corresponded, the less Phu Quoc sounded like a jolly Espíritu Santo of slaphappy *South Pacific* sailors. In our last exchange, he asked me to find out what happened to some civilians his unit had wounded, saying, "They walked into our sensors by mistake and we blew them away. I sure wish I knew if they were okay." He had helped lay out battery-powered lights on the landing strip so they could be medevacked to Saigon and had wondered about them ever since. And while I was at it, could I check on the wife of the local Vietcong commander? Some gung-ho Navy SEALs new to Phu Quoc had captured her, breaking the informal truce. He also felt guilty about what he and his buddies had done to some kids. "Some of it was expecting little kids to pull a gun on us, and some of it was just being plain mean and hateful to the weakest people on the island," he wrote. "Little kids at the dump would get in the way as we dumped slop from the mess hall—this was a few miles from the compound and we were in a hurry to get back—so we dumped the slop right on top of them, laughing as we did it. . . . Those kids were five to ten years old then, now they would be nearly forty and might not care for Americans too much."

The small propeller plane I took from Saigon descended over the beach where Sayle had surfed and taxied past the obelisk marking the graves of Coconut Jail's inmates. I had bought a packet of Phu Quoc postcards from a souvenir stall near the "pig cages" in the museum. They showed fishermen framed against a red sunset, wavy ridges of green hills, and some lovely beaches. The caption sounded a familiar alarm: "Geography, nature and location of Phu Quoc are very attractive to build up big tourist and special economic zone." But from the air I could see no evidence of any development, only a pretty island with a ridge of thickly forested hills and miles of empty beach.

A motorbike taximan grabbed my bag and drove me through Duong Dong, a tumbledown port hugging the last curve of a sewage-blackened stream. Two miles later, we turned down a track to the Kim Linh Hotel where I paid eight dollars for a room with a bed and mosquito net and found what may be the best island beach and restaurant on earth. The beaches of Ko Samui, a Thai island 250 miles across the Gulf of Thailand from Phu Quoc are as lovely as the Kim Linh's, but are lined with package tour resorts and backpacker bungalows, and patrolled by boys selling handicrafts, and women pestering you to have a massage. The Kim Linh's beach stretched for miles. It was undercrowded, but not lonely. The boats anchored just offshore belonged to families living in thatched huts under the palms.

Fishermen landed their catch on the sand and children splashed in the water. They accepted the Kim Linh's guests as temporary residents, and the guests, mostly expatriates from Saigon, tolerated their cooking fires, squabbling dogs, and squealing babies.

Fifty yards down the beach, Mrs. Hieu's little restaurant sat perched on bamboo poles above a two-foot escarpment of sand marking high tide. It was wood and thatch, so flimsy that every gust of wind sent it rocking like a ship. There were five tables, three on a shaded deck and two on the sand. The Hieus slept in the rear and cooked over charcoal. Mr. Hieu caught the restaurant's fish. His teenage children, Anh, Tho, and Hai, bought vegetables in the market on their way home from school and helped in the kitchen. For my first meal, Tho cooked shrimp soup with lemongrass, basil, and coconut while her mother grilled baby squid to serve in a light garlic sauce. The gas lamps hissed and the water lapped below the floor. When I went to pay, Tho and her sister Hai were bent over their schoolbooks. Hai wore a long-sleeved red tunic and black trousers, the same outfit I had noticed on a dead girl in a My Lai massacre photograph at the War Remnants Museum.

I was in no hurry to visit the Coconut Jail or find the men Roger Sayle had showered with slops. I liked the Kim Linh's beach so much that for four days I never left it. I lay in a hammock reading, napping, and watching the boys sport like dolphins. I walked down the sand for miles without seeing another foreigner. I ate whatever Mrs. Hieu suggested: fluffy omelets, creamy coconut-based soups and fiery ones with whole chilies, red snapper rubbed with ginger, and delicate imperial rolls with fish sauce from Phu Quoc's own factory. I pulled bottles of beer and water from a Styrofoam cooler and kept my own tab, paying about ten dollars a day for my drinks and three meals. I could happily have followed this routine for weeks. My metabolism fell to hibernation level and I became increasingly incurious about the rest of Phu Quoc. Mrs. Hieu's food was lotus.

I shared Mrs. Hieu's with a young Frenchwoman from Saigon

who was a good candidate for an Isla Robinson Crusoe exile. She spent her days reading *romans policiers* and patting the stray dogs. Her own pockmarked doggy face stayed frozen in a tragic expression. She looked daggers at children who wandered too close, and she chain-smoked Marlboros, stamping out the butts like a Nazi putting in the boot. Every evening she sat motionless, eyes fixed on the setting sun, dabbing at tears and downing a beer in quick gulps. She dined alone, always on grilled squid, and discouraged conversation. I asked if she had been to Phu Quoc before. She sighed and said, "Many, *many* times."

The other regulars were a French couple in their fifties who suggested Yves Montand and Simone Signoret gone to seed. He was walrus-sized, with a curly mane of gray hair. She was fey and flirtatious. Their building in Lyon provided enough income to allow them to winter in what they called "Indochine," and they had been here three months, staying at the Kim Linh and eating at Mrs. Hieu's. "Why move?" he asked. The Hieu family was very *sympathique*, Tho was the best cook in Indochine, this was the best restaurant in Asia, and the people were kind and welcoming. No, he did not mean the people of Phu Quoc were kind, just those living on this beach. What could they know about the others since they went to town only once a week to check the *poste restante*? The roads were unpaved and dusty, so traveling by motorbike was a horror. Besides, there was nothing to see.

To support this judgment he handed me a file of historical articles about Phu Quoc culled from the Lyon public library. A 1960 article described it as "wild forest surrounded by a perfect beach."

"We are *on* this perfect beach," he said, "so why go anywhere else?"

They had become champions of the lazy life travel brochures would have you believe is Crusoean, although it is really the antithesis. They lived in their bathing suits and lay in hammocks for hours smoking Gitanes and staring at the ocean, breathing at the rate of wintering bears. They slurped Tho's exquisite soups in silence and rationed their books, reading a few pages a day and often falling asleep with one open on their gently heaving stomachs. He ran his fingers through her sun-streaked hair. She absent-mindedly massaged his thigh. Every day at four they disappeared into their room for a marathon of lovemaking.

They worried I might overpay the motorbike taximen or tip the Hieus and ruin Phu Quoc—for them. But they were pleased to discover I spoke French and asked me to act as translator between themselves and Pham Thi Kiem, their favorite Kim Linh chambermaid. They believed she was too intelligent to be cleaning rooms (she was), and were making it their charitable project to introduce her to a mainland businessman who needed a secretary. Despite spending five winters in Vietnam, they had not bothered learning Vietnamese, and Kiem's only foreign language was English. They said this made her one of only two English-speakers on this island of thirty thousand or seventy thousand people, depending on whom you believed.

Had I been an American soldier based in Saigon in 1969 I might have fallen for Pham Thi Kiem, too. Like many Vietnamese women, she was coquettish and tough, part geisha and part Bangkok bar girl. Her body had widened with age but her teeth were perfect, and she had preserved the pretty, unlined face of the teenager who fell in love with the American soldier who had taught her English. "Jim Koch, Jim Koch, Koch, Koch, Koch," she repeated. "See, say it fast and it sounds like cash."

When they met she was living with an uncle and working as a waitress. He had blue eyes and blond hair, "very, very curly," she said, twirling her fingers. "His lips were like mine, not too fat, not too thin. Think, the same lips! Oh, he was perfect for me!"

He proposed marriage a month before leaving Vietnam and they became engaged, *really* engaged. His parents announced it in their hometown newspaper in Idaho and mailed her a clipping. His father wrote a letter welcoming her to the family. His mother said she would be proud to have her as a daughter. His baby brother sent finger paintings. During their last week together, he bought her a motorbike and took her on vacation. He fell off while teaching her to ride it and she saw him for the last time in a military hospital. He had promised to send for her the moment he returned home. Six years later, Saigon fell and she burned his letters and photographs, even the clipping announcing their engagement. Any evidence of an American friendship was enough to send you to a reeducation camp, so all across the city little backyard fires blazed, turning thousands of American-Vietnamese love affairs into smoke.

Kiem told me all this as we sat at one of Mrs. Hieu's tables. It was an hour before dark on the only west-facing, sunset beach in Vietnam. At the next table Yves and Simone were pawing and rubbing thighs.

I could not bear to ask her why Jim Koch had not sent for her. He had probably met someone at home or decided she was a wartime infatuation. Who cared? All I had done was compliment her English, and now I knew all this, and had more reason to feel guilty.

She finally noticed Yves and Simone. When they headed for their room, she said, "I came to Phu Quoc to escape my husband, my *Vietnamese* husband." Until two years ago, she had lived with her husband and three teenage children near the mainland town of Rach Gia. When he left her for a younger woman, it became too painful to remain in their village. She ruled out Saigon as too noisy and crowded, and chose Phu Quoc for the usual island reasons, silence and solitude. She had also wanted to place some water between herself and the tragedy of her marriage. She had quit her first job of waiting tables at the government-owned Hong Bien Hotel because it was too noisy and she hated making conversation with the customers.

■

Mrs. Hieu's was like Rick's in the movie *Casablanca*: sooner or later everyone turned up there. One night, two teenagers named Hiep and Minh invited themselves to my table to practice the English Kiem was teaching them. They drank Cokes and strung together one unintelligible sentence after another. Kiem stopped to say, "These are *very* charming boys, don't you think?" Maybe. But in a different country, I might not have humored them for so long.

I drank beer with an Australian shaped like a punching bag who had fought in Vietnam. Now he was house-sitting for the manager of a joint Vietnamese-Australian cultured pearl venture that was being strangled by red tape. He said dozens of former Australian and American veterans had retired to Saigon, sometimes living in the same neighborhoods they had known as young men, even frequenting the same bars. Why not? Where else could you enjoy a deluxe life on a sergeant's pension? He paid six dollars a night for a hotel room with clean sheets, and he could bring up a girl whenever he wanted. Saigon was coming back full circle to what it had been during the war.

Everyone at the Kim Linh and Mrs. Hieu's agreed that Phu Quoc's only English-speakers were Kiem and a fixer and jack-of-all-trades called "Billy," so I was surprised to hear flawless American English being spoken by two Vietnamese teenagers who were drinking Cokes with their parents. The boy said, "Mister, I learned my English in Dodge City, Kansas."

His father, Nguyen, wore khaki trousers and a striped polo shirt over his middle-American paunch. His mother had a dragon lady silk dress, heavy makeup, and long nails. He was relaxed, she was edgy. She disparaged her children as "lazy," which they were, compared to their parents, who had fled Phu Quoc in 1977 at the age of seventeen. Most young people left then, Nguyen said. He was about to be drafted and did not want to live under Communism. He and his wife spent two days in an open boat, then six months in a Thai refugee camp before flying to the United States, where they had both worked ever since in a meat-packing plant. They had returned two months ago to bury her dying mother. "We come for her funeral," she complained, "but she won't die!" The children had missed school and their airline tickets were about to expire. Refugee children were often summoned back to Phu Quoc like this, for a last reunion with sick parents who refused to die.

Nguyen would have been nine in 1969—the age of the boys Sayle covered with slop. But how do you ask a man if he once scavenged for food in a dump? Finally, I asked if he had any contact with the American soldiers on Phu Quoc.

"They lived at the airport so we rarely saw them," he said.

"Do you remember where they took their garbage?"

He shot his wife a worried look. After twenty years in Dodge City they had probably encountered their share of wiggy Vietnam vets, and here, on Phu Quoc of all places, was one more.

■

A 1908 monograph of the Indochinese Study Society that Yves gave me predicted that the "indolence" of Phu Quoc's population and its lack of good transport facilities would keep it a backwater. Despite the line on the War Remnants Museum postcard about tourist and economic zones, this prediction held true, and as I swung in Mrs. Hieu's hammock I congratulated myself on finding such a perfect anti–Pleasure Spot, although to be honest all I had found was the Kim Linh beach. It had taught me nothing about island prisons, but lots about island sloth, and how islands encourage it for the same reason they encourage sensuality, because you can spend all day in a hammock on Phu Quoc, or recline with lovers on orgy couches in Capri, and no one will see you.

The Kim Linh beach was a Capri of sloth. I forgot about skin cancer and picked up the best tan of my life. I drank midmorning beers and dozed until lunch. I spent hours watching a circle of women fishing with nets and became friends with one of the distinctive Phu Quoc dogs that have a line of hair growing forward along their backs. (They are related to the Rhodesian Ridgeback, and because Phu Quoc is the only place where they are found outside southern Africa it is assumed they were introduced by African slave traders, making them another typical island relic.) I convinced myself I was becoming an accepted member of the community because the locals smiled and waved and Mrs. Hieu brought *amuse-geules* to my table. I was in no hurry to return to Saigon and check out the bars popular with the retired Allied soldiers and watch its graceful colonial-era architecture being jackhammered to smithereens to make space for chain hotels and skyscraper apartments for expatriates. To be honest, now that I had found this paradise I was in no hurry to climb onto a motorbike and bounce over the washboard roads back to filthy Duong Dong, or poke around whatever remained of Coconut Jail.

A line of afternoon clouds and showers finally persuaded me to see Phu Quoc's showplace, the government-owned Huong Bien Hotel in Duong Dong. It was a phenomenally ugly pile, the twin of those cheap apartment buildings that surround Moscow. On an island with beaches to spare, the government had built its hotel on the only polluted one, where a black line of offal from the mouth of the Duong Dong river marked high tide. Six clocks showing the time in cities like Paris and Hong Kong hinted at the plugged-in future the People's Committee of Kien Giang province was planning for Phu Quoc.

The next day I walked a quarter mile north from the Kim Linh and found a bulldozer preparing the ground for an even larger government hotel. Nearby was the Club Tropicana, a Kim Linh–sized hotel whose owner and manager, the dapper Mr. Cuong, had been a pilot in the South Vietnamese air force. He said he had moved to Phu Quoc because he loved islands and this was the most natural and beautiful one left in Asia. He had sold his hotel in Da Lat and was betting everything on the Club Trop. He had widened its beach with a tractor, sited its restaurant on a bluff with sunset views, sent his son to study hotel management in Switzerland, and insisted on thatched roofs. "Go on, monsieur, look around," he challenged. "I defy you to find plastic at the Club Trop."

His sixteen rooms and bungalows were empty except for a Swiss couple, his *fruits de mer* tank was cracked and leaking, his future swimming pool a dusty hole. He said he would be repairing the tank so its dragonhead fountain would again spray water onto langoustines and crayfish. And soon the hole would be a freshwater swimming pool, backed by tennis courts. But as we drank Cokes and admired the sunset, I noticed that the "Club Trop" patch on the waiter's green uniform hung by a thread.

"Sure, I'm a dreamer," Mr. Cuong admitted. "But how can Club Trop fail?" Europeans loved the sun and the beach, and Phu Quoc had the best beach in Asia. It was that simple. He feared only that Phu Quoc might become too popular. He wanted enough guests to fill his rooms, no more. Thailand's Ko Phuket and Ko Samui had once been like this, but now they were horrors. If the same thing happened here, he would move to a smaller island, and if it happened there, he would move again, and again, until there were no islands left, or he was living on a rock.

I hired Kiem to accompany me to Coconut Jail as an interpreter. When she appeared the next morning dressed like Hai, in a long-sleeved red tunic and black trousers, I almost asked her to change. "Jim gave me a Yamaha like this," she said, climbing onto the motorbike taxi. "He left it as a present but I sold it when I saw the film he made in Taiwan."

Before I could ask "What film?" we started off. An island with no paved roads and less than a dozen cars sounds great until you try traveling anywhere. Phu Quoc's roads were obstacle courses of washboard, dips, and holes. El Niño had brought a scorching drought and motorbikes traveling in the opposite direction threw up walls of red dust. The country south of the Kim Linh looked ravaged by forest fires, and after half an hour I was ready to concede that Simone might be right, there really *was* nothing to see on Phu Quoc, and no reason to leave the Kim Linh.

A few miles before An Thoi, a port at the southern tip of the island, we sped past the Coconut Jail. I caught a glimpse of an ugly colonial-era brick church whose windows and doors had been filled in with cinder blocks and mortar, then a line of new wooden buildings I took for housing for sailors from a nearby naval base.

Our taximen refused to stop, claiming that the Coconut Jail lay within a prohibited area, the An Thoi naval base. When we halted a few miles later for sodas, they insisted there had been nothing to see anyway. The South Vietnamese government had bulldozed the barracks in 1972 (after the Paris peace accords), and after the Communist victory the church became a reeducation center for the South Vietnamese guards. The new barracks were a replica of Coconut Jail the government was building for the tourists who would arrive on jets and fill the Huong Bien Hotel.

An Thoi was even filthier and shabbier than Duong Dong, with stained and crumbling concrete shop houses and open sewers running black, as if fleets of trucks had just changed their oil in them. The children wore rags, but the sailors promenading with their families and girlfriends looked healthy and scrubbed.

Kiem and I were coated with red dust and had perspired through our clothes. We stopped at a café for beer and squid, and I finally asked the question puzzling me all morning, "*What* film made you sell Jim's Yamaha?"

"The film his best friend made me watch." Her voice was flat. "It showed them both making love to prostitutes in Taiwan during their leave. His friend thought if I saw it I would be so mad at Jim I would make love to him." Instead, she had screamed, broken crockery, and beaten Jim's friend with a chair. He had massacred her love. She cried for three days and considered suicide. Finally she recorded a cassette tape and mailed it to Jim in the United States. She said nasty, unforgivable things on it. He never replied, and never sent for her.

"Maybe he never married. Maybe he's divorced. Oh, I hope so!" She clapped her hands. Could her life turn around again? If she had never seen that film, never made that cassette, she might be an Idaho housewife with an American husband and American children, and if she found Jim again, anything could happen.

I admitted the Internet made locating people easier.

"Maybe he tried to contact me after 1975, but all he knew was my uncle's address. Tell him I'm older and wiser. Tell him I was a child when he needed a woman. Tell him I understand men and I don't blame him for Taiwan. If he's married, tell him we can be friends.

"Help me find him," she whispered, "and I'll never forget you."

I bribed our drivers to take us to Coconut Jail on the way back. We turned down a track leading to the water despite a sign warning that it was a military zone. The guardhouse was empty and the drivers admitted that the military permitted tourists to swim at the beach on Sundays, but they said people would become suspicious if we wandered around.

We stopped at a line of ruined foundations, all that remained of one Coconut Jail compound. There was nothing to tell you four thousand people had died here, no plaque, no photographs of skulls pierced by nails, none of the menace of a Devil's Island or Alcatraz. I felt as disappointed as someone watching a horror movie that fails to deliver a good fright. The other decommissioned island prisons I had seen had been just that, I realized, good horror movies, and perhaps that explained their curious appeal, and the charm of other frightening islands. They were all safe scares. Instead of lights coming up in a theater, there was always a ferry or plane to the mainland.

I kicked the stony ground, looking for proof of what had once been here. Kiem found a piece of barbed wire. "Perhaps French, but more likely from the time of the American war," she said, turning away and slipping it into her purse.

■

The more everyone warned me about "Billy"—and even Mrs. Hieu made a face when I mentioned his name—the more determined I became to meet him. They said he met every plane to offer his services to foreigners, but he had not met mine. They said I should tell the motorbike taximen that I wanted Billy and he would be at my doorstep in an hour, but a week passed before a mascot-sized man with a wispy mustache limped across the sand to my table. His eyes darted and he cringed like a cur expecting a kick. "Call me Billy," he said. "It's the name my American father gave me."

Some people have their history written on their faces. Billy's was on his toes. They were cracked and gnarled, more like talons. A bloody bandage covered two he had cut in a motorbike accident. He had patched himself up ("no money for a doctor"), and today was the first time in days he could walk.

He pulled off a filthy baseball cap advertising the Guess line of designer clothes and asked me to help him find Captain Giddy, his American father. If you subtracted this Giddy from Billy's life story, Billy was just another member of South Vietnam's former army of teenage fixers. He had learned English hanging around an American camp in Da Nang and made himself useful by informing on drug dealers. Giddy had bought him clothes, sent him to a church school, and adopted him so he could become an American citizen. He was supposed to follow Giddy to America when he turned eighteen in 1973, but his mother became so distraught at the thought of losing her only son that he kept postponing his departure. When the Communists won, he burned his adoption papers and fled to Saigon, adopting disguises and frequently changing his name. He was careful to speak Vietnamese, but he dreamed in English.

He assumed I wanted his help in buying beachfront property for a small hotel, a service that had become his specialty. He scouted the land, interpreted, and closed the deal. He had helped a German purchase land for a bungalow colony and was working with some Canadians. A Korean had opened forty cottages. The wife of Hanoi's mayor was looking. Perhaps there would be a big French hotel. Everyone had plans for Phu Quoc. Mrs. Hieu, he said with satisfaction, was doomed.

I asked if he knew anyone who remembered the wartime Americans and Coconut Jail.

He believed all its former inmates had returned to the mainland, and many of the Phu Quoc people from those days had escaped to America. But he was acquainted with a former South Vietnamese military policeman who had been a guard and still lived near the prison, although he might be too frightened to talk.

But Billy was a fixer, so he fixed this, too, and the following morning found me sitting on the back of his motorbike, my arms wrapped around his twenty-eight-inch waist as he drove me back to Coconut Jail.

The former guard lived in a village within the military zone. While Billy went to fetch him, I traded stares with a military policeman in the guardhouse and watched workmen putting the finishing touches on the Coconut Jail replica. The new barracks were the best housing I had seen on Phu Quoc.

Billy had left me reciting the mantra of the third world fixer, "No problem, no problem," but of course there always is. For years the former guard had been cadging tips, beers, and meals from the relatives of his inmates in exchange for leading them to the mass graves containing their loved ones, where they left flowers and sometimes returned after dark with shovels to dig. But I was his first American, Billy said, and this was making him nervous. He would talk to me, but not lead me to the graves or walk me through the ruins.

He impressed me as a man who had never experienced a nervous day in his life, and he was as animated as a sleeping lizard. The lids of his owly eyes had taken over his face so it resembled an African mask. He had enlisted in the French army in 1953 and still carried himself as if General de Gaulle were about to pin a medal on his tunic. He ended so many statements with "Fucking Communists!" I began to suspect a verbal tic.

I promised never to reveal his name and we all three jammed ourselves onto Billy's motorbike. He leaned back and said, "I saw a documentary about Coconut Jail on television. It said we burned prisoners alive, but I promise you, sir, we never did *that* thing."

His favorite café was deserted at 10:30 A.M. Without being asked, the waitress set down three beers, a glass of ice, a cold beef salad, and some fish and rice, his traditional revealing-the-grave-of-a-loved-one meal.

He downed the beers in quick succession and attacked the television documentary again, saying, "We never roasted prisoners on a spit or tied them in sacks. Fucking Communists!" He was not just any guard, he boasted, but head guard from 1971 to 1973, when Coconut Jail held ten thousand prisoners. Because Phu Quoc was an island, few of his "clients" ever escaped for good. Once his prisoners had protested their conditions. "But they became too noisy so we fired on them and some died." He shrugged. "Fucking Communists!"

He ordered three more beers and said he preferred entertaining relatives of dead prisoners to meeting his former "clients" in person. They were ungrateful and cheap, refusing to buy beers or tip him— "Fucking Communists!"

I asked about the incidents Sayle had described. He did not recall any wounded civilians but remembered the Americans arresting the wife of the VC commander. They had been too soft and released her. Too bad.

Two Vietnamese sailors in uniform entered the café. Immediately the guard stiffened and fell silent. Billy cringed. There was a roomful of empty tables but the sailors sat next to us. They ordered coconuts and glanced at us sideways as they sucked milk through pink straws. A foreigner drinking in here with two Vietnamese had made them suspicious. Billy gestured for me to hide my notebook and whispered, "No English."

As the sailors left they gave us backward glances. Billy said: "You see how it is with us. A sheet of glass that's invisible to outsiders separates the Communists from anyone in our generation who supported the South. Those boys sensed it. We can never feel comfortable with them."

The guard chugged his last beer. He insisted the police still followed and watched him. It would continue until he died. The sailors would report him and the owners of the café would be questioned. "Fucking Communists!"

"They may question me, too," Billy added. "You're lucky to be leaving tomorrow, Thurston. They may stop you at the airport, but they'll let you go."

I thought they were paranoid and that I was unlikely to be interrogated, but the possibility gave my last day on Phu Quoc a not entirely unpleasant frisson of danger.

Only five planes a week connect Phu Quoc with Saigon and their arrival and departure are major events. Many of the people I had met were at the terminal when I left, and Billy was limping through the concourse, handing out his business card to new arrivals. No one had questioned him, not yet, and his last words to me were, "You spell my father's name G-I-D-D-Y."

As the plane gained altitude I saw the white obelisk marking the graves of a thousand Coconut Jail prisoners. I had liked Phu Quoc, but I was relieved to be leaving. If all islands, by virtue of their geography, echo Devil's Island and Alcatraz, then another of their charms may be the curious feeling of escape and liberation that sometimes accompanies your departure from them.

12

PLEASURE SPOTS — GRAND CAYMAN
AND ROATÁN

I looked for Captain Giddy and Jim Koch, calling people with similar names I found through Internet searches, but no one was the right age or had served in Vietnam.

Six months before, the Internet had almost nothing about Phu Quoc; suddenly the search engines provided dozens of hits. A Saigon investment newsletter reported that ground had been broken for a government resort at the airport beach and advised, "Go to Phu Quoc. Go quickly. . . . It's developing fast." The schemes "pending" or "under construction" reminded me of plans for making Niihau the Las Vegas of the Pacific. A Singapore investment group proposed a $500 million development of resorts and offshore banks. A Vancouver outfit was offering to make Phu Quoc the "Asian Bermuda." Some Frenchmen called their hotel and casino scheme "Phu Quoc— A Monaco of Vietnam."

Aside from Nantucket, Kuda Huraa, and the Taj Lagoon, I had so far avoided Pleasure Spot islands. But finding an island in the Caribbean that was not a mooring block for cruise liners or a mass tourism playground was a challenge. I had liked Bequia in the Grenadines when the only way to reach it was a slow-moving and infrequent schooner from St. Vincent, but now it had an airport and direct flights to Barbados. Cozumel, once a backwater of pensiones, azure waters, and virgin reefs, saw a million and a half day-trippers a year, and a new cruise liner dock was being constructed four hundred yards from its most popular dive site, Paradise Reef. I had been stunned by St. Lucia's lush and jagged mountains in the early 1980s, but many of its hotels had since become all-inclusive resorts whose guests paid one price for everything (to the despair of local merchants), seldom left the grounds, and had inspired a calypso that ended:

> *Buying up every strip of beach,*
> *Every treasured spot they reach.*

The words "island" and "discovery" have had a tricky relationship. The history of European exploration teaches that islands, by their very geographic nature, demand discovery, yet most island-lovers, by their nature, want undiscovered islands. When I hear about an undiscovered island my head tells me it is probably too late but my heart says: Who knows? Perhaps it's a Bali in 1900. Or Key West in 1970.

When I offered "undiscovered island" or "Crusoe" to the Internet, it produced George Nowak, a German calypso singer living on Grand Cayman who is known to his fans as "Barefoot Man," and to his friends simply as "Foot." He sounded like someone who would know about undiscovered Caribbean islands. The editor of a diving magazine praised him as "a modern-day Magellan," searching out islands "unknown and untouched by commercial development" whose cultures had avoided being "diluted or destroyed." And I liked it that, like me, he had spent his early years bent over library atlases and *National Geographic*s as he imagined traveling to small and remote islands. We even shared an early fondness for *An Island to Oneself*, the autobiography of Tom Neale, the New Zealand beachcomber who during the 1950s and 1960s had marooned himself for a total of five years on uninhabited Suwarrow in the Cook Islands.

I reread Neale's book before going to Grand Cayman to meet Barefoot and was disappointed to discover that my hero had been a rather monochromatic beachcomber. His story had no shipwrecks, acts of heroism, or Polynesian beauties. His principal accomplishment had been living alone on Suwarrow. He had chosen this island out of admiration for Robert Dean Frisbie, who had preceded him there, but Frisbie had also sired a rambunctious half-Polynesian family, contributed to *The Atlantic Monthly*, and written two well-received novels.

Despite Barefoot's professed admiration for Neale, his own book, *Which Way to the Islands?*, made him sound more like a Frisbie. He had moved to North Carolina with his German mother after she married an American serviceman, and at eighteen headed to Nashville, where he swept floors in recording studios while attempting to become a country-and-western star. He hitchhiked to the Virgin Islands, taught himself to sing calypso, wandered to Hawaii, settled on a Bahamian out island, married a fifteen-year-old girl, and arrived on Grand Cayman in 1971, carrying his possessions in a paper bag.

Then, the island had six taxi drivers instead of a thousand, and 3 banks instead of 286. Its docks handled fish instead of cruise passengers, and its Seven Mile Beach, the Caribbean's longest and most beautiful, was just palm trees and empty sand, at least until one morning in 1975 when Barefoot saw a yellow bulldozer knocking down lines of palms. When the driver said he was clearing land for a Holiday Inn, Barefoot thought it was the end of Grand Cayman, never imagining his band would play at this Holiday Inn for twenty-three years, singing "Yellow Bird" 5,400 times.

"Yes, readers, I know what you're thinking," he wrote in his book, anticipating my question. "I wish this guy would make up his mind; does he want to be Robinson Crusoe or play in the cocktail lounge of a Holiday Inn?"

When we spoke on the phone, Barefoot urged me to hurry. Some

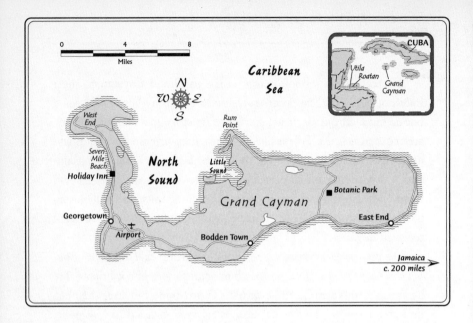

investors had just bought the Holiday Inn and planned to tear it down for a Ritz-Carlton. Most Caymanians were outraged. The Holiday Inn had become a beloved landmark, the only hotel with genuine island character, and the last place left for Caymanians and visitors to rub shoulders. Demolishing it for a Ritz-Carlton would be the final nail in the Caymanian coffin.

I did not expect much from an island whose most gemütlich gathering place was a 1975 Holiday Inn. Even so, I was astonished to land in such a perfectly realized anti-island. Its terrain was dull as a mowed lawn, so featureless even Columbus sailed past without stopping. Much of the scrub pine and sea grape had been cleared for a Sunbelt catastrophe of slapdash minimalls and gimcrack condos. Cruise liners might dump as many as five thousand passengers a day (on an island whose population was only forty-five thousand), and I assume this was why taxi drivers rebuffed my attempts at conversation, clerks stared through me, and everyone I met in the first twenty-four hours, black, white, expatriate, or Caymanian, was surly, bored, or both.

Prices were astronomical because the government imposed a hefty sales tax instead of an income tax. I paid a hundred dollars a night at a backstreet motel for a garden shed–sized room smelling of old cheese, ate mushy grouper at a restaurant under the airport flight path, and drank five-dollar beers at a downtown bar with soft-featured expatriates working in various offshore banks and enterprises. They had mops of blond hair and wore striped shirts with white collars, and their conversation was as nourishing as cotton candy. The gist of it was that because Grand Cayman had no income tax it attracted the world's rootless wealthy, people with so few ties to family and community they cheerfully relocated to this British crown colony for the pleasure of watching their money pile up, tax free. They lived in houses and condos that could cost over a million dollars if they came with gates and security guards. The Caymanians, "lucky buggers," filled cushy jobs in the government or the offshore financial industry and enjoyed the highest per capita income in the Caribbean. White ex-pats got high-priced office jobs. Jamaicans and Puerto Ricans mixed drinks and made beds. "Believe me," a yuppie white man said, "this island is paradise."

The next morning, I inched through Georgetown, the capital, with another morose cabbie, past the automobile dealerships that had foisted so many cars on Grand Cayman that during rush hours it might take an hour to travel three miles, and past the smoked-glass offices of attorneys representing 45,000 companies and the 592 banks holding $600 billion in deposits that made Grand Cayman the fifth-largest banking center in the world.

Seven Mile Beach was lined with condominiums and noisy with Jet Skis captained by children. It reeked of Coppertone and hamburger fat sizzling on charcoal. Cigarette butts and pop-tops littered the sand and NO TRESPASSING signs guarded lines of empty lounge chairs.

I ate the twin burrito lunch special at a Taco Bell while outside the window traffic crept down Seven Mile Beach Road. I thought about the Sentinelese, the last uncontacted islanders on earth who live on North Sentinel Island in the Andamans, an archipelago off the east coast of the Indian subcontinent. They are legendary for their hostility to trespassers, and their customary greeting is a shower of arrows. When anthropologists push canoes loaded with coconuts and eye-catching trinkets toward the shore, they shoot arrows at those, too.

Someone had left on my table a copy of *Key to Cayman*, a free magazine aimed at visitors. A letter of welcome from Mrs. L. Angela Martins, director of tourism, said, "Caymanians take pride in preserving the spirit of our heritage and culture. . . . We look forward to welcoming you . . . today and tomorrow, with an honest spirit of hospitality and warm, friendly smiles." Six months before, her government had banned a Norwegian Caribbean liner from dropping anchor because its passengers were homosexuals.

Back in Georgetown, the passengers off three Wal-Mart-shaped cruise liners were climbing into sightseeing buses or fanning out on foot to buy Coach handbags, Wedgwood dishes, Waterford crystal, and Dunhill knickknacks from tight-lipped blondes and yawning Caymanians. They gaped at ground-to-ceiling brass plates listing the names of phantom companies and searched for sights worth seeing in a city scraped clean of its history, architecture, and relics. The only attractions were a museum in the old courthouse whose principal mission was retailing souvenirs, a 1939 library and post office built from whitewashed cinder blocks, and a Caymanian National Trust marker beside a crumbling coral wall that announced, "The fort was demolished in 1972 following a battle between a developer and the planning authority."

Georgetown was a moribund little tax haven capital. The princes managing its money were invisible, specters in another dimension. Tinted glass protected their air-conditioned cars and office suites, their homes were gated and guarded, and their conscious minds were deeply buried in Wall Street, London, or Hong Kong.

I was sitting on the patio of a Georgetown snack bar, surrounded by passengers from the *Carnival Imagination*, when the sound system began blasting "Big Yellow Taxi." As the sky turned conch-shell pink, Joni Mitchell sang, "They paved paradise and put up a parking lot." But none of these hangdog seniors with their "Is this all there is?" scowls, or dough-faced frat boys (and when did college kids start taking cruises?) seemed to notice they were surrounded not just by parking lots, but by multistory garages.

Cruise liners are the most fearsome attack dogs the leisure industry looses on islands. What chance does a Grand Cayman, or especially a more naïve and simple island, have against the *Carnival Imagination*, or the higher-than-Niagara, longer-than-three-football-fields *Grand Princess*, or the yet unnamed 200,000-ton multihulled vessel said to resemble "four condominium complexes on a raft" that has its own wave machines and beaches, or the Royal Caribbean liner that entertains its four thousand passengers with a rock-climbing wall, water slide park, Rollerblading track, television studio, and ice rink, complete with a Zamboni resurfacing machine? Shipyards were turning out more and larger liners, but no one was building more islands, and even the smallest and most obscure were suddenly being added to itineraries. A thousand cruise passengers were flooding Caribbean islands with populations in the hundreds. In the Mediterranean, the liners had started calling at Pantelleria and Ischia, staples of guidebooks promising undiscovered islands. The *QE II* had even stopped at Funafuti, the capital of Tuvalu.

The shortage of visitable Caribbean islands was so serious some companies had bought or leased uninhabitable ones where they could land passengers for a few hours of beachcombing and snorkeling—ostensibly the full Crusoe experience. Orwell could have written the lines spoken by a *Sovereign of the Seas* passenger who, after disembarking on one of these islands for what the company called "a controlled shore experience," told a reporter for *Time* magazine, "There's nothing here but some palm trees. I'm going back to the ship to watch a movie."

I patronize Holiday Inns because when I was a civil rights worker in the South in the mid-1960s, they were the only hotels accommodating interracial parties. The Grand Cayman Holiday Inn was a flimsy motor hotel with floor-to-ceiling windows and lots of bright orange plastic, but I would have stayed there happily had Barefoot's nostalgic fans not booked all the rooms. Its staff was Caymanian and the waitresses, all gray-at-the-roots grandmothers, spoiled the children and fussed as if the food came from their own kitchens. When I asked about the impending sale they looked terrified. They were too old and slow for a Ritz-Carlton, and they knew it.

Lines of picnic tables surrounded the outdoor bandstand where Barefoot played. There was no cover or minimum and many people walked in from the beach. Fairy lights twinkled in trees and a waxing moon threw palm shadows onto a small dance floor. The temperature was a perfect tropical neutral.

Barefoot had a smooth face capped by a bowl of Beach Boy hair. He opened with "Matilda" and "Yellow Bird" before moving into his own mischievous compositions. His put-down of the popular calypso "Big Belly Man" was called "Big Panty Woman." It went, "I want to dance with a big panty woman, I want to give that big lady a whirl." My favorite lines in his song "Jimmy Swaggert and Jimmy Bakker" were, "While I'm living in a one-room shack, chasing away the mouse / You're eating T-bone steak in an air-conditioned house."

By the beginning of his second set the bar was three deep and a hundred dancers jammed the floor. The bank yuppies did a python wriggle. Gummy-mouthed Caymanian fishermen flapped their arms like chickens. Young female American office workers went pelvis-to-pelvis with predatory Englishmen. Barefoot slammed out "Hot, Hot, Hot" and an interracial forest of arms waved in the air like palms.

I wanted to dance with my wife and daughters, or sit at a table with a pitcher of beer and some good friends, then come back tomorrow and the next day. If Grand Cayman was an anti-island, this was the ultimate anti-anti-island event, almost enough to make you forgive everything else.

I met a young Englishman who worked for the television station. He said his father had incorporated dozens of offshore banks but *he* was devoting himself to documenting the Caymans' vanishing culture. The demolition of this Holiday Inn would be a catastrophe. Nowhere else could you find so many island characters. He pointed out the fisherman that Peter Matthiessen had described in *Far Tortuga*, and a trio of pirates in oiled hair who specialized in American widows. An old bird doing a loosey-goosey fox-trot went by the nom de guerre "Silver Fox" and picked up young girls. "He's even taught me some tricks," the Englishman said. "What happens to him when the Inn closes, or to the Caymanian waitresses? They're too wrinkly for the Ritz. Where else will Caymanians and visitors mix? Where else will I get a good rum punch? No other hotel has got it right. Just imagine, the last genuine place in the Cayman Islands is a Holiday Inn, and now even *it's* finished!"

The next morning, I drove against stop-and-go traffic to Barefoot's home in the village of Breakers. Once I turned down his dirt road, the wind and surf muffled the highway noise. It was a house I would wish for myself, a two-story wood-and-stucco structure overlooking breakers crashing on a reef, where I could not imagine ever tiring of the view or having a bad night's sleep. There was plenty to envy in Barefoot's life, too. Every night he returned here from the Holiday Inn and rowed out to the reef, lit a cigar, and fished until sunrise. (A pair of lobsters caught this morning rattled around in his sink.) He was the most famous white calypso singer in the Caribbean, and had performed one of his songs in *The Firm* and still received royalty checks that, because he had become a Caymanian citizen, were tax free.

I asked him why someone who claimed "keeping things the way they've always been is the type of progress I like to see," and who had written, "tropical islands should not consist of satellite dishes, traffic jams, and fast-food outlets" and "I would gladly turn back the hands of time . . . not to seek my youth, but to once again live on that placid sun-drenched island bursting with charm and tranquility"—why that man stayed on Grand Cayman.

He propped his famous feet on a deck chair and admitted to the contradictions. Sure, he remained because his business was here, and he had profited from the Caymanian boom, but he would sacrifice it all to live in the undiscovered Grand Cayman of 1971. It was the island time forgot. Astronauts had gone to the moon but no one in Georgetown had a radio or television. Cows wandered through town and when you heard a car in the distance you knew who was coming by the sound of its engine.

"I like telling Caymanians about Nauru," he said. This was the phosphate-rich Pacific island midway between Abemama and Kosrae that had become one of the wealthiest nations on earth by turning its interior into a strip-mined moonscape. Nauruans owned more cars than they could drive and more televisions than they could watch. To get them they had destroyed their island, and when the phosphates ran out, they would have to move to Australia. Barefoot related this story and asked his friends, "Does it remind you of anywhere?"

The laid-back beachcomber attitude fell away when he discussed Grand Cayman. He spat out "Burger King" like a curse, saying "Now we have two Burger Kings, *two,* and one on prime oceanfront property." He mocked the expatriates who came for just enough time to make their fortunes and leave, and recited lines from his song, "It's My Beach, Jack," about a local man ejected from a hotel beach for trespassing. He lifted his arms heavenward, saying, "So, what's the limit? How many cruise boats do we need? We've got the highest standard of living in the Caribbean. Why do we need a Ritz-Carlton? For the politicians and the ex-pats, the big money men!"

He had caught his neighbor filling in a swamp prior to subdividing it for condominiums. This man—a member of the planning board, yet!—had bulldozed mangrove trees without a permit. "I took the bastard to court!" Barefoot shouted. "I won because I photographed him, and because I'm a Caymanian citizen." But despite his victory, the parrots never returned, and cranes no longer glided over the beach.

Every summer he went searching for the ideal island, a 1971 version of Grand Cayman. He wanted "Freedom! No rules! No people! No oily bodies or footprints!" He wanted "The full Crusoe experience!"

One year he cruised the South Pacific on a chartered sloop. The climax was a pilgrimage to Suwarrow, Tom Neale's island. As it appeared on the horizon, Barefoot stood on the deck, gripping the dog-eared copy of Neale's book he had filched from a North Carolina library as a boy. He was too excited to wait for a dinghy and swam ashore. Three Cook Islanders greeted him on the beach. One, a policeman, said: "Good day and welcome to Suwarrow. Do you have your documents?"

When I asked Barefoot to recommend a non–Pleasure Spot Caribbean island, he praised the Bahamian out islands as a last frontier, but then made them sound doomed to a Caymanian future. While cruising through the Bahamas he had found Guana Cay. It seemed perfect, just ninety people and eight miles of beach. He bought a waterfront lot and returned the following year only to discover a multimillionaire had purchased the adjoining property and was installing a helicopter pad. He sold out and bought land nearer the village. The next year, his new neighbor constructed a bar and dance hall against the property line. Barefoot shook his head. "I was jumping from the Caymanian frying pan into the Bahamian fire. Progress just seems to follow me from island to island, sticking to my ass."

■

The story of Bishop Holme on Roncador Cay indicated that only a century before, the busiest and most explored sea in the world after

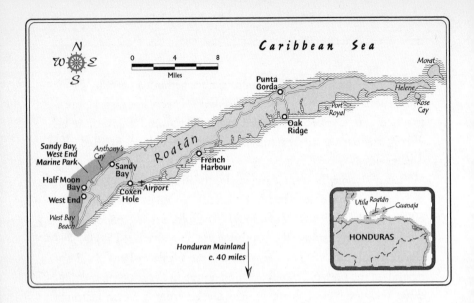

the Mediterranean had an "empty quarter" where you could be ship-wrecked on a desert island for almost a week. I hoped the islands near Roncador would still be less discovered than those in the busier eastern end of the Caribbean. Roncador is an uninhabited possession of Colombia, and what Eliza Holme called "Old Providence Island" is Isla de Providencia, another Colombian island. But reaching them meant an expensive detour through the Colombian mainland, so I decided to try the nearby Bay Islands (Islas de la Bahía), an arc of six islands lying between twenty and forty miles off the coast of Honduras.

Few islands have been discovered, lost, and rediscovered again more often than Roatán, the largest and most populous Bay island. Columbus sighted it during his fourth voyage and his brother went ashore to meet its first discoverers, an aboriginal people from Central America who brewed an excellent beer. It was discovered again by Spanish conquistadors, Puritan farmers from Maryland, English buccaneers, and English colonists from the Caymans, who stumbled on it while hunting turtles. But for most of the nineteenth and twentieth centuries it was forgotten again, and even though Britain ceded the Bay Islands to Honduras in 1859, many of their inhabitants continued speaking English and as late as the 1920s still believed themselves British subjects.

I was encouraged when I read *Blue Blaze: Danger and Delight in Strange Islands of Honduras*, published in 1934. The author, the 1920s adventurer Jane Harvey, described the Bay Islanders as "intolerant of interference" and living "entirely outside legal restrictions." I was even more encouraged when the only recently published article I could find about Roatán was a 1988 one in *Americas* magazine by a man who called it an "undiscovered Eden of unspoiled people" and "a secret seaside den" of heavily forested mountains and palm-fringed beaches that was unknown to travel agents and tourists, and unadorned by commercial clutter. Its roads were unpaved, and its airport could accommodate nothing larger than a DC-3. After one visit, he had decided to retire to it.

I began to suspect Roatán had changed during the short flight from the mainland when two California couples with gray-streaked ponytails and bush vests shouted over the roar of the engines that they had heard it offered retirement on the cheap and were coming to check out the deals. A jumbo-sized wheeler-dealer from Orlando yelled back, "This little island is going crazy!" The runway had been lengthened to accommodate nonstop jets from Houston and Miami, and the European Union had built a "world-class airport." Kevin Costner had been sighted. Chain hotels were stalking the beaches and Julio Iglesias and Oscar de la Renta might open a resort. Everyone was crossing their fingers for a Ritz-Carlton.

As we landed, passengers off a Miami jet were filing into a new glass-and-concrete terminal. A billboard across the street advertised time shares in the future Airport Plaza Hotel, Suites, and Convention Center. Through the rain-soaked windshield of a taxi I saw satellite dishes large enough to contact Mars and the gates of new waterfront subdivisions. Signs screamed LUXURY BEACHFRONT VILLAS! and PRE-CONSTRUCTION PRICES!

Rain bucketed down for the next two days and I was marooned in the Lost Paradise Inn, a hotel I had chosen on the strength of its name. It was owned by a coffee-colored, English-speaking family with Spanish names and wise faces. Carlos tended bar in the cavernous, dimly lit restaurant and reception area. His sister Pilar, nervous and cynical, kept one eye on the television screen while brushing back imaginary strands of hair and explaining how Roatán had gone from lost paradise to paradise lost in a single decade.

She said her family had owned this waterfront land for generations and had built a hotel on it in 1972 that was the first in the fishing village of West End, and only the second on Roatán. When electricity came to the island in 1985 and the government paved the track from West End to Coxen's Hole that was previously impassable during the rainy season, everything changed fast. Hondurans from the mainland flooded the island and in five years its population grew from thirteen thousand to thirty thousand. The newcomers threw up shantytowns, laid out soccer fields, slashed and burned hillsides, and planted subsistence crops. They used so much water the town of French Harbor had started rationing it. Meanwhile, magazines aimed at American retirees sponsored tours to Roatán, and American developers acquired the best waterfront land. They filled in wetlands and laughed at the fines.

Pilar's mother had given the Lost Paradise to her and Carlos on the condition that it remain in the family. Neither minded this restriction. He had once lived in St. Croix. There, he said, "People sold their land to Americans and spent the money, and now their descendants clean rooms in the hotels built on their ancestors' land."

When I asked Pilar how to reach West Bay Beach, she sighed. "I hate that beach. Five years ago, there were no buildings. Now I feel like I'm sitting in someone's front yard."

I asked her to recommend a taxi driver.

"Forget it," she snapped. "They are all Hondurans and know *nothing* about our island."

We spoke over a television that was never silent. Pilar could name all the Chicago Bulls, and she knew more about what was happening in Atlanta than down the road in Coxen's Hole. She knew snow was heading into the Dakotas and Southern California was bracing for mud slides, but she had no clue when it would stop raining outside the Lost Paradise. She sensed this was wrong, but that was the way things were in Roatán.

■

West End was the island's most pleasant village. It had a narrow, palm-lined beach, wooden guest houses buried in gardens, and cafés that stood on pilings over the lagoon. Its rutted road slowed taxis to a horse-and-carriage speed, and many of its visitors were backpackers recovering from weeks of rough travel on the mainland. Around noon on the day it stopped raining, a column of taxis and minibuses arrived with passengers from a Royal Caribbean Line boat that had this morning made Roatán history by becoming the first large liner to call there. Some people stayed in the bus, staring bug-eyed out its mud-spattered windows, but most plodded down the muddy road. West End had no duty-free shops, folklore shows, or rickshaws yet (although no doubt it would soon have all these and more), so they ogled the Danish lesbians, bought amulets from a gypsy German, and paused in front of a bulletin board that displayed an article from *Honduras This Week* reporting waterfront property prices had doubled in two years, some Iranian investors were erecting a condominium complex, and some Taiwanese were planning a resort with a swim-up bar.

Pilar had told me about a wealthy American resident who committed suicide by chaining himself to a piece of underwater coral. His note asked his family to understand the appeal of dying on such a beautiful island, but I saw nothing worthy of this devotion. Roatán had some sandy beaches and pleasant offshore cays, but its freshly slashed and burned hillsides resembled the coat of a mangy dog.

Coxen Hole's sandy alleys and West Indian gingerbread houses had been overwhelmed by pocket shantytowns with a filth and desperation approaching a Port-au-Prince level, and when I followed signs to waterfront developments I found raw lots or the stucco-and-red-tile villas of any Sunbelt sprawl, jammed together because Honduran law prohibited foreigners from owning more than three-quarters of an acre. American retirees lived suburban lives here, climbing into their cars whenever they needed to post a letter, fill a prescription, or buy groceries at one of the new strip malls.

One of the island's best beaches, Punta Gorda, remained in the hands of the Garifuna, a twice-marooned Afro-Indian people who have a bizarre provenance even for the Caribbean, where islands are a patchwork of castaway cultures and races. The Garifuna traced their ancestors to the survivors of two Spanish slaving ships wrecked off St. Vincent in 1635. The slaves found refuge among the island's Carib Indians and intermarried. The result was a Creole people known as the Black Caribs, or Garifuna, and a culture that is a mélange of Carib Indian and West African. The Garifuna became numerous and prosperous in St. Vincent, growing their own cotton and enjoying a good relationship with French planters. In 1775, British forces defeated the French and their Garifuna allies and exiled five thousand Garifuna, almost their entire population, to Baliceaux Island, where half died of yellow fever. Two years later, eight British ships dumped the survivors at Punta Gorda. The Garifuna lost their tools and food when a supply ship hit the reef, and it was too late in the season to plant crops. Many continued on to the mainland, where they spread along the coast, becoming smugglers, woodcutters, and merchant seamen. Of the 200,000 people considering themselves Garifuna, the most traditional may be the 2,000 who still cling to the Punta Gorda beach where the British marooned their ancestors, like a colony of Pilgrims living within sight of Plymouth Rock.

Punta Gorda was a mile of concrete bungalows and grass shacks whose hammocks, dugout canoes, and manioc patches could have floated in yesterday from West Africa. Its people played African drums and spoke a patois of French, English, Carib, and several African tongues. They kept the location of their manioc plots secret, because that is what their ancestors did on St. Vincent to hide them from the British, and lived, like all castaways, with their backs to the land. The interiors of their homes were furnished with Barca-loungers, televisions, and shag rugs, but their exteriors were a shambles, as if their owners expected to return to St. Vincent, or Africa, at a moment's notice.

Punta Gorda was a highlight of the mainland taxi drivers' tours, and the previous day dozens of Royal Caribbean passengers had jammed Robbe Castro's New Chicken Shack to watch a troupe of rubber-limbed boys dance. Castro, a gap-toothed leprechaun who had been a steward on the United States Lines, said the dancers were in school today, but he unlocked a bin so I could run my hands over mahogany drums identical to those I remember seeing in a Togolese village.

He had recently returned from St. Vincent, where he had visited Sandy Bay, one of its two remaining Garifuna settlements, and witnessed a classic demonstration of how remote islands preserve eccentric peoples and cultures. Punta Gorda and Sandy Bay were like twins who are separated at birth yet lead identical lives. They were two thousand miles apart and had had no contact for two hundred years, but their women dressed their hair in identical braid patterns, prepared the same plantain and breadfruit dishes, and used the same technique to wash clothes. Castro felt as if he had never left Punta Gorda.

I asked about the ornamental gate workmen were erecting up the road.

"People sell their land, get money, spend money, then no property, no land, and their children clean toilets," he replied. Punta Gorda's beach and lagoon were ideal for a resort and offers had been made for its waterfront. So far, he and other community leaders had persuaded owners not to sell. He said, "We threaten to make them ashamed of themselves in front of everyone."

But the more Castro talked the more precarious Punta Gorda sounded. The African superstitions were dying and fewer sick people were asking for dancing and dead chickens. Fleets of commercial boats had overfished its reef, and livestock belonging to mainland immigrants had destroyed the gardens of the Garifuna, forcing them to buy more of their food in the market. They had a tradition of sharing food, but this custom was fading now that they were not growing or catching it themselves. "We hope everyone still believes in the old ways in their hearts," he said, but he looked pessimistic.

A group of boys surrounded me as I was leaving, chattering in their strange language, yanking on my sleeves and insisting I admire some crawfish in a plastic milk jug they had caught. Their fathers swung in hammocks and their mothers sat gossiping in puddles of shade cast by palms. In six hours here I had seen no one doing anything resembling work. Castro might shame a few people into keeping their land, but how could the Garifuna continue to enjoy this leisurely life on an island that had nonstop jets to Miami, even if this beach was their Plymouth Rock?

■

"Roatán's becoming a great place for recycling retirees," Candace Hammond said over dinner in a West End restaurant. They arrived on a retirement magazine tour, bought property, joined the transitory community of American oldsters, and imagined themselves making local friends because they exchanged pleasantries with store clerks. Eventually they sickened, discovered that Roatán's medical facilities were rudimentary, and returned to the States. Another couple would buy the house and repeat the pattern. These timid retirees could not compare with the expatriates of the early 1980s, including some tough old birds who would walk six hours through the mud during the rainy season to buy supplies in Coxen's Hole.

I compared the expatriate real estate agents, with their Rotary Club manners and razor cuts, to Hammond. She had a Sargasso Sea of blond hair anchored by lacquered chopsticks and was the sort of feisty Southern woman, flirtatious one moment, cussing like a sailor the next, who takes over her daddy's faltering business, fires her lazy brothers, and turns it into a conglomerate. She had quit her job at a college in North Carolina and headed for the tropics because, she said, she grew tired of sleet storms and kissing ass. She hitched a ride to Roatán from Belize on a timber boat and bought a house that was cheap because its North American owner had drunk himself to death in it.

From the beginning she considered Roatán her special island, her Bali-ha'i. She liked how her neighbors spent their time promenading, sitting on stoops, and gossiping late into the night. On moonless nights she even learned to recognize them by their laugh and their walk. It was the kind of community she remembered from her North Carolina childhood—where no one took anything too seriously, every kid gave you a hug, and you knew the pets by name. "The storytellers are so good, it's almost worth dying to have them come to your wake," she said.

She had become an expert on the local superstition and patois, writing a pamphlet, *"Wee Speak—How to Understand and Speak Like an Islander,"* that translated expressions such as "country pay" (trade for sex), "fast hands" (thief), "nervous puddin' " (Jell-O), and "puff puff" (sex with all the frills).

She worried that the Honduran immigrants and North American retirees threatened this slang just as they threatened the West Indian architecture, and the security of knowing your neighbors. She worried about the shady American developers. "Sometimes I think there's a big sleaze slide funneling them down here," she said. "They sure have turned this little island into a place of major land dreams."

After this remark, I began picturing the Roatán dreams as a fleet of colorful hot-air balloons, crowding the sky, nudging each other, and casting long shadows. Scuba divers dreamed of virgin reefs stretching to Belize, locals of selling a few scrubby acres for big bucks, developers of jetloads of holidaymakers, retirees of six-dollars-a-day maids, and Candace Hammond of the Roatán she discovered when she stepped off that timber boat.

The most perfectly realized dream had belonged to Paul Adams, who had glimpsed Roatán's crescent beaches and undulating hills from the deck of an American troopship bound for the Panama Canal and the bloody battles of the Pacific war. He worked and saved over twenty Minnesota winters so he could open a hotel on the same perfect, palm-fringed islet he had seen from the ship. The result, Anthony's Key, was a resort so unobtrusive and ecologically sensitive it was obviously a labor of love. There were wood-and-thatch bungalows perched over the water, a Swiss Family Robinson maze of stairs, walkways, rooms, and decks, a wildlife sanctuary, and a marine biology education center attracting students from across the Caribbean and North America. After his death the Galindo family took over the hotel and ran it in his spirit, hiring workers from nearby Sandy Bay in order to reduce traffic on island roads, and founding the Sandy Bay–West End Marine Reserve, a ten-mile stretch of reef where spearfishing and coral gathering were prohibited, dive boats used moorings instead of anchors, and diving gloves were forbidden because they made it too tempting to touch the coral.

You can find old codgers weeping for the good old days in any small town overwhelmed by newcomers and sprawl. But Samir Galindo, whose parents now owned Anthony's Key, was a brisk young businessman who had attended an American military academy. Even he missed what he called "that simple, clean, and happy time on Roatán when conch shells covered beaches, deforestation hadn't dumped sediment onto the reef, and you could swim in clean water anywhere."

That simple time had been any time before 1985, the golden pre-electricity age, he said, looking up as if his childhood were being projected onto his office ceiling. People organized outings for their kids, ate big family meals, swept their yards, and respected the elderly. They not only attended church, they dressed for it, too.

Then, Bay Islanders had lived in a state of gentle anarchy, managing their own affairs. But once Roatán was electrified and its roads paved, mainland authorities began collecting taxes, imposing fees, and facilitating immigration, ushering in a more destructive anarchy. Immigrants with a continental attitude toward natural resources burned land and used water as if those resources were limitless. The government did little to stop them, or to enforce rules against spearfishing and harvesting coral in the Marine Park. Once the island got round-the-clock satellite television, people wanted to eat, drink, and have what they saw on it. Teenagers had started dressing in Los Angeles gang clothes, graffiti were appearing on walls, and Roatán had just had its first antidrug march.

"What we have here," he said, "is Snow White confronting Buck Rogers."

It was also, I thought, Pilar's lost paradise pitted against the Royal Caribbean Line, the ecological sensitivity of Anthony's Key against the Airport Plaza Convention Center, escapists like Candace Hammond against penny-pinching retirees, Garifuna accustomed to spending half the day in their hammocks against squatters burning forest land as if this were the Amazon, the lilting West Indian English of a few thousand Bay Islanders against the stiletto-sharp mainland Spanish of millions, and "puff puff" versus "sex."

I asked Galindo how many Bay Islanders thought Roatán was a better place to live before electricity, paved roads, and the Florida wheeler-dealers.

"I don't even have to *think* about the answer to that," he snapped. "Poll everyone who lived here in 1985. They all want to go back."

UNDISCOVERED ISLAND — UTILA

Samir Galindo suggested that if I wanted to see what Roatán was like before 1985 I should visit Isla de Utila, a smaller and less populated Bay island. I doubted an island even closer to the Honduran mainland could be that different but changed my mind after browsing through a guidebook in a West End bookstore and reading how some Utilans believed Robinson Crusoe had been a real man who was marooned on their island.

I flew there next morning, the sole passenger on an eighteen-seater whose kiddie pilots smoked and ignored their seat belts. We landed on a coral strip that anchored one end of the main street and I walked through a ramshackle town that reminded me of Key West in the good old days. Here were the same undrained swamps, rickety houses, dubious well water, and sand flies so vicious I was soon wearing socks underneath my sandals. And here was another lost tribe of Caribbean whites, bleached-out, lank-haired, and crocodile-skinned, rocking on peeling verandas and drinking in evil bars, although unlike Key West's "Conchs," who traced their ancestry to white immigrants from the Bahamas, they looked to pirates and Caymanian turtle fishermen. The buildings crowding the curve of Utila's lagoon were as haunted and neglected as any in Key West had once been, with sagging porches and broken shutters, and their hedges and fences promised a Key West and Patmos–like balance of solitude and community.

Hemingway had called Key West "the last place to run to," and Utila too was an end-of-the-line island, more welcoming and tolerant than anywhere you passed through to reach it. It also shared Key West's disappointing beaches and its custom of making the sunset a social occasion. Every evening, elderly ladies with dandelion-seed hair sat rocking or swinging on front porches while their children and grandchildren gathered in the road to exchange news and, as Hawaiians would say, "talk story." As the sky darkened, naked bulbs glowed in shoebox-sized stores, the shutters of roadside stalls flew up, and the descendants of the pirate Henry Morgan sold Sno-Kones.

Utila was not the prettiest island, but it was one of the most communal islands I visited. No one was very rich or poor, and to give mainland immigrants a stake in the community the municipality offered them plots of reclaimed swampland and urged them to build homes. Most everyone lived together along a single road, lost electricity together when the generator shut down every night, and shared a distant view of the mainland's towering mountains that reminded them how different their island was.

Key West had been famous for its colorful characters. Utila had Shelby McNab, a tall and sweet-tempered bald eccentric who told me, seconds after we met, "It's simple, really. *Robinson Crusoe* is too good a book to be some fictitious piece of bullshit. Crusoe was a real sailor who was shipwrecked on Utila, and Defoe bought or stole his diary and plagiarized it. Sure, he changed things to throw people off, but most of it happened, and happened right here. I have proof, artifacts from his boat, and I know where to find more. When the time is right, our mayor will tell the world we are Crusoe's island!"

He jutted out his lantern jaw, defying me to contradict him.

His story was that an elderly Englishman had appeared on Utila in 1917 and related the Crusoe story to Dwight Hunter, one of his relations. Hunter became a Crusoe fanatic, memorizing the book,

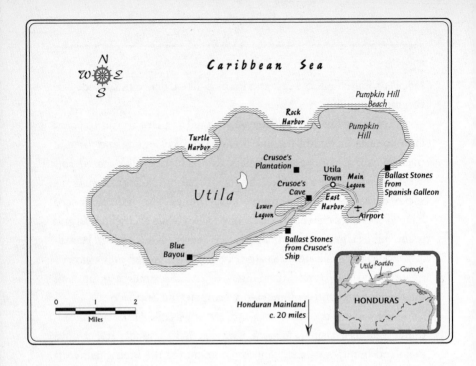

passing the story down to McNab, and showing him the Crusoe sites. The resemblance between these sites and the ones mentioned in Defoe's book was so strong McNab feared that once the truth was known, treasure hunters and developers would descend upon Utila.

When I mentioned the Juan Fernández Islands and Alexander Selkirk, he scowled. Those islands were in *entirely* the wrong place, and had I seen that ridiculous cave with the rock wall? Anyone who knew *anything* about Crusoe—and he reread the book once a month—knew that the *real* Crusoe had dug a hole in a hillside. Stones, never! And besides, Crusoe's stuff had been biodegradable, he said, giving me a hint that he was not only Utila's foremost Crusoe expert but also its most passionate environmentalist, and that the similarities between him and Keith Robinson went beyond a vague physical resemblance.

He would show me the Crusoe sites, but first he had to satisfy himself that I was not a treasure hunter, a stalking horse for the Roatán real estate sharpies, or a journalist planning a quick article.

He was negotiating to buy some waterfront land himself, and feared the price would skyrocket once Utila's Crusoe connection became known. He was sure investors would buy up the best Crusoe sites for their hotels, turning Utila into a Crusoe Disneyland.

McNab's paranoia was justified, considering the huge impact small outside forces have had on Utila. In 1969, just ten San Francisco hippies had demolished its racial taboos. Like McNab, most of the island whites were descended from Caymanians who had arrived in the 1830s, attracted by its fine turtling grounds and anxious to escape the Caymans before their newly emancipated slaves sought revenge. But their slaves, reasoning that if this island was good enough for their former masters it was good enough for them, followed them here and settled near the present Methodist church. Relations between the two groups were cordial but distant for over a century, until those ten hippies danced with black Utilans at the Bucket of Blood bar. Once that taboo was broken so publicly, the races became more intimate. Mixed marriages followed, and now Utila's blacks were disappearing as a distinct race.

In the late 1980s, the telephone had changed Utila's social life. At first everyone thought phones were a senseless luxury for an island whose two thousand people lived on top of one another. But slowly they became accepted, and now news took longer to travel through town. Last week, McNab had heard a tolling church bell and been shocked to learn it was for one of his friends. "She passed away the day before, and I didn't know about it!" he said, slapping his forehead. "That would *never* have happened before. We know what's happening around the world, but not when our neighbors die!"

Two Norwegian sailors, just two, had launched a modest tourist boom that would be negligible elsewhere, but was rocking Utila. They had visited the island after hearing about it from Utilans serving on their ship. They returned to Norway and praised it as an undiscovered paradise. The news spread and the island was soon attracting European scuba divers and backpackers. Utilans began repairing dilapidated buildings and building new ones, opening small cafés, guest houses, and dive shops, and returning from economic exile in Florida and New Orleans. McNab said most people welcomed this small-scale tourism because every family made a little, but it was also hard on the environment.

Utilans had scraped sand off their narrow beaches and spread it across the yards of their guest houses and cafés to make them more appealing. Visitors wanted to eat turtle steaks, so turtles were vanishing from nearby waters. Before, Utilans had dumped modest quantities of paper and cardboard refuse into their lagoon, where it decomposed. After the scuba divers and backpackers discovered the island, plastic bottles and cans could be seen floating in the lagoon and mangrove ponds, and people began shoveling refuse under their houses or piling it in their backyards. The number of dive shops increased from three to thirteen in five years, sedimentation and pollution from detergents and waste raised the water temperature, and the reef was showing signs of bleaching. Utila had one mile of paved road and a dozen cars, but there was talk of more roads, more cars, and courting the cruise passengers whom McNab dismissed as "robots who never leave any money behind."

He had become an environmentalist on a night in 1972 when he and his cousin watched as American treasure hunters dynamited Utila's reef and hauled up chests of what he believed was pirate treasure. The following night, the same men dug holes on Pumpkin Hill, looking for Crusoe's treasure. Shortly after that, McNab moved to Florida, where he managed a health club for the next fifteen years. When he returned to live on Utila he saw its reef was being menaced again and he founded the Bay Islands Conservation Association (BICA). Under his leadership it imported sand from the mainland to discourage the excavation from Utila's beaches, charged visitors five dollars for a pass and used the receipts to finance a garbage truck and landfill, installed buoys along the reef, persuaded the municipality to outlaw spearfishing, and gave turtle eggs to schoolchildren so they would become attached to the baby turtles and beg their parents not to eat the turtles' mommies. But after these triumphs BICA's influence had waned. Six of its dive buoys had disappeared. People became lazy about bringing their garbage to the landfill and started dumping it on the beach near the airport. McNab resigned from BICA following death threats from fans of turtle steak, and his successor worried that its reef had already been so damaged the island was more vulnerable to global warming hurricanes and rising sea levels.

I spent several days following McNab around as he tilted at Utila's environmental windmills. We handed out endive and black-seeded lettuce plants from his garden so Utilans would become less dependent on imported foods, visited people he had persuaded to turn their broken washing machines into planters, and gave wisteria plants to anyone building traditional West Indian houses with columns, verandas, and gingerbread. He pointed out a mango tree where hummingbirds swarmed like flies, and the cacao, whose flowers tasted like snap peas and whose stems Crusoe had woven into baskets.

We poked our heads under buildings to watch cockfights and stopped at the restaurant whose owner had infuriated McNab by whispering at passing tourists, "Hey, mister, turtle soup!" We lingered opposite two woebegone houses so he could recount the endless feuds between their occupants, whom everyone knew as the "Piranhas" and the "Scorpions" because one family swarmed and bit while the other attacked singly, and with great stealth.

I heard this word, "everyone," often on Utila, and on islands like it. McNab said "everyone" had decided the best way to incorporate the mainland immigrants was to give them land, "everyone" knew pirates had buried treasure on Utila, and "everyone" had gathered outside the one-room jail when a boy was arrested for burglary, not to protest or demand a lynching, but because crime was so rare. On Campobello, everyone had admired the Roosevelts. On Fishers Island, everyone went to the pit parties. On Santo, everyone wished the Americans would return. On Niihau, everyone opposed its becoming

a gambling den. On Jura, everyone was against the Overland Route.
Not everyone had actually voted against the Overland Route, or attended the pit parties, or gathered outside Utila's jail, but this word
indicated a communal outlook, opinion, routine, and habit, and it reminded you that on a small island everyone really *did* know everyone
and watch out for everyone, and to be slightly controversial and outside the community, as McNab seemed to be, indicated either great
courage or recklessness.

When businessmen had complained that BICA's visitor pass was
discouraging tourists, McNab had angered them by saying, "Good!
Who needs tourists who can't afford five dollars!" The people he reported for selling turtle soup had not forgiven him. One of his most
implacable enemies, a Mr. Bush, traced his ancestry back to the turtle
fisherman who had rescued McNab's great-great-grandfather after a
hurricane demasted his ship in 1832. Now McNab repaid this kindness by tattling on Mr. Bush for serving turtle soup.

I suspected McNab had also meddled in the affairs of the fishermen who congregated outside a popular café every afternoon. They
scowled when we passed, and one shouted, "King of England!" as if
it was a curse. This puzzled McNab. But he was over six feet, taller
than the average Utilan, and he had ramrod posture and a regal habit
of wearing his half-glasses low on his nose.

The Utilans seemed stunned that the world had discovered them.
They squinted when we met or did a Rip Van Winkle blink, like
someone emerging from a theater on a bright summer afternoon.
They were friendly but wary, and unable to shed the habit of considering anyone from the mainland a snoop or a threat.

Viola Bodden, who had taught English to McNab and several generations of Utilans, invited me into her house so I could admire her
needlepoint and glass figurines. She confirmed McNab's story about

the American treasure hunters and had also heard them dynamite the reef. She believed treasure could still be found on the island, and that was why Utilans walked with their eyes down, hoping for a gold coin. Her sister had found a bloodstained jade tomahawk on Utila that was finer than the one in the National Museum in Tegucigalpa.

McNab interrupted, saying it must have belonged to Indians who paddled over from the mainland to sacrifice captives, like the ones who were planning to eat Crusoe's Friday.

Bodden worried about keeping her splendid nineteenth-century antique desk. It was made of seventeen different woods, with dozens of compartments and pigeonholes, and had belonged to an American consul stationed on Utila at the turn of the century, when the island was a banana plantation and freighters brought the fruit directly to New Orleans. Her father bought the desk when the consulate closed, but now that Americans were rediscovering Utila perhaps the embassy in Tegucigalpa would demand its return. She produced her father's 1909 bill of sale from a compartment and asked, in a tremulous voice, if I thought this was enough to prove her ownership. The consul had also left his official seal in a compartment. If she returned that, did I think the Americans would let her keep this desk?

As we left her house, a lady rocking on a nearby porch veranda shouted, "Hey, Robinson." McNab waved back. Some islanders believed he *was* Crusoe, he explained, and who knows? Perhaps he *was* his reincarnation.

He lacked anything concrete to support his Crusoe theory, but the more time I spent with him, the less fantastic it seemed. He sprinkled every conversation with so many references to Crusoe's cave, Crusoe's wreck, and Crusoe's hill I began thinking of them that way, too, and the physical similarities between Utila and the island Defoe gave Crusoe were so uncanny I wondered if Defoe could have read a description of it somewhere.

As we paddled a canoe into the interior, heading for the "low moorish ground" where Crusoe slept while salvaging supplies from his wrecked ship, McNab shouted, "Remember this is not some joke for tourists. It's all true. No bullshit!"

We glided through channels shaded by giant mangroves and past termite nests bigger than doghouses. After beaching the canoe, we followed a path to its end and McNab whispered, "You're standing on the most incredible spot." It was where Indians had grown the food they sold to pirates, Captain Flood had buried his treasure, and Crusoe had planted his "country bower," cultivating sugarcane, grapes, tobacco, and limes.

"How do you know this?" I asked.

"On Utila, everyone knows these things. No bullshit."

He pointed out that Crusoe's dietary habits matched those of Utilans. "He ate wild grapes in July, just when they appear in Utila! He hunted wild pigeon, and we still hunt them!"

We paddled into a pond bordering the airport. McNab claimed the creek connecting it to the lagoon was the "little opening" through which Crusoe poled a raft loaded with supplies from the wrecked ship. Defoe described him heading for "a little cove on the right side of the creek" and landing on a steep shoreline. We did the same, going ashore on an islet known as Tabow Cay that was, exactly as Crusoe reported, the only high-rising ground near this pond. The view of Pumpkin Hill from here also matched Crusoe's description of a hill "not above a mile from me, which rose up very steep and high." Tabow Cay, McNab pointed out, also lacked fresh water, the reason Crusoe left it after thirteen nights.

Many illustrations of Crusoe show him holding a goatskin umbrella. McNab always carried a furled red-and-white umbrella with an Estée Lauder logo. On Tabow Cay he poked the ground with its tip, searching for relics and muttering, "Amazing! There could still be stuff Crusoe buried here!"

Crusoe's next home had been what Defoe called a flat "green" near the shoreline where he erected his "castle," a tent made from sails. Behind it lay a hill, "steep as a house-side" with a "hollow place worn a little way in like the entrance or door of a cave" that afforded him shade.

McNab believed Crusoe's castle had been next to a limestone cliff bordering the road near the Methodist church. Everything was here, he insisted, "the steep hill, even the flat land for his tent."

Earthquakes had obliterated the cavelike entrance, but the rest really did match, even down to the ledges where Crusoe stored gunpowder in small sacks. McNab scooped out a handful of limestone and shouted, "See how easy it was for Robinson to dig his cave!" He jabbed his umbrella at the ground, saying, "I am still finding things all over the island. There are pirate bottles everywhere—the same ones they held to their mouths four hundred years ago."

From here we walked inland to Crusoe's farm, the "well-watered ground" where he grew barley and wheat. It had Utila's only artesian well, and McNab said finding it had been the clincher, "the discovery that made me flip out."

We returned to the plateau where Crusoe had looked down at the beach while thinking, "I was lord of the whole manor." The three hardwoods, the giant fig, even the thorny-trunked tree where he spent his first night—they were all here, too. The thorny tree, the only one I saw on Utila, grew where Crusoe placed it, one furlong, or 220 yards, from shore. The cay where the storm had tossed his skiff ashore was two miles north, separated from the main island by a half-mile inlet, just as he described. To the south was the creek Friday swam across while escaping his captors and where he jumped for joy. "Like this," McNab said, leaping in the air, his arms and legs akimbo.

Some Texans had attempted to build a hotel on Crusoe's hill. They had planned five high-rise buildings, acres of formal gardens, and a swimming pool. They hired Garifuna to carve decorative totems, and imported tiles from the United States. They left behind crumbling foundations, worm-eaten doors, and unfinished patios covered in trumpet flowers.

"Know what their problem was?" McNab asked, referring to the Texans. "They neglected the Crusoe connection."

The next morning, we walked to Shipwreck Cove along beaches covered with plastic flotsam. Some of it came from the mainland or boats, but most was local. McNab swept it aside with his umbrella. Despite the garbage truck and landfill, Utila was drowning in trash.

Defoe wrote of a Spanish galleon breaking up in a heavy sea before being hurled onto the rocks of Crusoe's island, where it was "stuck fast, jammed in between two rocks." From this wreck Crusoe salvaged liquor and "three great bags of pieces of eight which held about eleven pieces in all, six doubloons, and some bars or wedges of gold."

We stopped at a crevice in the rocks near the shoreline where McNab believed the galleon's forecastle had been stuck fast. Its stern had floated onto the beach by the airport, explaining why you could sometimes find cannonballs there. The only apparent Crusoe relics remaining here were ballast rocks. McNab picked up two that were lying twenty yards from the water and said, "River rocks from the mainland, unlike any you can find on Utila." They were round and smooth, and nearly identical.

We tramped through acres of thick bush near the water, searching for evidence of treasure hunters. McNab believed Utila was honeycombed with treasure left by Crusoe and pirates and he had stopped giving tours to visitors because one party of Germans had returned after dark to a Crusoe campsite with shovels. Other tourists had stolen ballast stones.

I was ready to dismiss McNab as a hopeless crank when I almost tumbled into a freshly dug hole big enough for two graves. There was no reason for an excavation like this here. Someone had been searching for something, and since they had dug just one hole, they had probably found it.

McNab's face went rigid with anger. He cursed the invention of the metal detector and spoke darkly of mysterious sailboats moored off the airport. "This is our *heritage*," he cried, "and we are losing it to these damn treasure hunters."

The next day, we bicycled to the beach where Crusoe walked on his first day on Utila, and where Fred McNab, Shelby's father, owned a backpackers' hostel called the Blue Bayou. We stopped on the way so McNab could show me a prominent mound that he said was the final resting place for the inedible remains of numerous cannibal feasts. Pottery shards and clamshells lay scattered about and he had once found a child's skull. Friday had feasted on twenty adults and a child. Perhaps it was that child? Anyway, it gave him the shivers.

It really did. He fidgeted and circled the mound, but refused to cross it. He was convinced it contained the remains of people eaten by the real Friday. No bullshit.

He believed this, just as he believed Utila was Crusoe's island, and just as earnestly and fervently as the cargo cultists of Espíritu Santo believed American planes would land again on Bomber Two, as Selkirk imagined himself as a child again back at Largo, and as the ninety-eight Americans captured by the Japanese on Wake Island at the start of World War II had believed, on October 7, 1943, that an American task force would rescue them that day.

Wake is one of the loneliest places in the Pacific, a three-square-mile atoll made up of three islets lacking fresh water, vegetation, and indigenous inhabitants. The Japanese evacuated most of the seventeen hundred American Marines and civilian technicians responsible for building, operating, and guarding its airstrip, keeping behind only a hundred to operate the machinery. Two of these died of natural causes, the other ninety-eight became the most physically and psychologically isolated prisoners of the war. After the U. S. Navy blockaded Wake, the Japanese garrison and their prisoners ate land crabs, morning glory vines, and the atoll's rats. Following an attack by carrier-based fighter planes on October 6, 1943, the prisoners convinced themselves an American task force would arrive the next morning on the leeward side of the island. That night, they murdered their guards and crept across the island. At dawn the Japanese counterattacked, killing fifty Americans and ordering the survivors to dig a communal grave. The late author Eugene Burdick, who pieced together their story from the postwar trial records of the Japanese officers, described them digging "calmly and without protest or remorse," pausing occasionally to "gaze confidently out at the horizon." They smiled at one another, and stared back impassively at their executioners. They had passed a psychological point of no return, Burdick said, and believed, against all empirical evidence, that rescue was imminent.

As I paced around this cannibal burial mound with McNab, I got the shivers, too. Not because I was scared, but because I thought I was witnessing a demonstration of the "Mystery of the Ninety-Eight" phenomenon, the ability of a remote island to create not just its own version of time, but its own reality, and to encourage the most fantastic but firmly held delusions.

Shelby's father had a coffee-bean face but walked like a teenager, perhaps because of the vitamin shots Shelby gave him. Fred had once been as controversial as his son. After serving in the U.S. Merchant Marine and marrying a child bride in New Orleans, he had opened a hotel that Shelby claimed was Utila's first brothel. During a ferocious 1978 hurricane he became a foxhole Christian, making the usual bargains with God. When the Blue Bayou was spared he converted it into the kind of hostel that made me wish I was twenty-five. Its hammocks overlooked Utila's best beach and there was a swimming pier where some young Scandinavian women were rubbing oil into each other's bodies.

"What the hell are you doing way out here?" Fred asked, as if we had come from New Orleans.

"We're searching for Crusoe," Shelby said.

Fred sighed. "I sure wish you'd find him."

An hour later we had.

Midway between the Blue Bayou and town we waded into the lagoon. When the water reached our knees, McNab fished out a cross-shaped piece of metal, a decoration from the prow of Crusoe's boat. I was the first non-Utilan he had brought here, he said, and next he would show me Crusoe's wreck, although I would have to swear not to reveal its location for two years.

After an hour, I gave up and sat on the beach, shivering and slapping at sand flies, watching McNab's snorkel moving back and forth in a patient pattern.

The sun was setting when he began to shout and wave. I joined him and we floated together over a pyramid of smooth boulders. He carried one ashore. He insisted it was a river rock from the mainland, completely different from Utila's porous volcanic stones. Had I seen how many were there? What could they be except ballast stones from Crusoe's wreck? He handed the stone to me slowly and reverently, as if passing the Communion host, and announced, "Now you have found Robinson Crusoe."

But what I had really found was another Des Alwi, Keith Robinson, and Barefoot Man—another person obsessed by an island—and another fragile island that could be turned upside down by the visit of ten hippies, two Norwegian sailors, or the revelation that it was Robinson Crusoe's true home.

BACK AT THE FOUR BROTHERS

When I returned home at the end of my travels I did not bewail my return to the world, dig a backyard cave, seek solace in solitude, or sleepwalk through the mainland because my conscious mind was buried on an island. Instead, I stared at the Four Brothers, noticing how the one shaped like a rocky thumb resembled the islet Keith Robinson's father swam to while kicking away sharks, the granite cliffs of another echoed Campobello, and another's oval of sand capped by low shrubbery was almost Maldivian. I saw how different and distinctive they were and thought, forget John Donne, every man *is* an island, and we love islands because they are the only geographic features that echo our isolation and individuality.

My islands often reappeared in my memory like old friends, and as with old friends, I fretted about them and followed their news. I can tell you that the Robinson family still owns Niihau, the Friends of Tílos Association is alarmed at a plan to improve and widen the island's main road because it may encourage speeding and attract more automobiles, and the Overland Route Company (now the Islay and Jura Ferry Company) has not abandoned its proposal to operate direct ferry service between Jura and the mainland.

I turned out to be wrong about all the evil being tapped and drained from the Bandas. Riots between Christians and Muslims swept through the Moluccas and two hundred people died on Ambon. Refugees fled to the Bandas, bringing the violence with them. After Christians on a Bandanese out island murdered a Muslim youth, Muslims on Banda Neira smashed churches and burned eighty houses. Des Alwi faced down angry Muslims and helped hundreds of Christians escape. Flights to Banda Neira were suspended and, according to a Reuters dispatch, a mob on Banda Besar butchered five members of "an old Dutch colonial family" named van den Broeke.

Shortly after I left Grand Cayman the Holiday Inn was razed. One Barefoot fan said its passing signaled "the end of romance on Grand Cayman." Two of Barefoot's songs have made the British pop charts and he now plays at the Rum Point Hyatt, but indoors rather than on the beach and under the stars.

Hurricane Mitch devastated the Garifuna settlement at Punta Gorda. Utilans fled to concrete buildings on high ground and emerged to find streets under water and trees toppled, and I fear many of McNab's Crusoe sites, including the burial mound, cave, and ballast stones, were washed away.

There was an explosion in a Barentsburg coal mine three months after I left Svalbard. After thirteen bodies were recovered and ten men remained missing, the Russian consul, echoing Tami's last words to me, told the Moscow *Times*, "Hope dies last." Three months later, he warned that Moscow had failed to deliver emergency aid and food supplies had shrunk to some rotten vegetables and a few chickens. I had no way of knowing whether Tami's husband had died or if they were both gnawing on a chicken wing. So much for coming to Barentsburg to eat.

Eigg has prospered. The Highland Council gave the Trust a grant to renovate two island houses and the National Lottery Charities Board funded an administrator and a project officer. More grants are paying to build a pier and fence woodland areas. The new tearoom and craft shop is flourishing and the Royal Commission on the Ancient and Historic Monuments of Scotland is surveying Eigg's buildings.

Madison Nena received the Indigenous Conservationist of the Year Award from the California-based Seacology Foundation for outstanding achievement in preserving Kosrae's environment and culture. A press release praised him for working with island elders to revitalize historic construction methods and said: "Fourteen structures have been built, combining traditional exteriors constructed with local materials with modern interiors. There is now a core group of young builders trained in traditional skills, insuring that more of these structures reflecting Kosrae's past will be constructed. Traditional canoe-building techniques have also been resurrected, and the boats are now used for fishing and recreation throughout the lagoon area."

I had never expected to see Isla Robinson Crusoe again, but a year later I spotted an advertisement in *National Geographic* showing a panoramic view of the island, photographed on a cloudless day from a hill overlooking the airport. A green sport utility vehicle dominated the foreground and the copy beneath it read: "Breathtaking, awe-inspiring, powerful, rugged, towering, vast, unparalleled, and boundless. The promise of adventure and the capacity to tackle it. It's the only way to go." I remembered only a dozen rattletrap vehicles on Isla Robinson Crusoe, and there was no way to drive to that rugged spot. But sometimes I wonder.

The appetite for Pleasure Spot islands has remained insatiable. A twelve-page advertisement for the Atlantis, a resort complex on Nassau's Paradise Island, fell out of my *New York Times* one morning, trumpeting, "If ever there was a place that embodies the spirit of the new century and the new millennium, this is it." Instead of real nature, it had a thirty-four-acre interlocking waterscape of artificial lagoons, swimming pools, and bogus waterfalls; instead of real history, a six-story Mayan temple with five water slides; instead of real relics, the Dig, an aquarium where fish swam through the toppled pillars and ruined streets of an imaginary Atlantis; instead of the genuine security of an island community, a children's day camp equipped with digital cameras, pagers, and radios, "to ensure that youngsters and their parents feel comfortable and safe at all times"; instead of silence, the Thriller, a fifty-foot racing boat powered by four 250-horsepower engines that would entertain its passengers by "showing cruise ships a thing or two about making tracks."

The fascination with islands, and with the Crusoe story, is as strong as ever. The BBC was advertising for volunteers to participate in *Castaway 2000*, a "living experiment" in which a hand-picked group would spend twelve months on an uninhabited Scottish island with no contact with the outside world or means of escape (although I will wager that if one of the BBC Crusoes develops appendicitis, he or she will be evacuated faster than Mary Gillies was from St. Kilda). The producers would supply shelter and a small budget for essentials; otherwise the Scottish Crusoes would have to produce their own food and energy.

In the United States, CBS was launching *Survivor*, a thirteen-episode mixture of *Robinson Crusoe*, *Lord of the Flies*, and *Gilligan's Island* in which sixteen Americans would be stranded on Pulau Tiga, an uninhabited island off Borneo in the South China Sea. Every three days they would decide by secret ballot which of their number should be expelled. When only two remained, those most recently expelled would vote which survivor would win one million dollars. A CBS publicist talked about the island's pythons and wild animals. The producer said, "I'm sure there's going to be major conflicts, but I don't expect them to be hunting each other with spears." *Survivor's* participants would experience very little silence or solitude, and the program promoted competition and low cunning rather than community. The CBS Crusoes might shake hands every day, but they would be holding knives behind their backs.

■

Sometimes I gazed at the Four Brothers and imagined them covered by the lawns and houses of an Astor estate, and remembered how a single shipwreck, or the visit of twelve travel writers or ten hippies, can have such momentous consequences for a small island and make predicting its future very tricky. Still, I will bet that by the time you read this there will be a Ritz-Carlton on Grand Cayman, more garbage washing ashore on Eigg and Utila, more cruise liners visiting Roatán, more carpenters from the Adirondacks building more houses on Nantucket, and more Pleasure Spots.

But I will also bet that the Octagon House has survived, Kosraeans are building more traditional houses and canoes and remain just as friendly and religious, and Shelby McNab is continuing to hand out the seeds and cuttings he believes will make Utilans more self-sufficient. I will bet you can still find silence and wilderness on Jura and Isla Robinson Crusoe, and community on Eigg and Svalbard, immerse yourself in D. H. Lawrence's "dark and wide mystery of time" on Espíritu Santo, and acquire the "spirit of peace" on Patmos and countless other islands that have the potential to save the soul of a continent, if you believe Robert Lax.

Before I began traveling, there had been numerous jokes about my "never-ending vacation" and "Carnival Cruise route." In reply I had argued, without entirely believing it, that an all-island journey was as logical as a trip down a great river, across a desert, or through any region unified by culture and language. Now I knew this was true. I also knew that not only did islands share similar traits and face similar threats, but islanders themselves were a distinct psychological race. Like Robbe Castro, who had found Garifunas with identical customs on Punta Gorda and St. Vincent, I had found island people with similar tastes and sensibilities from the Arctic to Vietnam to Maine, from the Hebrides to the Aegean to the Pacific. Like Carolyn Marsh on Narrows Island, they were comfortable with simplicity and silence; like the Kosraeans greeting Duperry, they were instinctively friendly and welcoming; like Bill Jones on Jura and the people of Walung, they preferred good places over cheap goods and would not trade their isolation for a paved road, electricity, and more choices in the island store; like the inhabitants of Eigg and Svalbard, like Orwell pitching a tent for his guests, like Lax living as a part-time hermit surrounded by busy Skala, they were as hungry for community as they were for solitude; like Selkirk and Crusoe, they confined their wants to "the natural necessities."

When I was asked what all my islands had in common I remembered George Murphy's motto, "May you live in the most interesting of places." My islands had all been interesting individualists, yet all shared certain characteristics. They were silent and wild, so they encouraged reflection or, as Marietta would say, "hearing yourself." They had preserved their relics and history, and their rocks "remained in the same place." They left indelible memories, and were friendly places that encouraged their inhabitants to become, as Tami had said, "better people."

When I saw the Italian film *Mediterraneo* I was reminded of Tami's comment, and of the Japanese soldiers who refused to massacre the Kosraeans. The film's story, which has the feel of being based on actual events, concerns a squad of Italian soldiers ordered to occupy Megisti, a remote Greek island off southern Turkey. Their ship explodes after putting them ashore, their radio is disabled, and they are marooned for four years. The Greeks soon weave them into the island community. The sensitive young lieutenant paints frescoes in the church and says, "For the first time since I left home I feel good." His men drink, dance, and fall in love. As with Selkirk on Isla Robinson Crusoe, their nights are untroubled, their days joyous, their lives one continual feast. Megisti is a Bali-ha'i, an island outside time, a refuge from war, and a paradise where the soldiers regain their humanity. One soldier marries and stays behind. In the final scene, the lieutenant returns decades later only to discover his sergeant came back soon after the war and also considers Megisti his true home.

Orwell concluded his "Pleasure Spots" essay by arguing that we need solitude, creative work, and a sense of wonder as much as warmth, society, leisure, comfort, and security, and that "man only stays human by preserving large patches of simplicity in his life."

I believe islomanes sense that islands nudge us toward becoming more human—"better people"—by providing this simplicity, and making us shake hands with our neighbors, listen to ourselves (and perhaps to God), respect history and natural limits, and live surrounded by wilderness and beauty. They do not always do this, but they are more likely to than a similar-sized fragment of continental land, which is why when an island is lost to the Global Village or global warming, more is lost than an inhabited piece of earth where at least one sheep can graze.

In his book *The Insights of Solitude*, author Peter France quotes Robert Lax as saying, "All through history most of the bad stuff quietly eliminates itself in its particular form from generation to generation. It may be replaced by other bad stuff, but the fashion disappears. Whereas the good stuff renews itself." As an example, Lax points out how in Elizabethan England bear-baiting was vastly more popular than Shakespeare's plays.

I hope Lax is right, and this principle applies to islands, too. If it does, then long after Pleasure Spots like the Atlantis have eliminated themselves, there will still be islands capable of making us more human, and people intoxicated to be in a little world surrounded by the sea.

NOTES

The purpose of these notes is to acknowledge major sources and direct readers to books and articles mentioned in the text. I have tried to cite the most recently published edition of a book since this is the one likely to be available from stores and dealers.

INTRODUCTION: THE FOUR BROTHERS

The Thoreau quotation can be found in *A Week on the Concord and Merrimack Rivers* (New York: Thomas Y. Crowell, 1961), pages 303–304. The Lawrence Durrell quotation is from his *Reflections on a Marine Venus: A Companion to the Landscape of Rhodes* (London: Faber & Faber, 1960 ed.), page 1.

Everything you could want to know about Christmas Island can be found in Eric Bailey's *The Christmas Island Story* (London: Stacey International, 1977).

The imaginary islands are identified by Henry Stommel in *Lost Islands: The Story of Islands That Have Vanished from Nautical Charts* (Vancouver: University of British Columbia Press, 1984), and by Rear Admiral G. S. Ritchie, R.N. (Ret.), in his foreword to Stommel's book.

The story of Samuel Comstock and the Globe mutineers is recounted by James Michener and A. Grove Day in *Rascals in Paradise* (New York: Random House, 1957).

For the material on Father Laval I relied on Robert Lee Eskridge's *Manga Reva: The Forgotten Islands* (Indianapolis, Indiana: Bobbs-Merrill, 1931; Honolulu: Mutual Publishing, 1986). The book gives a detailed account of the construction of Laval's cathedral.

Anyone wishing to learn more about Key West in the "good old days" should read *The Key West Reader: The Best of Key West's Writers, 1830–*

1990 (Key West: Tortugas, 1989), a collection of fiction set in Key West that comes with an excellent introduction by George Murphy.

CHAPTER 1. CRUSOE'S ISLAND—MÁS A TIERRA

For the material about the importance of Defoe's novel I am indebted to the following: Maureen Corrigan's "Tales of Toil," an article in the April 9, 1991, *Village Voice* that points out that Defoe's book was the first to depict everyday work and an individual's daily routines as worthy of being the subject of literature; Michael Seidel's *Robinson Crusoe: Island Myths and the Novel* (Boston: Twayne, 1991); J. R. Hammond's *A Defoe Companion* (Lanham, Maryland: Barnes & Noble Books, 1993); and Martin Green's *The Robinson Crusoe Story* (University Park, Pennsylvania: Pennsylvania State University Press, 1991). Green follows the Crusoe theme through several hundred years of literature, showing its influence on generations of novelists and readers. His perceptive analysis of the importance of the Crusoe story has influenced my own observations.

I found the quotation from Rousseau in the introduction to Diana Loxley's *Problematic Shores: The Literature of Islands* (New York: St. Martin's Press, 1990). Her book follows the Crusoe story through the novels it has inspired in the following centuries.

One of the best essays that I found about *Robinson Crusoe* was the introduction by Angus Ross to my now dog-eared Penguin edition (London: Penguin Books, 1965; reprinted numerous times). Woodes Rogers's account of the rescue of Selkirk is an appendix to this edition.

Edward E. Leslie's *Desperate Journeys, Abandoned Souls: True Stories of Castaways and Other Survivors* (Boston: Houghton Mifflin, 1988; 1998) is a fascinating compendium of stories about island castaways. Leslie says his book was inspired by the story of Alexander Selkirk, and not surprisingly, his chapter about Selkirk is one of his best. It provided the foundation for some of my own observations.

The article about the Juan Fernández archipelago by James and Mayme Bruce appeared in the spring 1993 issue of *The Explorers Journal.*

Joshua Slocum's account of his single-handed circumnavigation of the globe, *Sailing Alone around the World,* originally published in 1900, is a classic sea story and has recently been reprinted (New York: Penguin Books, 1999).

CHAPTER 2. SPICE ISLAND—BANDA NEIRA

Very little has been written in English about the Banda islands. For most of my historical material I relied on four sources: interviews with Tamalia Alisjahbana and Des Alwi; the excellent summary of Bandanese history in Dr. Kal Muller's *Spice Islands: Exotic Eastern Indonesia* (Lincolnwood, Illinois: Passport Books, 1990); and Willard Hanna's *Indonesia Banda: Colonialism and Its Aftermath in the Nutmeg Islands*. Dr. Hanna, an American academic, lived in the Bandas for many years and became a friend of Des Alwi. His book is out of print in the United States, but Des Alwi's Rumah Budaya Museum reprinted it in 1991, and it can be ordered from Yayasan Warisan dan Budaya Banda Neira, Moluccas, East Indonesia.

CHAPTER 3. BALI-HA'I AND THE OCTAGON HOUSE—ESPÍRITU SANTO

More information about the importance of Michener's *Tales of the South Pacific* (New York: Macmillan, 1947) and the musical and film based on it can be found in Michael Sturma's article "South Pacific" in the August 1997 edition of *History Today*.

For material about Michener's wartime experiences in Santo I relied on his *The World Is My Home: A Memoir* (New York: Random House, 1992), and on A. Grove Day, *James Michener*, 2d ed. (Boston: Twayne, 1964; 1977); John P. Hayes, *James A. Michener, a Biography* (Indianapolis, Indiana: Bobbs-Merrill, 1984). Michener's fondness for Santo's "zany life" is evident in his chapter on the island in his *Return to Paradise* (New York: Random House, 1951; Fawcett, 1993). I also relied on this chapter and on *Building the Navy's Bases in World War II: The History of the Bureau of Yards and Docks and the Civil Engineer Corps, 1940–1946*, vol. 2 (Washington, D.C.: United States Government Printing Office, 1947) for my description of the U.S. bases in Santo.

The effect of the huge World War II American military presence on the ni-Vanuatu and other Pacific Islanders is described by Geoffrey M. White and Lamont Lindstrom in "War Stories," the first chapter in a book they also edited, *The Pacific Theater: Island Representations of World War II* (Honolulu: University of Hawaii Press, 1989).

For the history of the 1980 rebellion in Santo I relied on press accounts of the time and on Matthew Gubb's narrative account of the uprising, *Vanuatu's 1980 Santo Rebellion: International Responses to a Microstate Security Crisis* (Canberra: Australia National University, 1994).

CHAPTER 4. ATLANTIS—THE MALDIVES

Journey through Maldives (Nairobi: Camerapix Publishers International, 1992) by Mahamed Amin, Duncan Willetts, and Peter Marshall is a large-format photographic essay on the islands with a colorful and informative text by Marshall that is the best account of Maldivian history and customs I found. Marshall mentions the English traveler T. W. Hockly, who commented on the extraordinary cleanliness of Male in 1934. Stuart Bevan's *Maldives* (Avoca Beach, Australia: Other People Publications, 1982), and Clarence Maloney's *People of the Maldive Islands* (Bombay: Orient Longman, 1980) also provided good background material on the Maldives.

Barbara E. Brown's essay "Disturbances to Reefs in Recent Times," in *Life and Death of Coral Reefs*, edited by Charles Birkeland (New York: Chapman & Hall, 1997) describes the damage caused to Maldivian reefs by the mining of coral.

CHAPTER 5. BELOVED ISLANDS—FISHERS AND CAMPOBELLO

The *New York* magazine article about Fishers Island, "We Happy Few," was written by Jesse Kornbluth and appeared in the July 1–8, 1985, issue. The drop in Fishers's year-round population is described in "A Fragile Balance— Year-Rounders' Exodus Threatens Life on Fishers Island," by Bill Blyer in the December 29, 1998, *Newsday*.

Elisabeth Ogilvie's charming memoir, *My World Is an Island*, was first published in 1951 and then an updated version was published in 1990 by Down East Books (P.O. Box 679, Camden, Maine 04843).

Franklin Roosevelt's years at Campobello are covered in considerable detail by Geoffrey C. Ward in the first two volumes of his splendid biography of FDR, *Before the Trumpet: Young Franklin Roosevelt, 1882–1905* (New York: Harper & Row, 1985) and *A First-Class Temperament: The Emergence of Franklin Roosevelt* (New York: Harper & Row, 1989), both republished in 1998 by Book-of-the-Month Club.

Most books about Campobello recount Roosevelt's summers on the island. I depended on Alden Nowlan's *Campobello: The Outer Island* (Toronto: Clarke, Irwin, 1975; North York, Canada: Stoddart, 1995), and Stephen O. Muskie's *Campobello: Roosevelt's "Beloved Island"* (Camden, Maine: Down East Books for the Roosevelt Campobello International Park Commission, 1982).

In addition to Jim McDougal's own *Arkansas Mischief: The Birth of a National Scandal* (New York: Henry Holt, 1998), I am indebted to several newspaper articles for my account of McDougal's attempt to develop Campobello, among them "Development Threatens US–Canadian Bond— Islanders Fear Ruination of Campobello," *Boston Globe,* June 30, 1985, and "Off Maine, A Whitewater Link—Clintons' Partner McDougal Bought Much of Island in Deal That Weakened Arkansas Thrift," *Boston Globe,* April 4, 1994, both by Michael Kranish.

Eleanor Roosevelt's fondness for Campobello is described by Blanche Wiesen Cook in *Eleanor Roosevelt*, vol. 1, *1884–1933* (New York: Viking Penguin, 1992) p. 182. In *My Parents: A Differing View* (Chicago: Playboy Press, 1976) James Roosevelt writes of the family summers on Campobello.

CHAPTER 6. SILENT ISLAND—ISLE OF JURA

For more about Jura's history and archeology I recommend *Hebridean Islands: Colonsay, Gigha, Jura* (Glasgow: Blackie & Son, 1974), by John Mercer, who lived on Jura for several years. Among the book's photographs is one of Mclaine's skull.

Gordon Wright, Jura's historian, has written and published several excellent pamphlets about the island, including *Jura: A Guide for Walkers*; *Jura's Heritage: A Brief History of the Island*; and *Jura and George Orwell* (D.G.B. Wright, Craighouse, Isle of Jura, Argyll, Scotland). This last publication also has a long reminiscence about Orwell's years on the island by Jamie Fletcher's mother, Margaret Nelson.

For my account of Orwell's life at Barnhill I relied on Bernard Crick, *George Orwell: A Life* (Boston: Little, Brown 1980). The comment by T. R. Fyvel comes from Crick's *George Orwell: A Memoir* (New York: Macmillan, 1982).

Orwell's letters from Barnhill and his "Pleasure Spots" essay can be found in *The Collected Essays, Journalism, and Letters of George Orwell*, vol. 4, *In Front of Your Nose, 1945–1950*, edited by Sonia Orwell and Ian Angus (New York: Harcourt, Brace & World, 1968; Boston: David R. Godine, 2000).

CHAPTER 7. HOLY ISLAND—PATMOS

The most recent edition of Axel Munthe's *The Story of San Michele* (London: John Murray, 1929) I could find was published by Carroll & Graf, New York, 1984, and by the Folio Society, London, 1991.

There are numerous references to Robert Lax in Thomas Merton's *The Seven Storey Mountain* (New York: Harcourt, Brace, 1948). The quotation about St. Antonin is on page 37.

Robert's Lax's *Love Had a Compass: Journals and Poetry* (New York: Grove Press, 1996) is the best introduction to Lax and his work. It contains an informative introduction by the editor, James J. Uebbling, a collection of Lax's poetry, including his "One Island," and his journals from the 1960s that describe his thoughts and experiences while living on Patmos and Kalymnos. Another good Lax collection is *A Thing That Is* (Woodstock, New York: Overlook Press, 1997), thirty-three previously unpublished Lax poems, edited by Paul J. Spaeth, the curator of the Lax archives at St. Bonaventure University. Robert Lax's gentle sense of humor is on display in *A Catch of Anti-Letters* (Mission, Kansas: Sheed, Andrews & McMeel, 1978; Kansas City: Sheed and Ward, 1994), the playful correspondence between him and Thomas Merton during the 1960s.

In addition to my own conversations with Lax I relied on two interviews with him that appeared in the *New York Quarterly*, issue no. 30 (1986), and Peter France's *Hermits: The Insights of Solitude* (London: Chatto & Windus, 1996). Lax is France's only known island-dwelling hermit, but France's observations about isolation and solitude furthered my own understanding of islomania, and I would urge island-lovers to read his thoughtful and enlightening book.

CHAPTER 8. FRIENDLY ISLANDS—ABEMAMA AND KOSRAE

A fuller description of Abemama, Christmas Island, and other equatorial islands can be found in my own *Equator: A Journey* (New York: William Morrow, 1988). The most recent paperback edition was published in 1997 (New York: Avon).

The only history of Kosrae I have found is *Kosrae: The Sleeping Lady Awakens*, by Harvey Gordon Segal. It is a detailed and well-researched work that provided most of the historical background appearing in this chapter. It was published in 1989 by the Kosrae Tourism Division and can be ordered by writing the Tourism Division, Department of Conservation and Development, Kosrae State Government, Federated States of Micronesia, FM 96944.

A fuller account of the Snows and their mission on Kosrae can be found in David and Leona Crawford's *Missionary Adventures in the South Pacific* (Rutland, Vermont: Tuttle, 1986).

The Book of Puka-Puka: A Lone Trader on a South Sea Atoll, by Robert Dean Frisbie (New York: Century, 1929), has been reprinted by the Mutual Publishing Company of Honolulu, and is one of the great island books of the twentieth century.

The Kosrae Village resort on Kosrae is constructed entirely of local materials and is one of the most unusual and pleasant hostelries in Micronesia. Its Web site (www.kosraevillage.com) is also a good source of information about the island.

Louis Becke describes his stay in Walung (or Leassé, as he calls it) in *South Sea Supercargo*. The University of Hawaii Press (Honolulu) republished his book in 1967 with an informative introduction by the noted historian of the South Pacific, A. Grove Day, who has also written a biography of Becke.

CHAPTER 9. PRIVATE ISLAND—NIIHAU

Allan Beekman's *The Niihau Incident* (Honolulu: Heritage Press of the Pacific, 1982) explains how a single Japanese pilot was able to terrorize the population of Niihau for several days following the attack on Pearl Harbor.

For the history of Niihau in this chapter I am indebted to Ruth M. Tabrah, who twice visited the island and has written its most complete history, *Ni'ihau: The Last Hawaiian Island* (Kailua, Hawaii: Press Pacifica, 1987).

The quotation from Ilei Beniamina is from a May 17, 1987, feature article in the *Wall Street Journal* by Carrie Dolan, "On Hawaii's Niihau, Present-Day Life Is a Relic of the Past."

Niihau: The Traditions of a Hawaiian Island (Honolulu: Mutual Publishing, 1989), by Rerioterai Tava and Moses K. Keale Sr., provides the most authoritative description of the culture and traditions of the island (Keale is a native Niihauan). The 1998 report on Niihau by Philip A. Meyer, *Niihau: Present Circumstances and Future Requirements in an Evolving Hawaiian Community,* is available from its publisher, Hoomana Ia Iesu Church, Niihau, Hawaii.

A series of articles about Niihau, the Robinson family, and the Kauai Nature Preserve by Catherine Kekoa Enomoto in the July 1997 issues of the *Honolulu Star-Bulletin* described the controversy surrounding the Robinsons' ownership of Niihau.

The Kauai Movie Book (Honolulu: Mutual Publishing, 1996), by Chris Cook, recounts the production history and plot of every movie filmed on Kauai and is beautifully illustrated with stills from the films and photographs of their locations. It also makes a good guidebook to the island.

CHAPTER 10. UTOPIAN ISLANDS—EIGG AND SVALBARD
Camille Dressler's *Eigg: The Story of an Island* (Edinburgh: Polygon, 1998) is a perceptive and scholarly history of the island that is particularly good on the peculiarities of its lairds and the early clan battles.

Eigg (Edinburgh: Canongate Publishing, 1987), by Judy Urquhart, is a shorter and less detailed history, but also well written; it benefits from some fine black-and-white photographs by Eric Ellington, as well as the inclusion of several evocative poems about the island.

Most of my discussion of the abandonment of St. Kilda is based on Charles Maclean's *Island on the Edge of the World: The Story of St. Kilda* (Edinburgh: Canongate, 1972; 1977), a classic work of island history that remains in print and should be part of any islomane's library.

Russell Kirk's pessimistic article about Eigg, "Eigg, in the Hebrides," appeared in issue no. 3 of the 1950 *Yale Review.*

I found the reference to Dr. Petrukov in "The End of the Game: Russian Science," in the January 20, 1996, issue of *The Economist.*

Tim Greve's *Svalbard: Norway in the Arctic* (Oslo: Grondahl & Sons Forlag, 1975) is dated but remains the best overall book about these islands.

CHAPTER 11. FRIGHTENING ISLANDS—MALEKULA AND PHU QUOC
All of the *Odyssey* quotations and references are from Robert Fagles's marvelous translation (New York: Viking, 1996).

The 1974 double murder was the subject of Vincent Bugliosi's *And the Sea Will Tell* (New York: Norton, 1991).

The bizarre story of the German colony in Floreana is told in John Treherne's *The Galapagos Affair* (London: Jonathan Cape, 1983).

My account of the Johnsons' experiences on Malekula is based on Osa Johnson's *I Married Adventure: The Lives and Adventures of Martin and Osa*

Johnson (Philadelphia: Lippincott, 1940), and the article "They Married Adventure," in *Zoogoer* 26, no. 4 (1997).

My own visit to Devil's Island is described in *Equator: A Journey* (New York: Morrow, 1988).

CHAPTER 12. PLEASURE SPOTS—GRAND CAYMAN AND ROATÁN

Tom Neale's account of his life on Suwarrow, *An Island to Oneself* (London: Collins, 1966) was reprinted in 1990 by Ox Bow Press of Woodbridge, Connecticut.

George Nowak's book, *Which Way to the Islands?* (Canton, Ohio: Daring Books, 1988) as well as his CDs can be purchased through his Web site (www.barefootman.com), or by writing him at Barefoot Records, P.O. Box 1249 GT, Grand Cayman, Cayman Islands. Nowak described his experiences on Rum Cay, an uninhabited island in the Bahamas in "An Island of My Own—From Ultimate Fantasy to Utopia Found," in the February 1990 issue of *Skin Diver Magazine*. Barefoot also expresses his dismay with recent changes in Grand Cayman in his foreword to *Under Tin Roofs: Cayman in the 1920s* (Grand Cayman: Cayman Islands National Museum, 1993), Aarona Booker Kohlman's memoirs of growing up in the island.

The article about Roatán, "A Secret Seaside Eden," was written by William L. Dulaney for the January–February 1988 *Americas*.

I relied on William V. Davidson's *Historical Geography of the Bay Islands, Honduras: Anglo-Hispanic Conflict in the Western Caribbean* (Birmingham, Alabama: Southern University Press, 1974) for the history of the Bay Islands.

Candace Hammond's amusing pamphlet "Wee Speak: How to Understand and Speak Like an Islander" is available from Candace Hammond, Sandy Bay, Roatán, Bay Islands, Honduras. It includes local recipes and stories.

CHAPTER 13. UNDISCOVERED ISLAND—UTILA

Shelby McNab has written a pamphlet about his Crusoe theories titled "Robinson Crusoe Island Discovered." It was published and edited by Shirley Canther, a friend of McNab's living in Florida. To obtain a copy I would suggest writing to McNab directly at Utila, Bay Islands, Honduras.

© Jerry Bauer

About the Author

THURSTON CLARKE is the author of nine widely acclaimed works of fiction and non-fiction, including *California Fault*, a *New York Times* notable book; *Equator*; *By Blood and Fire*; *Pearl Harbor Ghosts*, the basis for the CBS documentary; and the bestselling *Lost Hero*, which was made into an award-winning NBC miniseries about Raoul Wallenberg. He has written for *Vanity Fair, Glamour, Outside, Travel Holiday, Condé Nast Traveler*, and numerous other magazines and newspapers. He is the recipient of a Guggenheim Fellowship, the Publication Award for the Geographic Society of Chicago, and a Lowell Thomas Award for travel literature. He lives with his wife and three daughters on Lake Champlain in upstate New York.